DR. RALPH PATAI is a noted anthropologist and author. He has been Director of Research at the Herzl Institute and Editor of the Herzl Press and has served as Visiting Professor of Anthropology at Fairleigh Dickinson University, the University of Pennsylvania, Princeton, Columbia, and Ohio State Universities. He was also consultant to the Department of Social Affairs at the United Nations and director of the Syria-Lebanon and Jordon research project of the Human Relations Area Files. Dr. Patai's books include HEBREW MYTHS (with Robert Graves), MAN AND TEMPLE IN ANCIENT JEWISH MYTHS AND RITUAL, GOLDEN RIVER TO GOLDEN ROAD, SOCIETY, CULTURE AND CHANGE IN THE MIDDLE EAST, and WOMEN IN THE MODERN WORLD.

THE HEBREW GODDESS

RAPHAEL PATAI

A DISCUS BOOK/PUBLISHED BY AVON BOOKS

*To my mother
on her eightieth
birthday*

AVON BOOKS
A division of
The Hearst Corporation
959 Eighth Avenue
New York, New York 10019

Copyright 1967, 1978 by Raphael Patai
Published by arrangement with KTAV Publishing House, Inc.
Library of Congress Catalog Card Number: 67-22753
ISBN: 0-380-38289-5

First Discus Printing, August, 1978

DISCUS TRADEMARK REG. U.S. PAT. OFF. AND IN
OTHER COUNTRIES, MARCA REGISTRADA, HECHO EN
U.S.A.

Printed in the U.S.A.

CONTENTS

ACKNOWLEDGMENTS

Four of the chapters contained in this book were published originally, in a somewhat different or shorter form, in scholarly journals: Chapter I, "The Goddess Asherah," in the January-April 1965 issue of the *Journal of Near Eastern Studies;* Chapter IV, "The Shekhina," in the October 1964 issue of *The Journal of Religion;* Chapter VI, "Matronit—the Goddess of the Kabbala," in the Summer 1964 issue of *History of Religions;* and Chapter VII, "Lilith," in the October-December 1964 issue of the *Journal of American Folklore*. I wish to thank the editors of the four journals for their permission to reprint these papers in an altered and expanded form.

My thanks are also due to the following institutions who helped me in obtaining and reproducing pictorial material: the Bollingen Foundation, Inc., New York; the British Museum, London; the Israel Museum and Israel Department of Antiquities and Museums, Jerusalem; the Louvre, Paris; the Metropolitan Museum of Art, New York; the Oriental Institute, Chicago; the Palestine Museum of Archaeology, Jerusalem; the Princeton University Press; the Reifenberg Collection, Jerusalem; the Royal Ontario Museum, Toronto; the Semitic Museum, Harvard University, Cambridge, Mass.; the Syrian Directorate of Antiquities and Museums, Aleppo; the University Museum, Philadelphia.

In addition, Mr. R. D. Barnett, Keeper of the British Museum; Dr. Elie Borowsky, of Zurich; Col. Norman

Colville, London; Prof. Cyrus H. Gordon, of Brandeis University, Waltham, Mass.; my cousin Michael Klein, a graduate student at the University of Pennsylvania; Mrs. Inna Pommerantz, Research Secretary at the Israel Museum, Jerusalem; Prof. James B. Pritchard of the University of Pennsylvania; and Prof. Claude F. A. Schaeffer of Paris extended their help in securing illustrative material, and my thanks are herewith expressed to them.

As in several of my previous books, it is my most pleasant duty to express my gratitude to the New York Public Library, and in particular to Abraham Berger, head of its Jewish Division, and Francis Paar of its Oriental Division, without whose patient and expert help this book could not have been written.

Forest Hills, N.Y.
May, 1967

RAPHAEL PATAI

Note to the Avon Books Edition

For this edition, several pages of new material have been added to Chapters VI, VII, and VIII. The notes for the Introduction, inadvertently omitted from the 1967 edition, have been restored, and certain other printer's errors have been corrected.

Forest Hills, N.Y.
March, 1978

RAPHAEL PATAI

INTRODUCTION

1. THE UBIQUITOUS GODDESS

Goddesses are ubiquitous—this, in a nutshell, is the conclusion one reaches from a perusal of the voluminous and still growing literature on the history of religion.

They stood by the cradle of Homo Sapiens, and testified to his earliest known appearance in Europe, some thirty to forty thousand years ago, as evidenced by the discovery in Aurignacian deposits of statuettes of nude women with enormous breasts and buttocks and protruding abdomens. These figurines, representing in a highly stylized and exaggerated form women in an advanced stage of pregnancy, are usually refered to as paleolithic Venuses—of Willendorf, Menton, Lespugne, Laussel, to mention only a few—and are generally regarded by students of prehistory as having had religious significance.[1]

They are strikingly paralleled by finds of a later provenance, unearthed in Mesopotamia and Syria, and dating from the so-called Halafian age of the 5th millennium B.C. Both the European Old Stone Age and the Near Eastern Halafian figurines served the same purpose: to ensure fertility and delivery; in all probability, they served similar ends in relation to the animal and vegetable worlds as well. The earliest attested role of the goddess, therefore, was that of the numinous mother who endowed her worshipers with her own mysterious qualities.

At least as old as the Near Eastern nude statuettes are myths in which goddesses play a larger, more universal role. The earliest answers to the great question of "Whence?" all reiterate, in various forms, the same idea: it was out of the body of the primordial goddess that the world-egg emerged, or that the earth was born; or alternately, it was the goddess' body itself that provided the material from which the earth was made. Thus the oldest cosmogonies, like the oldest worship of concretely represented deities, typically start with a primal goddess.

Once these phenomena were ascertained, and long before the data were adequate, attempts at explanation began. One of the earliest was that of the 19th-century cultural evolutionist who posited an early matriarchal social order in which the supposedly general predominance of women was assumed to have been paralleled by a similar situation in the divine realm. The family was ruled by the mother, the people by queens, and the heavens by goddesses.

In a modified form this explanation recurs as late as the 1930's in Father Wilhelm Schmidt's theory on the origin of religion. He no longer adhered to the view of unilinear cultural evolution, but instead assumed the existence of several simultaneous "primitive cultures" of food-gatherers, whose religion was centered around a High God or a Supreme Being. Out of these developed, says Father Schmidt, the three "primary cultures": the matrilineal-agricultural, the patrilineal-totemic, and the patriarchal-nomadic. Since the cultivation of plants was first undertaken by women, their importance in the social structure greatly increased, which, in turn, gave rise to a cult of Mother Earth, as well as to a mythology of the moon conceived as a female. Under the influence of these factors, "the Supreme Being was often thought of as a female." [2] Thus Father Schmidt assigns an early but secondary place to the goddess in his multilineal scheme of religious evolution.

The Freudian position [3] on the goddess is that she represents that stage in the early development of the human individual in which the mother appears to the child as the all-powerful source of both gratification and deprivation. The goddess is a mother figure whose qualities are universal because they stem from unconscious fantasies common to all peoples from time immemorial, which have their primary source in the infantile mind. The child in its jealousy of the father repudiates his role in procreation, wishes to deny that the mother is a sexual being, preferring to think of her as pure and virginal—hence the virginity of the goddess image. When the child learns "the truth," its wish that the mother should be a virgin is frustrated, and it then unconsciously regards her as a harlot— hence the goddess is not only a virgin but a harlot. Moreover, in very early fantasy life the frustrated nursling wants to devour the mother's breast, imagines that he actually is destroying the mother, and, projecting his own hostility upon her, fears that she will devour him—hence the bloodthirsty character shared by the ancient Near Eastern virginal and wanton love goddesses.

Jungian analytical psychology considers the Great Goddess as a primordial image or archetype in the sense of an inward image at work in the human psyche and symbolically expressed in her figures as represented in the myths and artistic creations of mankind. The workings of the goddess-archetype can be traced in rites, myths, and symbols throughout history, as well as in the dreams, fantasies, and creative works of both the sound and the sick of our own day. The archetypal Feminine, designated only relatively late in the history of mankind as the Great Mother, was worshiped and portrayed thousands of years before the appearance of the term. A wealth of symbolic images surrounded her, and she herself appeared in numerous manifestations, as goddesses and fairies, she-demons and nymphs, sometimes friendly, sometimes hostile. An essential feature of the primordial goddess archetype is that it combines positive and negative attributes.

> This union of opposites in the primordial arche-types, its ambivalence, is characteristic of the original situation of the unconscious, which con-sciousness has not yet dissected into its antitheses. Early man experienced this paradoxical simul-taneity of good and evil, friendly and terrible, in the godhead as a unity; while as consciousness developed, the good goddess and the bad god-dess, for example, usually came to be worshiped as different beings.[4]

2. "CHURCH"-LESS JUDAISM

In view of the general human, psychologically de-termined predisposition to believe in and worship goddesses, it would be strange if the Hebrew-Jewish religion, which flourished for centuries in a region of intensive goddess cults, had remained immune to them. Yet this is precisely the picture one gets when one views Hebrew religion through the polarizing prisms of Mosaic legislation and prophetic teaching. God, this view maintains, revealed Himself in suc-cessive stages to Adam, Noah, Abraham, Isaac and Jacob, and gave His Law to Moses on Mount Sinai. Biblical religion, in this perspective, is universal ethical monotheism, cast in a ritual-legal form.

Historical scrutiny, however, shows that for many centuries following the traditional date of the Sinaitic revelation, this religion, idealized in retrospect, re-mained a demand rather than a fact. Further study, undertaken in the present volume, indicates that there were among the Biblical Hebrews other religious trends, powerful in their attraction for the common people and their leaders alike, in which the worship of goddesses played as important a role as it did any-where else on comparable stages of religious development. It will also be attempted to show that the female deities of the early, monarchic period did not subsequently disappear but underwent transformations and succeeded in their changed forms to retain much of their old sway over religious sentiments. How these different religious trends could coexist requires some explanation.

In contrast to the Roman Catholic faith with its single body, the Church, Judaism has never developed a monolithic structure which could superimpose its authority upon all Jewish communities in the many lands of their diaspora. Local variations exist, to be sure, between one Catholic diocese and another, as well as between folk belief and practice, on the one hand, and the official teachings and rites of the Church, on the other. Yet there is only one Catholic faith, one doctrine and one practice, which unites believers throughout the world. Doctrines and rites may change, as they did in the course of centuries; but when they do, it is because the Church, as embodied in the Pope and the Roman Curia, decides on a modification and makes it, from that time on, the rule equally mandatory upon the entire far-flung body of the Church.

No such unity exists in Judaism, nor has it ever existed, with the possible exception of a brief period when the Great Sanhedrin exercised central authority in Jerusalem. Prior to that time and after it to this day, Jewish doctrine and practice, although derived from one ultimate source, the Bible, differed from place to place, because, lacking a coordinating and sanctifying central authority, their precise formulation was left to local religious leadership. For example, European Jews, in obedience to a certain medieval rabbinical authority, accepted the religious ban on marrying two or more wives, while their brethren in the Middle East continued to consider plural marriages legal and to practice polygamy to the present time.

Differences in doctrine among Christians led to schism. Among Jews, they led to heterodox groupings without secession, because there was no organized religious body from which to secede or which might

have cut off the offending limb. There was, to be
sure, disapproval of the views and conduct of groups
other than one's own, there were even arguments and
conflicts; but however erroneous the ways of others
appeared, such errors were never considered serious
enough to warrant a formal break. Jewish history
contains examples of excommunication of individuals
because of apostasy—Uriel Acosta's case comes readily
to mind—but no body of religious leaders ever used
the weapon of the *herem* ("ban") against any Jewish
group, however great the disapproval provoked. A
case in point is the situation that developed in the
18th and 19th centuries when the Jews of Eastern
Europe became sharply divided into *Hassidim*
(roughly, Mystics) and *Mitnagdim* (Opponents). The
antagonism between the two groups increased to such
a degree that intermarriage between them was completely out of the question. Yet, at no point during
the great struggle, did any Hassidic or Mitnagdic leader
go so far as to cast a doubt upon the Judaism of the
opposing group. Similar furcations have occurred repeatedly in Judaism, before and since, but without
ever splitting Jews into rival, discrete groups.

The relevance of these observations to the subject
of the present study is as follows. Whatever formulation was given to the Jewish faith by any local religious leadership, simultaneously and side by side with
it existed divergent faith-variants within the broad
and flexible overall framework of Judaism. Consider
the situation in Palestine in the days of the great
Hebrew prophets. There was Yahwism, preached by
the prophets; there was an official cult, organized by
the court and headed by the king; there were local
variants, combining elements from these two as well
as from other sources, practiced by the simple country
folk; and there were sects such as the Rechabites who
constituted an early example of what religious historians call primativists. Yet all these trends were part
of the "Hebrew religion" of the Biblical period.

The average layman, whether Jew or Gentile, still
believes that the official Hebrew religion was a strict

monotheism beginning with God's revelation of Himself to Abraham. Scholars date the origin of Hebrew monotheism a few centuries later, during the days of the great prophets. As we shall see, even this qualified statement must be modified somewhat in view of certain doctrines, which succeeded in being admitted into the literary depositories of the official religion during Talmudic times, and in view of the Kabbalistic adumbration of a plurality of persons in the deity. Let us here stress the fact that in addition to "official" Judaism—that crystallization of the religion which represented the consensus of most of the religious leaders of a certain time and place—Judaism has always comprised heterodox variants as well. Moreover, since there was no hard-and-fast dividing line between official and non-official versions of the faith, there was constant interaction between the two. The feminine numina discussed in this book must, therefore, be considered part of the Hebrew-Jewish religion, whether they were admitted into the "official" formulation of the faith or accepted only by the simple people, against whose beliefs and practices the exponents of the former never ceased to thunder.

3. THE MASCULINE GODHEAD

Let us now proceed to look at the person of the deity as He appeared, first of all, in the Biblical and Talmudic writings. To begin with, let us restate that the legitimate Jewish faith, beginning with the earliest formulations of its belief-system by the great Hebrew prophets, down to its various present-day versions (e.g., those of the Orthodox, Conservative, and Reform Judaism in the United States), has always been built upon the axiom of One God. This credo had its complementary corollary in the denial of the very possibility of other gods.

As for God, He is not merely the One and Only God, but also eternal, omnipotent, omnipresent, omniscient, aphysical (and therefore invisible), inscrutable, and incomprehensible, as well as just, good, compassionate, merciful, and benevolent. Since, being pure spirit, he is without body, he possesses no physical attributes and hence no sexual traits. To say that God is either male or female is therefore completely impossible from the viewpoint of traditional Judaism. As Maimonides, the greatest medieval Jewish philosopher, put it, "God is not a body, nor can bodily attributes be ascribed to him, and He has no likeness at all."

Yet one factor, a linguistic one, defied all theological repugnance to the attribution of bodily qualities to God. It is in the nature of the Hebrew language that every noun has either the masculine or the feminine gender (except a very few which can take either). The two Biblical names of God, *Yahweh* (pronounced, out of reverence for its great holiness, as "Adonai" and usually translated as "the Lord") and *Elohim* (or briefly *El*, translated as "God"), are masculine. When a pronoun is used to refer to God, it is the masculine "He"; when a verb describes that He did something or when an adjective qualifies Him, they appear in the masculine form (in Hebrew there are male and female forms for verbs and adjectives). Thus, every verbal statement about God conveyed the idea that He was masculine. Most people, of course, never stopped to think about this, but every Hebrew-speaking individual from early childhood was imbued with the idea that God was a masculine deity. No subsequent teaching about the aphysical, incomprehensible, or transcendental nature of the deity could eradicate this early mental image of the masculine God.

In fact, during Biblical and Talmudic times, no efforts were made to counteract the popular image of a masculine God. On the contrary, while the Bible stresses that man cannot see God and survive, and the Talmud contains the axiom that "God sees but cannot be seen," both of these great source-books of Judaism contain innumerable references to God which reinforce belief in His masculinity. The Biblical prophets, psalmists, moralists, and historians, as well as the sages, scribes, theologians, rabbis, and teachers of the Talmudic period, constantly use unmitigated anthropomorphisms in referring to God. He is a "Man of War," a "Hero," "Lord of Hosts," "King," "Master of the Universe," and "Our Father in Heaven," to mention only a few expressions. Needless to say, these appellations all carry a pronouncedly masculine connotation, and, together, with the words of the prayer, "We are Your sons, and You are our Father," or "Have mercy upon us as a father has on his sons!" indelibly impressed all Jews not only with the Kingship and Fatherhood but also with the Manhood of God.

Theologians will point out that none of these expressions are indicative of an actual belief in, let alone a doctrine of, the masculinity of God. Human imagination, they will argue, needs symbols to fasten on. The fatherhood of God (which connotes His masculinity) is merely such a symbol. We do not mean, when we pray to Our Father in Heaven, that He actually is our male progenitor, but that we feel that we are dependent on Him, as we were on our father in childhood. We certainly have no quarrel with this argument. The God of Judaism is undoubtedly a father-symbol and father-image, possibly the greatest such symbol and image conceived by man. Nor can there be any doubt as to the greatness of the psychological need answered by this image. This, together with the great moral imperatives, was the unique contribution of prophetic Judaism to mankind.

Comparative religion, however, teaches us that there is in man an equally great, or possibly even greater, need for yet another symbol: that of the divine woman who appears in many different forms throughout the world, yet remains basically the same everywhere. Most familiar to us in the Western world is the figure of Mary, who rose to such prominence in Christianity, and especially in Catholicism. Did Judaism, the mother-religion of Christianity, fail to fulfill this need?

Is it conceivable that the human craving for a divine mother did not manifest itself at all in Judaism?

It is true, of course, that official Judaism, to a greater extent than Christianity, let alone the ancient Near Eastern religions, stressed the moral and intellectual aspects of religion, to the relative neglect of its affective and emotional side. The prophetic demand for justice and mercy and the knowledge of God as the core of religion, rather than ritual observance, points in this direction. By the beginning of the Talmudic period, Judaism was characterized by an emphasis on the study of the Law as the essence of religion, as against mere belief expressed in traditional and emotion-laden images. It is characteristic of this development, as well as of the incipient reaction to it, that as against the thousands of new religious laws contained in the vast compendium of the Talmud, one finds in it only one single significant addition to the realm of religious faith: the loosely sketched, vague aspect of God's Presence, called *Shekhina*, of whom more anon.

4. THE GENIUS OF IDOLATRY

The Biblical God-concept, intuitively grasped by the prophets and gropingly reached by the people, reflects the strictly patriarchal order of the society which produced it; this patriarchal society gave rise to a religion centered around a single, universal deity whose will was embodied in the Law, but who was abstract, devoid of all physical attributes and yet pronouncedly male, a true projection of the patriarchal family-head. But, among the simple people, old popular religious traditions were too strong to be easily overcome. According to a Rabbinic tradition "the instinct of idolatry was eradicated" in the days of Mordecai and Esther, or in those of Hanania, Mishael, and Azaria,[5] that is to say, well after the destruction of the Jerusalem Temple by Nebuchadnezzar which took place in 586 B.C. According to another tradition, the idolatrous instinct, or "the Genius of Idolatry," as the name can be equally translated, was overcome only as late as the days of Nehemia, that is, in 445 B.C., when the Levites among the Judaeans "cried with a loud voice unto the Lord their God." [6] Their request, a Talmudic myth recounts, was:

> . . . 'Woe and woe! It is he [the idolatrous instinct, or the heavenly Genius of Idolatry] who destroyed the Sanctuary, burnt the Temple, killed the pious, and exiled Israel from their land, and yet he still jumps about among us. Is it not that You [God] gave him to us only in order to grant us a reward [if we overcome him]? We want neither him nor his reward!' . . . .
>
> [In response] a tablet fell down from heaven and upon it was written 'Truth,'. . . which is the seal of God. Thereupon they sat in fasting for three days and three nights, until he [the Genius of Idolatry] was delivered up to them. He emerged from the Holy of Holies like a young fiery lion, and the prophet Zechariah said to Israel: 'This is the Genius of Idolatry,' as it is written, 'This is Wickedness.' [7] As they got hold of him, a hair was torn out of his mane and he let out a roar which was heard over four hundred parasangs. They said: 'What shall we do, lest, God forbid, they take pity on him from heaven?' The prophet said to them: . . . 'Lock him into a leaden kettle and seal its mouth with lead, for lead absorbs the voice. . . .' [8]

What happened to the fiery lion embodying the idolatrous instinct after he was thus rendered harmless, we are not told. What is, however, most remarkable in the above story is that it makes the leonine Genius of Idolatry dwell in the adytum, the Holy of Holies itself, in that innermost sacred chamber of the Temple in which God Himself was believed to dwell. Historically this means that the adytum, and the Jerusalem Temple as a whole, were recognized in the retrospect of Talmudic times as the very center of the idolatrous enticements to which the people succumbed throughout the days of the First Temple and down to the time of Nehemiah, some two generations after the return from the Babylonian exile.

In a more general sense, too, there can be no doubt that down to the very end of the Hebrew monarchy the worship of old Canaanite gods was an integral part of the religion of the Hebrews. As we shall see in the first two chapters, the worship of goddesses played a much more important role in this popular religion than that of gods. The reason is not far to seek. The image of Yahweh, in the eyes of the common people, did not differ greatly from that of Baal or the other Canaanite male gods. Often it would have been difficult to determine whether a certain cult was legitimately Yahwistic, heretically Yahwistic, or unequivocally pagan. The worship of Yahweh thus easily merged into, complemented, or supplanted that of the Canaanite male gods.

But Yahwism lacked the female touch which was such an important part of Canaanite religious life. Nothing it could offer replaced the Canaanite goddesses. Therefore, the prophetic denunciations of these idols had little effect. The devotees of the goddesses could not be swayed to give them up and to concentrate instead exclusively on the worship of a male god.

5. THE HEBREW GODDESS

Were Asherah, Astarte, and the other goddesses served by the Biblical Hebrews, *Hebrew* goddesses or merely foreign abominations as labeled by the prophets? Gods are rarely invented or discovered; rather they are taken over by one group from another. Even Yahweh had pre-Hebrew antecedents, and so had the deity called El and identified by the Hebrews with Yahweh. The Roman Jupiter goes back to the Greek

Zeus Pater, who, in turn, is derived from the Sanskrit Diaus Pitar. As long as a god is alive, he can easily cross international frontiers and establish himself in a new country in superficially changed but basically identical image and function. This is what probably happened to Asherah, Astarte, and Anath: they arrived, at different times no doubt, among the Hebrews, and although foreign in origin, they soon adopted the Hebrews as their children, and allotted them all the benefits man finds in the worship of a goddess. There can be no doubt that the goddess to whom the Hebrews clung with such tenacity down to the days of Joshiah, and to whom they returned with such remorse following the destruction of the Jerusalem Temple, was, whatever the prophets had to say about her, no foreign seductress, but a Hebrew goddess, the best divine mother the people had had to that time.

Following the death of the "spirit of idolatry" in the days of Nehemiah, the Hebrew goddess succeeded in surviving. She underwent, to be sure, an astounding metamorphosis, but then that, too, is the mark of a living deity. In one of her manifestations she penetrated—in what period we can only conjecture—the rebuilt sanctuary as a female Cherub, poised in marital embrace with her male partner in the dark cell of the Holy of Holies. In another, she became the manifestation of God's presence, the Shekhina—a feminine name just as God's is masculine—the loving, rejoicing, motherly, suffering, mourning, and, in general, emotion-charged aspect of deity.

Her role thereafter was minor and restricted, difficult to trace, for several centuries. One can, however, surmise that she must have gained strength in the course of that time, and gradually asserted her independence, because during the 13th century, when Kabbalism invested Judaism with a new vitality, she emerged as a distinct female deity, possessing a will and desire of her own, acting independently of the traditional but somewhat shrunken masculine God, often confronting and occasionally opposing Him, and playing a greater role than He in the affairs of Her children, the people of Israel. Corresponding to this reassertion of her personality, she, although often still called by her old name Shekhina, assumed another name as well, more fitting to her new and high status: Matronit, the Matron, Lady, or Queen.

The new mythology of the Kabbala, revealed in the writings of the Jewish mystics of the 13th century and amplified in those of the 16th, knows evil goddesses in addition to the good ones. They are the she-demons of yore, Lilith, Naamah, and Igrath bath Mahalath, who first appear in Talmudic literature as lowly and hairy female ghouls and who managed to work themselves up to much higher position, until their queen, Lilith, became God's consort. This happened following the destruction of the Jerusalem Temple and the subsequent exile of Israel, which came to be regarded as catastrophic events not only for the people but also for God. The Shekhina, or Matronit, as she now was called, in her motherly love of her children went into exile with them. This brought about a separation between her and the King, who thereupon allowed Lilith, queen of the demons, to attach herself to him and take the place of the Matronit as his spouse. The similarity between Matronit and Lilith is one of the rather uncanny aspects of Kabbalistic mythology.

The Matronit, meanwhile, continued to be closely concerned with her children. Like a true goddess, she played the role of spouse as well as mother to her people. She also assumed the form of a divine queen and bride, who joined them every Friday at dusk to bring them joy and happiness on the sacred Sabbath. To this day, in every Jewish temple or synagogue she is welcomed in the Friday evening prayers with the words "Come, O bride!" although the old greeting has long been emptied of all mystical meaning and is regarded as a mere poetic expression of uncertain significance.

Is the Hebrew goddess dead, or does she merely slumber, soon to awaken rejuvenated by her rest and reclaim the hearts of her sons and lovers? No one can say. But should she manage to revive, we can expect this to take place only in the Land of Israel. It was there that she first clasped to her bosom the wild Hebrew warriors who irrupted from the desert. It was there that most of her life-history, including her amazing metamorphoses, took place. And it was there—less than four hundred years ago!—that her Rachel and Leah forms revealed to the pious and the learned the divine meaning of earthly love, the last of her great motherly-wifely acts, and that her identity with the ancient Biblical goddess Asherah was recognized [9] in a remarkable flash of intuitive insight. It will be there, therefore, if at all, that she will re-emerge, in who knows what surprising old-new image, to mediate, as of old, between man and God and to draw the returning faith-bereft sons with new bonds of love to their patiently waiting Father.

Chapter I

THE GODDESS ASHERAH

In embarking now upon an examination of the various forms in which the feminine principle was conceived by the Biblical Hebrews and their successors, the Jews of the Hellenistic, Talmudic, and Kabbalistic periods, we begin, so as to proceed in chronological order, with the Goddess Asherah, who was the earliest female deity known to have been worshiped by the Children of Israel.

1. THE PROBLEM

The beginnings of the period we are dealing with here go back to the time following the arrival of the Israelite tribes in Canaan. For about six centuries thereafter, that is to say, down to the destruction of Jerusalem by Nebuchadnezzar in 586 B.C., the Hebrews worshiped Asherah (and next to her also other, originally Canaanite, gods and goddesses) in most places and times. Only intermittently, although with gradually increasing intensity and frequency, did the prophetic demand for the worship of Yahweh as the one and only god make itself be heard and was it heeded by the people and their leaders. This much is apparent, although the religious history of the period as a whole—in spite of the numerous studies devoted

16

to its untangling—is still obscure, due to the inadequacy of the available sources.

The primary literary sources pertaining to the period are contained in the Biblical canon. While undoubtedly based on ancient oral tradition, some of it reaching back into the Mosaic period, or even as far as the patriarchal age, the Biblical accounts are preserved in relatively late reworkings and are therefore not contemporary, in a strict sense of the word, with the events they describe. Editorial revisions were especially thorough when the subject matter pertained to the non-monotheistic phases of early Hebrew religion. References felt to be offensive were toned down or abridged, and we have, of course, no way of knowing how many were excised altogether. In the narratives which deal with the subsequent period of the Hebrew monarchy, the monotheistic point of view is even more stringent, so that all references to non-monotheistic forms of popular worship are not only consistently derisive and unrelentingly condemnatory but are kept purposely in vague and general terms.

The archaeological data, while obviously suffering neither from subsequent modification nor from contemporary tendentious representation, are disappointing because of their paucity or lack of clarity. The temples, sanctuaries, high places, altars, and other religious structures which were unearthed from the early Hebrew period, contain, as a rule, no clear-cut evidence as to the identity of the deity to whom they were dedicated. From a comparison of Biblical references and archaeological discoveries we know that the rituals of both Yahweh and the Canaanite gods followed the same general pattern, and it is precisely this circumstance which makes the identification of the deity worshiped at any particular archaeological site extremely difficult.

In the case of the small figurines and statuettes, of which many hundreds were found all over Palestine, and a considerable percentage of which can be attributed without any doubt to the Israelite monarchic period, there is a difficulty of another kind. While it can be taken for granted that these figurines, mostly nude females, were used in some religious-ritual context, in many cases we cannot be sure whether the goddess so represented was worshiped by the Hebrews or by the Canaanite population who lived side by side in early Palestine. The greatest frustration, however, for the historian of religion is the absence of contemporary literary documents, such as inscribed tablets, monuments, statues, or walls, which would contain clear evidence of the nature of popular Hebrew religion in the early period ending with the Babylonian captivity of 586 B.C.

Having stated what we do not have, let us now turn to the extant evidence on which one can nevertheless base an attempt at reconstructing early Hebrew popular religion. This can be divided into four categories:

1. The evidence of the Bible, which, in spite of the efforts of its monotheistically oriented authors and/or editors, contains incidental information as to the court ritual and popular religion which a few judges and kings and all the prophets strove to suppress, eliminate, and replace by monotheistic Yahwism.

2. Local archaeological evidence, admittedly limited, but nevertheless useful and, with the intensive work going on in Israel, daily increasing in volume and variety.

3. The considerably more ample data contained in Canaanite, Syrian, Mesopotamian, Iranian, Anatolian, and Egyptian archaeology and mythology, with their detailed information about the deities who, according to Biblical evidence, were worshiped by the Hebrews.

4. Literary sources of post-Biblical Judaism, which flow richly especially in the first few centuries of the Christian era; which, because of their less sacred character were not subjected to the same meticulous scrutiny as the Holy Book; and in which, therefore, many references and recollections of early Hebrew polytheism were able to pass muster.

This enumeration of the types of source material bearing on early Hebrew popular religion indicates the amount and nature of the information we can expect concerning the female deity whose person, image, and worship form the subject of the present chapter. We are forewarned that the data will be neither ample nor explicit, neither exhaustive nor detailed, and, in some cases at least, neither conclusive nor irrefutable.

As far as the Biblical books are concerned, their anti-polytheistic attitude manifests itself in, among other things, a pronounced reluctance to allow any ritual detail of pagan worship to enter the references they contain to Israel's religious transgressions. Nevertheless, it is from Biblical sources that we know the names of the three goddesses who were worshiped by the ancient Hebrews down to the days of the Babylonian exile: Asherah, Astarte, and the Queen of Heaven, who was probably identical with Anath. It is with the first of these three that the present chapter deals. Let us begin by reviewing what extra-Biblical sources tell us about Asherah.

2. THE CANAANITE ASHERAH

That Asherah was the chief goddess of the Canaanite pantheon we know from the rich mythical material unearthed a few decades ago at Ugarit, the modern Ras Shamra, near the northeastern corner of the Mediterranean. In Ugaritic mythology, as preserved on numerous tablets, written in a language quite close to Biblical Hebrew and dating from the 14th century B.C., Asherah figured prominently as the wife of El, the chief god. Her full name was "Lady Asherah of the Sea"—apparently, her domain proper was the sea, just as that of her husband El was heaven. She was, however, also referred to simply as Elath or Goddess. She was the "Progenitress of the Gods": all the other gods, numbering seventy, were her children, including Baal, Anath, Mot, and the other chief protagonists of the Ugaritic pantheon. One of her servants was Qadesh wa-Amrur, called the "fisherman of Lady Asherah of the Sea," who fished at her bidding and, in his capacity as her equerry, saddled her donkey and helped her to mount. Asherah's relationship to her husband El was not unlike that of an Oriental queen to her master: when entering into his presence, she would prostrate herself, whereupon El would kindly inquire after her desire. When Baal wished to obtain permission from El to build a house, he sent his mother Asherah to intercede with El. Upon the death of Baal, El asked Asherah to name one of her sons to succeed him as king.

Asherah was a motherly goddess and as such she, together with her daughter Anath, served as the wetnurse of the gods. She suckled even human princes who were exceptionally deserving, such as Yassib, the son of King Keret. She also seems to have foretold the fortunes of her devotees, for in a 14th-century B.C. letter, found at Taanach near Megiddo (in Palestine), reference is made to a "wizard of Asherah" through whom she seems to have spoken.[1]

Little is known of Asherah before the period of the Ugaritic myths. In a Sumerian inscription, set up by an Amorite official in honor of Hammurabi and dating from ca. 1750 B.C., and other contemporary documents, she is called Ashratum (i.e., Asherah), the bride of Anu.[2] Since the Sumerian and Akkadian deity Anu closely corresponded to the Canaanite El in being the god of heaven, it appears that Asherah held the position of the chief or mother goddess for at least three centuries prior to the Ugaritic period. She was also known in Southern Arabia, where her name had the form Atharath, as in the Ugarit tablets.[3] In the 14th century B.C. Amarna tablets, containing letters written by Canaanite petty chieftains to their overlords, the king of Egypt,[4] the names Asherah and Astarte interchange, which may indicate a lack of clear distinction between the functions and personalities of these two goddesses. As we shall see below, the same confusion between Asherah and Astarte is found in the

Bible and persisted even among scholars down to our days.

Asherah was associated with several cities where she was worshiped in her local manifestations. She was the "Asherah of Tyre" and the "Elath [Goddess] of Sidon"—both Tyre and Sidon having been for long periods not only the capitals of independent states but also important Mediterranean seaports whose prosperity depended on the bounty of the sea and the good graces of its ruling lady. A third port, Elath, far to the south on the Gulf of Aqaba, may have been named after her. There were thus Asherahs of many localities (just as there are a Virgin of Fatima, a Virgin of Guadalupe, etc.), and when the Biblical references state that the Israelites served "the Asherahs," this can only mean that they adopted the worship of several of these local manifestations of the great goddess.

A king of the Land of the Amorites, mentioned in the Amarna letters, was called Abdu-Ashirta, i.e., "Slave of Asherah," [5] clearly showing that he was a devotee of her cult, which included the sacrificing of cattle and flocks.[6]

3. WHAT WAS THE HEBREW ASHERAH?

It was almost inevitable that the cult of this great Canaanite mother-goddess, who was venerated also in many other parts of the Ancient Near East,[7] should penetrate Hebrew religion as well. In fact, it was not long after the Israelite conquest of the Canaanite hill country, in the period of mixed Israelite-Canaanite settlement, that this development took place, together with intermarriage between the Israelites and the Canaanites, Hittites, Amorites, Perizzites, Hivites, and Jebusites, "among whom they dwelt." The establishment of family and religious ties went hand in hand, and "the Children of Israel . . . served the Baals and the Asherahs." [8]

While it is not easy to reach a definite conclusion as to the physical shape in which Asherah was represented among the Hebrews, a careful perusal of the numerous Biblical references to the "Asherahs" [9] seems to indicate that they were carved wooden images which were set up by implanting their base into the ground. In early times they often stood next to altars dedicated to Baal; [10] later, a "statue of Asherah" was set up in the Jerusalem Temple itself.[11] The word Asherah in Biblical usage can thus refer either to the goddess herself or to her image.[12]

From a story told in the Book of Judges about Gideon, who lived in the 12th century B.C., we learn that the Asherah worship in those early days was a communal or public affair. However, the wooden image of the goddess belonged to the town's chieftain who, at one and the same time, was also the priest of Asherah and Baal. This chieftain was none other than Joash the Abiezrite, Gideon's father. When Gideon, an early precursor of zealous Yahwist reformers, demolished the altar of Baal and cut down the Asherah, he incurred the wrath of the entire town of Ofra. His immediate punishment by death was demanded by the men of the city, and he was saved only because his father stood by him.[13]

Gideon's act remained, for several generations at least, an isolated incident. The cult of the Goddess Asherah continued among the Hebrews throughout the periods of the judges and the kings. Unfortunately, in the climate of Palestine, with its annual heavy winter rains, wooden objects do not survive. Therefore, however large was the number of the carved wooden poles or statues which represented the Goddess Asherah and around which her communal worship took place, as it did in the town of Ofra until its disruption by Gideon, no archaeological evidence can attest to their existence.

On the other hand, there is ample archaeological evidence as to the importance of Asherah as a household goddess, a variety of the Teraphim. This evidence consists of numerous small clay figurines of nude

women already referred to above. These were found
all over Palestine and can be dated with confidence as
deriving from all ages of the Israelite period. Many
of these figurines conform to types which can be taken
as stereotyped representations of Asherah. This seems
especially to be the case with those figurines which
show a woman with protruding breasts below which,
however, instead of torso and legs, the figure consists
of a straight cylindrical column with a flaring base.
One can assume that these figurines are the small clay
counterparts of the larger wooden Asherah poles which
were set up by implanting them into the ground. (See
Plates 1–7, and the Asherah figure on Plate 8). Judging from the frequent occurrence of these female
figurines, not matched anywhere by images of male
gods, the worship of the goddess must have been
extremely popular in all segments of Hebrew society.
One of the reasons for her popularity may have been
the belief that she promoted fertility in women and
facilitated childbirth. In a 7th-century B.C. Hebrew incantation text, found in Arslan Tash in Upper Syria,
the help of the Goddess Asherah is sought for a
woman in delivery.[14] Such an invocation of Asherah
may have been contained in the original form of the
exclamation made by Leah at the birth of Zilpah's
son, whom she named Asher.[15] If so, we have here a
testimony to the worship of Asherah in the early period
in which the patriarchal traditions of Genesis originated.

4. SOLOMONIC IDOLATRY

While the worship of Asherah was thus a central
feature of popular Hebrew religion in the pre-monarchic period, and her statues stood in many a local
sanctuary, it remained for King Solomon to introduce
her worship into his capital city of Jerusalem.

As is well known, the very manner in which Solomon's Temple was built in Jerusalem was conducive to

the establishment of a polytheistic-syncretistic cult. Solomon's religious proclivities are condemned by the Yahwist historian, who begins his account of Solomon's reign by stating that "Solomon loved Yahweh," but feels constrained to add in the same sentence that "he, nevertheless, sacrificed and burnt incense on the high places." [16]

The architects and builders who, at Solomon's request, were sent by King Hiram of Tyre to Jerusalem to build the Temple hewed close to the patterns familiar to them from their own temples. That this was the case is indicated by a comparison of archaeological discoveries with the Biblical description of Solomon's temple. Of the numerous Canaanite and Syrian temples excavated, the one most closely resembling Solomon's is that of Tell Tainat in Syria from the 9th century B.C. That temple, like the one of Jerusalem, was divided into three sections, a vestibule, a nave, and an inner sanctuary, and like it, had two pillars at its entrance. A much older Canaanite temple, which might be considered as the prototype of Solomon's, dating from the end of the Late Bronze Age, was found at Hazor.[17] In Solomon's temple, all the brass work, including the two pillars Jachin and Boaz, was executed by a Tyrian craftsman also called Hiram.[18] Again, archaeology teaches us that these brass furnishings of the Jerusalem temple were made in a manner customary in temples dedicated to "other gods" along the east-Mediterranean coast. It is probable that this similarity in structure and furnishings was matched by a similarity of the worship itself: the difference between Yahweh and other gods lay not in ritual, but in the ideology and morality, which was developed in his name by the great Hebrew prophets.

The chronicler of Solomon's reign reproaches him for having built places of worship for many gods, yet he does so in a curiously restrained manner: Solomon's heart, he says, "was *not whole* with Yahweh his god," and "he did what was evil in the eyes of Yahweh, and went *not fully* after Yahweh as did David his father." [19] In the passage in question, two extenuating circumstances are offered in excuse of Solomon's acts: he did what he did because his wives, to whom "he cleaved in love," turned his heart; and all this happened when Solomon was old.[20] Historical considerations, however, invalidate these excuses.

Firstly, we know that political marriages between a ruler and foreign princesses were an accepted means of strengthening alliances or friendly relations between states. Secondly, the introduction of a foreign princess into a royal household inevitably meant the admission of her gods as well. Thirdly, while such marriages may have taken place any time during the reign of a king, the most ambitious of Solomon's political marriages, that with the daughter of Pharaoh, was entered into at the very beginning of Solomon's reign.[21] It is reasonable to assume that he married the Sidonian princess [22] about the same time, when he set about to carry out his great building projects for whose execution he needed the friendship and help of the Phoenicians. A Hittite princess at his court—whose presence served as a living political bond between Solomon and the neo-Hittite states of Syria—was also valuable for him at the same time, as were daughters of his Moabite, Ammonite and Edomite vassals. These marriages were in the nature of guarantees of security, without which he would have had to keep powerful troup contingents in constant readiness at a time when he needed all the available manpower in the country for the construction of his grandiose religious and royal compounds. It is thus more than probable that all these marriages were contracted by Solomon soon after his succession, and that the introduction of the respective divinities worshiped by his wives also took place at the same time.[23]

Among the deities whom Solomon worshiped was "the Goddess of the Sidonians" who, as we have seen, was none other than Asherah. However, the historian recording this calls her " 'Ashtoreth, Goddess of the Sidonians." [24] Also the prophet Ahijah the Shilonite, an uncompromising Yahwist who flourished towards the end of Solomon's reign and in the years following it, reproaches the Israelites once with worshiping "'Ashtoreth, the Goddess of the Sidonians," and another time with serving Asherah.[25] However, such a confusion of Asherah and Astarte is not confined to the Biblical authors who equally detested both of them; it is found, as mentioned above, already in the Amarna letters written in the 14th century B.C. by people who should have known better because they believed in the two goddesses and worshiped them. But we have to keep in mind that in polytheistic cultures the prevalent tendency often was to identify one god with another, substitute one god for another, combine one god with another, or call one god by the name of another, as we know from many examples in the Egyptian, Babylonian, Hittite or Canaanite religions. In any case, there can be little doubt that it was the worship of Asherah, already popular among the Hebrews for several generations, which was introduced by Solomon into Jerusalem as part of the cult of the royal household, for his Sidonian wife.

5. ASHERAH IN ISRAEL

Close to the end of Solomon's reign, a dramatic encounter took place between the prophet Ahijah of Shiloh, and Jeroboam the son of Nebat, a young and brave foreman of Solomon's work force. As the two men met in the fields outside of Jerusalem, Ahijah grabbed the new mantle worn by Jeroboam, tore it into twelve pieces, and said to the astonished youth:

> Take ten of these pieces, for Yahweh, the God of Israel, will tear away the dominion over ten tribes of Israel from Solomon, because he forsook Yahweh, and served 'Ashtoreth, the Goddess of the Sidonians, Chemosh, the God of Moab, and Milcom, the God of the children of Ammon. If you will hearken to all that Yahweh commands you, He will be with you and give you Israel.[26]

As is well known, Ahijah's hopes in Jeroboam were bitterly disappointed. No sooner had Jeroboam established himself in the northern part of the country, when he set up two golden calves, one in Beth-el, just a few miles from Jerusalem, and the other in Dan, the northernmost point of Israel. "These are your gods, O Israel, who brought you up from Egypt," he proclaimed.[27]

One can imagine the pain and the anger felt by Ahijah. As soon as the stern Yahwist prophet had an opportunity, he prophesied the downfall of the house of Jeroboam, as he had foretold its rise some years previously. The charge was again the worship of "other gods and molten images" in general, coupled with a more specific accusation levelled against the people of Israel as a whole: "Because they have made their Asherahs, provoking Yahweh." [28] The fact that of all forms of idolatry only the cult of Asherah was mentioned specifically by Ahijah must mean at least that the one variety of religious worship in which the Israelites engaged more frequently than in any other was the cult of the Goddess Asherah, symbolized and represented by her carved wooden images.

The introduction of the Asherah worship into the ritual of the royal court had to wait for the arrival in the capital of Israel, Samaria, of another Sidonian princess, as bride of King Ahab (873–852 B.C.). She was Jezebel, daughter of Ethbaal, King of Sidon, in whose capital city the "Elath of Sidon," i.e., the Asherah of Sidon, had been worshiped as early as at least five centuries prior to his own time. Under Jezebel's influence, and in order to cement the alliance with her father, King Ahab of Israel built an altar to Baal in Samaria and "made" an Asherah.[29]

The extent of the worship of these Sidonian deities in Ahab's court is attested by the report that 450 prophets of the Baal and 400 prophets of Asherah ate at the table of Jezebel.[30] It was these prophets whom Elijah met on Mount Carmel, in a great public rain-making contest which ended with the utter defeat of the Canaanite god and a miraculous vindication of Yahweh.[30a] It is interesting to observe that Elijah did not accuse the people of having abandoned Yahweh for the foreign gods but merely of dividing their attentions between both.[31] Although the 400 prophets of Asherah seem to have attended the meeting on Mount Carmel, only the 450 prophets of Baal were challenged to the contest by Elijah, and no further word is said in the entire detailed narrative about the prophets of Asherah. The appeal of the Baal prophets to their god and that of Elijah to Yahweh are surprisingly similar, in fact, almost identical. When Yahweh's fire (lightning?) descends on Elijah's altar and thus proves His superiority, the people side with Elijah, and burst into shouts of "Yahweh is the god!" Thereupon the 450 prophets of the Baal are seized, dragged down into the valley, and slaughtered at the River Kishon.[32] No word is said about the fate of the 400 prophets of Asherah. The inference must be that, not being part of the contest, no harm befell them. If so, they must have continued unhindered to serve their goddess. Nor was the Asherah which Ahab had "made" and set up in Samaria removed or in any way harmed either as a result of Elijah's victory over the prophets of the Baal, or during the remaining years of Ahab's reign. It would appear then that only the Baal was considered by Elijah (and the strict Yahwists in general) as a dangerous rival of Yahweh, while the Goddess Asherah was regarded as his inevitable, necessary, or at any rate tolerable, female counterpart.

Ahab died ca. 852 B.C. and was succeeded by his son Ahaziah (ca. 852–851), who in turn was followed by his brother Joram. In 841–842 Jehu overthrew the dynasty and became King of Israel, to be followed, after a reign of 27 years, by his son Joahaz (814–798). It is from the days of this king that the next report about the Asherah of Samaria dates. The *Book of Kings* states tersely that during the reign of Joahaz the people of Israel "departed not from the sins of the house of Jeroboam, wherewith he had made Israel to sin, but walked therein; and also the Asherah remained standing in Samaria." [33]

The persistence of the Asherah cult in Samaria, indicated by this statement, is in marked contrast to the much lesser tenacity of the Baal cult. For we are told that Joram, son of Ahab, "removed the pillar [*masseba*] of the Baal that his father had made." [34] This pillar of the Baal must have been the same cult object which, when erected by Ahab, was referred to as "an altar for the Baal in the house of the Baal which he had built in Samaria." [35] The absence of any indication of what, if anything, Joram did with the other cult object, the Asherah, which his father Ahab had made,[36] could mean that he did not touch it, because the worship of Asherah was considered, as in the days of Ahab, a legitimate religious pursuit even by those who objected to the Baal cult.

Even more remarkable is the absence of any action on the part of Jehu and his zealous supporters, the Rechabites, against the worship of Asherah in Samaria. Against the Baal worship Jehu proceeded ruthlessly: by a clever ruse he induced all the prophets of Baal (evidently, the 450 prophets of Baal killed by Elijah less than two decades earlier were not all the Baal prophets in the country; or possibly, new ones arose in the interval), as well as all the priests and worshipers of Baal, to gather in the temple of Baal in Samaria and had them put to the sword there. Then he had the pillar (or pillars) of Baal broken into pieces and destroyed the Baal temple itself, desecrating its very site by making it a place of latrines.[37] The narrative concludes with a statement which both gives credit to Jehu for what he did and blames him for what he left undone:

Thus Jehu destroyed the Baal out of Israel; but the sins of Jeroboam the son of Nebat, wherewith he had made Israel to sin, Jehu departed not from them: the golden calves that were in Beth-el and that were in Dan.[38]

No word is said in this entire detailed account as to any action against the prophets of Asherah—most

of the 400 spared by Elijah must have been still alive
—the priests of Asherah, the worshipers of Asherah,
or the Asherah statue itself which still stood unharmed
in Samaria. When the reign of Jehu's son, Joahaz,
came to an end (798 B.C.), the statue of Asherah still
stood in Samaria,[39] and if it stood, it must have been
worshiped.

This state of affairs continued in the Kingdom of
Israel during the remaining three-quarters of a century of its existence after the death of Joahaz. Both the
court and the people continued to worship Asherah.
Only in the eyes of the post-exilic historian, looking
back at the period of the divided monarchy from the
vantage point of his advanced Yahwist monotheism,
does the Asherah worship appear as a sin. When he
gives his melancholy account of what brought about
the subjugation of Israel by Shalmaneser, King of
Assyria, in about 722 B.C., he lists several religious
transgressions: they set up pillars and Asherahs for
themselves upon every high hill and under every leafy
tree, and burnt incense there, on all the high places
("*bamoth*"), as did the nations whom Yahweh expelled before them; commited evil acts, thereby anger-
ing Yahweh; served idols; made themselves molten
images of two calves; made an Asherah; bowed down
to the host of heaven; served Baal; caused their sons
and daughters to pass through the fire; and used divi-
nation and enchantment. As we see, this list of ritual
transgressions, although given in two parts separated
by several verses,[40] contains no repetition with the exception of the worship of Asherah: first it is stated that
the Israelites set up pillars and Asherahs for themselves upon every high hill and under every leafy
tree; then, that they made an Asherah—this time in singular.
The context clearly shows the reason for this repetition: the first mention, in plural, refers to the Asherahs
of village sanctuaries on hilltops; the second, to the
statue of Asherah which stood in Samaria, in the
royal chapel of the capital. The twofold mention of
Asherah alone indicates the relatively great importance

of the worship of this goddess among all the deities served by the Israelites down to their Assyrian exile.

On the basis of the above rapid survey, one can summarize the history of Asherah worship in Israel. The Goddess Asherah was worshiped in Israel from the days of the first settlement in Canaan, the Hebrews having taken over the cult of this great mother goddess from the Canaanites. For public worship, the goddess was represented by carved wooden images, implanted into the ground, usually next to an altar dedicated to the god Baal, and located on hilltops, under leafy trees. For private religious use, innumerable small clay figurines of Asherah were in circulation, showing the goddess in the nude, with the characteristic gesture of holding her own breasts in emphasis of her fertility aspect.

During the reign of Ahab, under the influence of his Sidonian wife Jezebel, the worship of Asherah received added impetus: a statue of Asherah, probably much more elaborate and impressive than the wooden images simple villages could afford, was made and set up in Samaria, making that city, Ahab's capital, the center of the Asherah cult. At the same time, Beth-el in the south and Dan in the north of the Israelite kingdom remained the centers of the court-approved cult of Yahweh, identified with the Canaanite deity who manifested himself in the shape of a bull-calf and was related to either Bull-El or his son Hadd, the Baal (i.e., the Lord) of the Ugaritic pantheon.

The cult of Asherah escaped the popular anti-Baal and pro-Yahweh uprising which, led by the prophet Elijah, took place under Ahab. Several years later, when all the Baalists were massacred and Baal's temple in Samaria destroyed by Jehu, the Asherah of Samaria again escaped unharmed, and her worship survived down to the end of the Israelite monarchy.

The Assyrians put an end to the Kingdom of Israel in 721 or 722 B.C.; yet at least one center of Asherah worship and one statue of the goddess Asherah survived the national catastrophe by a hundred years. As part of his great Yahwist reform, King Joshiah of

Judah, in or after the year 621 B.C., purged Beth-el of the remainder of the religious buildings and institutions erected there by Jeroboam more than 300 years previously. The terse one-verse notice, in which the Book of Kings reports this,[40a] states that Joshiah destroyed the altar and the high place (*bamah*) that Jeroboam had made, "and burned Asherah." No word in this notice about the Golden Calf which Jeroboam had set up for worship in Beth-el and against which Hosea found it necessary to prophesy as late as the second half of the 8th century B.C.,[40b] only a short time prior to the destruction of Israel. The Golden Calf was, in all probability, removed by the Assyrian invaders, and in its place new gods and cults were established all over Samaria, brought along by the new settlers from all parts of the Assyrian Empire.

Beth-el, a town lying some ten miles to the north of Jerusalem, while traditionally a part of the Kingdom of Israel, came under the rule of Judah when Joshiah succeeded in pushing the boundaries of his kingdom a few miles to the north of the old frontier between the two sister-states. In the century that had elapsed between the Assyrian conquest of Israel and this modest expansion of Judah, some remnants of the Israelite population must have managed to hold out in Beth-el, and it must have been they who carried on the worship of their old goddess Asherah. Thus the goddess survived all the upheavals that passed over Samaria during the Assyrian invasion and following it, until she fell under the axe of Joshiah, that last great Yahwist reformer among the Judaean kings, who could tolerate the worship of no other god besides Yahweh in any part of the country under his control.

How are we to explain the extraordinary hold Asherah exercised over the people of Israel? We can only make an informed guess to the effect that she answered the psychological need for a mother-goddess which was keenly felt by the people and its leaders alike throughout the centuries following the conquest of Canaan. Equally intriguing is the question: why was the Yahwist opposition to the Asherah worship

so much milder and, at any rate, so much less effective
than the struggle against Baal?

Could it be that even in the eyes of those with the
strongest pro-Yahwist sentiments, who were ready to
put to death every Baalist and eradicate all physical
traces of Baal worship, the cult of Asherah did not
appear as an equal ritual sin? Was the goddess perhaps regarded as complementary to, rather than com-
petitive with, Yahweh, and her worship therefore
tolerated? Or was the cult and the accompanying
belief so strongly entrenched in the populace that even
zealous Yahwists like Elijah, Jehu, and the Rechabites,
however offensive Asherah was in their eyes, did not
dare take action against her? Wherever the answer
lies, the continuity of Asherah worship in Israel is a
fact which must be recognized and remembered in
any attempt to trace the subsequent role played by the
concept of a female divinity in the popular religion of
the people of Judaea and their heirs, the Jews.

6. ASHERAH IN JUDAH

As far as it is possible to reconstruct the history of
Asherah worship in Judah from the terse Biblical
references, the goddess first penetrated the Jerusalem
Temple itself under Rehoboam, the son of Solomon
(ca. 928–911 B.C.). His mother, Naamah, was the
Ammonite wife of Solomon, under whose tutelage
Rehoboam must have been introduced to the worship
of Milcom. Rehoboam's favorite wife was Maacah, the
daughter of Abshalom [41]—that is to say, she was his
paternal cousin. Maacah bore several sons to Rehoboam; her eldest, Abijah or Abijam, was his father's
favorite, whom Rehoboam appointed to be chief over
his older sons by his other wives, and made him heir
to his throne during his lifetime. In all this one recog-
nizes, of course, Maacah's hand; her position remained
equally strong after her son Abijam actually succeeded

Rehoboam, when she assumed the position of *Gevi-rah*, or queen-mother.[42]

Maacah used her influence to introduce the Asherah already worshiped in Jerusalem since the days of Solomon, into the Temple itself.[43] During the short reign of Abijam (911–908 B.C.) the image of Asherah remained in its place; but Abijam's succession by Asa (908–867 B.C.) [44] marked the end of both Maacah's dominance as queen-mother and the worship of her Asherah. Under the influence of a prophet—a certain Azariah, the son of Oded—Asa, in the fifteenth year of his reign, instituted the first religious reform in the history of the Judaean Kingdom.[45] He "put away the detestable things [i.e., the appurtenances of idol worship] out of all the land of Judah and Benjamin," removed the sacred male prostitutes, and all the idols, took away the strange altars and the sun-images, broke down the pillars and hewed down the Asherahs, and, finally, removed the Asherah made by Maacah, made dust of it and burnt it in the Kidron Valley, at the same time deposing Maacah herself from her exalted position of queen-mother.[46]

One notes that the setting up of the Asherahs which Asa removed from all over the land of Judah is nowhere mentioned in the Biblical sources. This leads to the conclusion that this popular form of Asherah worship was a heritage from the pre-monarchic period discussed above.

Asa's son and successor, Jehoshafat (870–846 B.C.), continued his father's cleanup work: he removed, we are told, all the Asherahs from the countryside.[47] Although this was already done by Asa, he either did not complete the job or the Asherahs had sprung up again soon after they were removed by him. The seer Jehu, son of Hanani, complimented Jehoshafat for his zeal,[48] but even this victory of Yahwism over Asherism was short-lived.

Some ten years after the death of Jehoshafat, Joash (836–798 B.C.) ascended the throne of Judah. At first, under the influence of Jehoiada the priest, he

"did what was right in the eyes of Yahweh," and engaged in extensive restoration work in the Temple.
But, following the death of Jehoiada, Joash gave in to
the demands of the princes of Judah and led the people
back to the worship of the Asherahs and the idols. In
all probability, it was during this period that an image
of Asherah was reintroduced into the Temple itself,
where it remained until, a century later, King Hezekiah
(727–698 B.C.) removed it. By that time, the countryside too was again overrun by the traditional Canaanite cult objects, such as high places and pillars, and
all these were also removed, and destroyed by Hezekiah. In the Jerusalem Temple itself, Hezekiah "cut
down the Asherah and broke into pieces the Brazen
Serpent which Moses had made, for unto those days
the Children of Israel used to burn incense to it, and
it was called Nehushtan." [49] The Asherah referred to
must have been a statue which stood in the Temple,
just as the Brazen Serpent did and was worshiped
like it.

We do not know what was the precise connection
between Hezekiah's reforms and the activities of Isaiah
and Micah, the two great Yahwist prophets of his
day. It is, however, probable that the king's work
echoed the prophetic demand. For, in keeping with
their monotheistic Yahwist point of view, the prophets,
within the general framework of their overall opposition to any form of idolatry, spoke up against the
Asherah cult in particular. Isaiah regarded the breaking of the altar stones into pieces and the removal of
Asherahs and sun-images as the prerequisites for the
expiation of the nation's sin, although he expected this
to happen only at a future, indeterminate, date.[50] In
the same future day, Micah too expected witchcraft,
soothsaying, graven images, pillars, and Asherahs to
be uprooted from the midst of the people.[51]

However, no sooner was Hezekiah dead than his
son and heir Manasseh (698–642 B.C.) reverted to
the old religious customs. The chronicler dryly enumerates the sins of which the young king was guilty:

He rebuilt the high places which his father Hezekiah had destroyed; he set up altars for the Baal,
and made an Asherah, as did Ahab King of Israel,
and he bowed down to all the host of heaven,
and served them. And he built altars in the House
of Yahweh . . . for all the hosts of heaven, in the
two courts of the House of Yahweh. And he
made his son to pass through the fire, practiced
soothsaying, used enchantments, and appointed
them that divine by a ghost or a familiar spirit;
he wrought much evil in the sight of Yahweh
to anger Him. And he set the statue of the Asherah that he had made in the house [of Yah-
weh].[52]

The similarity between this list of ritual sins and
the one which is given as the causes which brought
about the destruction of Israel is striking.[53] What
interests us in the present context is one detail; in
both lists of transgressions Asherah alone of all the
idolatrous appurtenances is mentioned twice. The
reference to King Ahab indicates that Manasseh was
considered to have in some way imitated Ahab's
Asherah. It is also noteworthy that the only image
said to have been introduced into the Temple in the
course of Manasseh's restoration of old forms of worship was that of Asherah. If Manasseh did not bother
to replace the Brazen Serpent, the other image removed from the Temple by his father, this was probably due to the fact that with the passage of time the
worship of a deity symbolized or represented by a
serpent figure had become obsolete. Not so Asherah,
whose motherly figure must have been dear to many
worshipers and whose restoration to her traditional
place in the Temple was therefore considered a religious act of great importance. It is tempting to
conjecture that the mythical motivation behind Manasseh's act was the conviction that Yahweh's consort,
the great mother-goddess Asherah, must be restored
to her old and lawful place at the side of her husband.
With Joshiah (639–609 B.C.), another reformer

came to the throne whose Yahwist zeal, stimulated by
the discovery of the *Book of Deuteronomy* in the
eighteenth year of his reign, surpassed even that of
Hezekiah. The Deuteronomic legislation had no such
leniency towards Asherah as Elijah, Jehu, and the
Rechabites had displayed. Its point of view was unequivocal; it commanded the complete destruction of
the seven nations that had inhabited Canaan, prohibited intermarriage with them, and ordered their
altars to be broken down, their pillars to be dashed
to pieces, their Asherahs hewed down, and their graven
images burnt.[54] In addition, it warned:

> You shall not plant for yourself an Asherah, any
> tree, beside the altar of Yahweh your god which
> you shall make for yourself. Neither shall you
> set up a pillar, which Yahweh your god hates.[55]

In the remaining twelve years of his life and reign,
Joshiah carried out these commandments faithfully.
He had all the vessels that were part of the service
of Baal, the Asherah, and all the host of heaven
removed from the Temple and burned in the Kidron
Valley outside of Jerusalem. Then, as if afraid that
even the charred remains of these idolatrous utensils
might have power to defile, he had the ashes carried
to Beth-el, a place which he seems to have regarded
as of old contaminated by idolatrous practices. Following this, he brought out the image of Asherah
herself from the Temple, had it burned in the Kidron
Valley, ground it up into powder, and cast the dust
over the graves of those who had worshiped her. Next
he demolished the quarters of the Qedeshim, the sacred
male prostitutes, which were in the Temple and in
which the women wove "houses" (clothes?) for the
Asherah. Finally, he turned his attention to the countryside and cut down the Asherahs wherever they
were found, filling their places with human bones. In
a similar manner he destroyed, removed, and defiled
all the other high places and objects of idolatry which
were originally set up by Solomon.[56]

However, not even the most thorough and zealous Yahwist reform was able to eradicate the tenacious worship of Asherah. Following Joshiah's death, her worship, and that of her consort, Baal, with whom Yahweh was popularly identified, sprang up again all over the countryside. Consequently Jeremiah, whose main prophetic activity fell into the 23 years between Joshiah's death (609 B.C.) and the destruction of Jerusalem by Nebuchadnezzar (586 B.C.), again found it necessary to prophesy against idolatry in general, and Asherah worship in particular. Most frequently, it is true, Jeremiah reproaches his people for their worship of Baal.[57] He never mentions Astarte, whose cult seems to have disappeared from Judah with Joshiah's reform.[58] But he speaks up against the "altars and the Asherahs by leafy trees and upon high hills." [59]

To sum up, we find that the worship of Asherah, which had been popular among the Hebrew tribes for three centuries, was introduced into the Jerusalem Temple by King Rehoboam, the son of Solomon, in or about 928 B.C. Her statue was worshiped in the Temple for 35 years, until King Asa removed it in 893 B.C. It was restored to the Temple by King Joash in 825 B.C. and remained there for a full century, until King Hezekiah removed it in 725 B.C. After an absence of 27 years, however, Asherah was back again in the Temple: This time it was King Manasseh who replaced her in 698 B.C. She remained in the Temple for 78 years, until the great reformer King Joshiah removed her in 620 B.C. Upon Joshiah's death eleven years later (609 B.C.), she was again brought back into the Temple, where she remained until its destruction 23 years later, in 586 B.C. Thus it appears that, of the 370 years during which the Solomonic Temple stood in Jerusalem, for no less than 236 years (or almost two-thirds of the time) the statue of Asherah was present in the Temple, and her worship was a part of the legitimate religion approved and led by the king, the court, and the priesthood and opposed by only a few prophetic voices crying out against it at relatively long intervals.

7. EZEKIEL'S "IMAGE OF JEALOUSY"

The years immediately preceding Josiah's reform or following his death must be the time recalled by Ezekiel in his great vision of the sins of Judah which, in his prophecy, appear as the cause of her impending doom. There is, to be sure, no consensus of scholarly opinion on the subject, and some Biblical scholars think that Ezekiel refers to the very time in which the vision came upon him, that is, the year 592 B.C., six years after the exile of Jehoiakim and six years before the destruction of Jerusalem.[60]

The vision itself, whether based on more than thirty-year-old memories or on fresh intelligence (such as a visit to Jerusalem or reports), contains the most detailed account of idolatrous practices in the Jerusalem Temple found in the entire Bible. The prophet, while being visited in his house in Chaldaea by the elders of Judah, suddenly feels the hand of the Lord Yahweh upon him, sees Him as a blinding fiery apparition, feels His hand taking hold of him by a lock of his hair, lifting him up between heaven and earth and taking him to Jerusalem, and depositing him there at the northern gate of the inner Temple court.

Then God points out to Ezekiel one by one the "abominations" being committed by the "house of Israel" in His sanctuary: first He shows him the "Image of Jealousy, which provokes to jealousy," standing near the northern gate which leads to the altar. Then, on the inside wall of the court, or of the Temple building itself, He shows him reliefs of creeping things and beasts and of all kinds of idols, being worshiped by seventy elders of Israel led by Jaazaniah, the son of Shaphan: each has a censer in his hand, out of which clouds of incense billow upwards. Thence God takes Ezekiel to the northern gate of the Temple

itself and there shows him the women sitting and
weeping for the Tammuz. The next stop is in front
of the Temple, between the hall and the altar, where
the prophet sees some 25 men prostrating themselves
to the rising sun, with their backs turned to the Temple
of Yahweh. All this, Ezekiel hears God tell him, provokes Him utterly: His punishment will be unspar-
ing.[61]

Ezekiel's visionary enumeration of idolatrous practices is arranged in a crescendo: every next rite
mentioned is a "greater abomination" than the preceding one.[62] Taken literally, this means that, in the
judgment of Ezekiel, the presence of the "Image of
Jealousy" was considered the smallest sin, followed
in increasing order by the burning of incense to creeping things, beasts, and other idols, the mourning of
Tammuz, and finally the worship of the sun.

Apart from the fact that the "Image of Jealousy"
is regarded by Ezekiel as the least of all the idolatrous
transgressions seen by him in his vision, there is one
significant difference between it and the rest: in speaking of all the other sins, he describes and condemns
idolatrous *acts*: the reliefs on the wall are worshiped
by burning incense to them; the Tammuz—by mourning; the sun—by prostrations. Only the "Image" has
no worshipers: it merely stands in its place, its mere
presence a sin of the house of Israel.

What was this "Image of Jealousy"?[63] Biblical
scholars generally accept the view that it was the statue
of Asherah set up in the Temple by King Manasseh.
If so, we have here some independent contemporary
testimony to the presence of Asherah in the last years
of the Jerusalem Temple. Since, as we have seen
above, following the death of Joshiah, the Asherah
worship was reestablished all over the countryside, it
was to be expected that it would be restored in the
Jerusalem Temple as well. This is borne out by the
testimony of Ezekiel's vision.

8. CONCLUSION

It is on this note that we take leave of the Biblical Asherah, this elusive yet tenacious goddess to whom considerable segments of the Hebrew nation remained devoted from the days of the conquest of Canaan down to the Babylonian exile, a period of roughly six centuries. In the eyes of the Yahwists, to whom belonged a few of the kings and all of the prophets, the worship of Asherah was an abomination. It had to be, because it was a cult accepted by the Hebrews from their Canaanite neighbors, and any and all manifestations of Canaanite religion were for them anathema. How Asherah was served by the Hebrews we do not know, apart from the one obscure and tantalizing detail of the women weaving "houses," perhaps clothes, for her in the Jerusalem Temple.

Yet whatever her origin and whatever her cult, there can be no doubt about the psychological importance that the belief in, and service of, Asherah had for the Hebrews. One cannot belittle the emotional gratification with which she must have rewarded her servants who saw in her the loving, motherly consort of Yahweh-Baal and for whom she was the great mother-goddess, giver of fertility, that greatest of all blessings. The Hebrew people, by and large, clung to her for six centuries in spite of the increasing vigor of Yahwist monotheism. From the vantage point of our own troubled age, in which monotheism has long laid the ghosts of paganism, idolatry, and polytheism, only to be threatened by the much more formidable enemy of materialistic atheism, we can permit ourselves to look back, no longer with scorn but with sympathy, at the goddess who had her hour and whose motherly touch softened the human heart just about to open to greater things.

Chapter II

ASTARTE-ANATH

It is a typical feature of Ancient Near Eastern and Mediterranean religions that the divinities who people their pantheons form family groups and belong to at least two successive generations. In Chapter V we shall have a closer look at the manner in which this old Near Eastern concept re-emerged in the Kabbalistic mythology of the 13th and 16th centuries. In the present chapter, we propose to discuss the goddess who was considered along the east coast of the Mediterranean the daughter of Asherah and her husband El, and who at times and in certain places overshadowed her mother in popularity and in the hold she exercised on human imagination and emotion.

Her proper name was Anath. However, she was equally well known, far beyond the boundaries of Syria and Palestine, by the name Astarte (Hebrew: 'Ashtoreth, or, in plural 'Ashtaroth), which seems originally to have been her most favored epithet. It is characteristic of the unsatisfactory state of our knowledge of the history of ancient Canaanite religion, that we cannot as yet be sure whether Anath and Astarte were originally one and the same goddess or two separate female deities who, in the course of gradual development, became identified. In the following we shall have to leave this problem unsolved and discuss separately first Astarte and then Anath, while presenting also the data which connect the two goddesses.

1. THE CANAANITE ASTARTE

Most of the chief gods of ancient Syria, to judge from the Ugaritic sources, had two names; occasionally one was a proper name and the other an epithet. As we have seen above, the Lady Asherah of the Sea was also referred to as Elath, that is Goddess. Her husband, properly named Father Shunem, was in most cases styled El (i.e., "God"), or Bull El. Asherah's son Hadd is most always called Baal or Master. The Divine Mot is also called El's Darling Ghazir. Another god is alternatingly called Prince Yamm (Sea) and Judge Nahar (River). In like fashion, Asherah's daughter seems to be called either Anath or Astarte ('Ashtoreth).

Two names for a deity are a prosodic requirement for classical Semitic poetry, a favorite device of which is the reduplication of significant statements without a repetition of the same words. In order to be able to express the same idea in two parallel sentences, using two sets of synonymous words, the Semitic poet had to have at his disposal two names for his gods who figure so prominently in his mythological poems. The following examples, all taken from the Ugaritic tablets, illustrate the point:

> Then came the messengers of Yamm,
> The envoys of Judge Nahar . . .[1]

Or:

> She penetrates El's field and enters
> The pavilion of King Father Shunem.[2]

Or:

> And say unto Divine Mot.
> Declare unto El's Darling Ghazir.[3]

Or:

> He cries to Asherah and her children,
> To Elath and the band of her kindred.[4]

In the same way, the names Anath and Astarte appear in parallel positions making it probable that the two names refer to one and the same goddess:

> Whose fairness is like Anath's fairness
> Whose beauty like 'Ashtoreth's beauty.[5]

Or in another passage where the first part of the crucial name Anath has to be conjecturally completed:

> His right hand (Ana)th seizes
> 'Ashtoreth seizes his left hand.[6]

Such Semitic refinements of style were lost on the Egyptians, and thus we read in a 12th-century B.C. hieratic papyrus that Neith, the Great, the God's Mother, demands that the Ennead (the nine great gods) should thus address the All-Lord, the Bull Residing in Heliopolis: "Double Seth in his property; give him Anath and Astarte, your two daughters . . ." [7] Other Egyptian documents, some as early as the 13th century B.C., also show that Anath and Astarte were accepted in Egyptian religion as two separate goddesses of war.[8] By the 18th Dynasty, Astarte had become a goddess of healing in Egypt, referred to as "Astar of Syria." [9] Rameses III calls Anath and Astarte "his shield." [10] Both Anath and Astarte, as well as a third goddess derived from the Canaanite-Syrian pantheon, Qadesh, bore the Egyptian title "Lady of Heaven." (See Plate 25.) An Egyptian stele erected in Beisan, Palestine, in the 12th century B.C., shows an Egyptian worshiping the goddess "Anath, Lady of Heaven, Mistress of all the gods." Of the three, Astarte seems to have been the most popular in Egypt; she had her own priests and prophets [12] as Asherah had in Israel. Also in Moab the name of Astarte appears with the omission of the feminine ending, as 'Ashtar and is coupled with Chemosh on the Moabite Stone of ca. 830 B.C.[13] Astarte seems to have been the consort of Chemosh, Moab's national god.

A Canaanite city, called 'Ashtarot or 'Ashtartu, in the Bashan, is mentioned in several Egyptian documents from the 18th century B.C. on, as well as in the Amarna letters which date from the 14th century B.C.[14]

At a much later period Astarte became the chief goddess of Sidon, replacing Asherah. When this transition occurred is unknown, but by the 4th century B.C. it was completed as can be concluded from the fact that at that time the kings of Sidon were also the priests of Astarte and their wives had the title "priestess of Astarte." However, the changeover could not have taken place much earlier, because a century later Sidonian king Eshmun'azar reports that he and his mother built a temple for Astarte in Sidon-by-the-Sea and Shamem-Addirim, two sections of Byblos; in other words, in his days the cult of Astarte was still spreading in Phoenicia. The same inscription of Eshmun'azar which contains the above details also tells us the full Sidonian name of Astarte: it was 'Ashtart-Shem-Baal, i.e., "Astarte of the Name of Baal." Astarte and Eshmun, "the Holy Prince, the Lord of Sidon," were termed "the gods of Sidon." [15] The name " 'Ashtoreth of the Name of Baal" occurred to the north of Sidon over a thousand years earlier: this is how the goddess, in all probability Anath, is called in two passages on the Ugaritic tablets.[16]

This is more or less the gist of what we know about Astarte from Canaanite and Phoenician sources.[17] As we shall see later, the Canaanite mythical material about Anath is much more abundant.

2. ASTARTE IN THE BIBLE

In passing now to an examination of the Biblical references to Astarte, let us begin with those which show the clearest correspondence with the extra-Bibli-

cal sources. The city of 'Ashtartu [18] in the Bashan is
referred to several times in the Bible, as a city of
Levites. Once it is called Be'eshterah,[19] once 'Ash-
terah,[20] but usually 'Ashtaroth, in the plural form
which is frequently employed in Biblical place names.[21]
'Ashtaroth was originally the capital city of Og, the
legendary giant king of Bashan,[22] and of his people
the Rephaim who were smitten by Chedorlaomer.[23]
This last mentioned detail is contained in an old semi-
historical, semi-mythical account which is the only reference to retain the full old name of the city:
'Ashteroth-Qarnaim (i.e., "Astarte of the Two Horns").
The concept behind this designation is graphically
illustrated by several Astarte-figurines found at various archaeological sites in Palestine and actually showing the goddess with two horns.[24] (See Plates 9 and
10.)

The original meaning of the name Astarte ('Ashtoreth) was "womb" or "that which issues from the
womb." [25] Such a meaning is most appropriate as an
appellative for a goddess of fertility: she is called
"she of the womb," i.e., the inducer, as well as
symbol, of female fertility, just as her brother-consort
Baal was the inducer and symbol of male fertility.[26]
Thus the primary meaning of the names of the divine
couple Baal and Astarte was begetter and conceiver,
man and woman, husband and wife.

This being the case, the name 'Ashtoreth or Astarte
must have originally been but an epithet of the goddess
whose proper name was Anath, just as Baal (Master)
was the epithet of the god whose proper name was
Hadd.[27]

Now as to the Biblical references to the goddess
Astarte, the first mention of her worship by the
Hebrews comes from the early period of the Judges,
soon after the penetration into Canaan: "And they
forsook Yahweh and served the Baal and the 'Ashtaroth." [28] A little later more explicitly:

And the children of Israel again did that which
was evil in the sight of Yahweh, and served the

Baalim and the 'Ashtaroth, the gods of Aram,
and the gods of Sidon, and the gods of Moab,
and the gods of the children of Ammon, and the
gods of the Philistines, and they forsook Yahwah
and served him not.[29]

The first purge of these Baals and Astartes took place
at the bidding of Samuel, and was immediately followed by a decisive intervention by Yahweh in favor
of His people in their battle against the Philistines.
As to the Philistines themselves, their Astarte must
have been a goddess of war as well as that of love
and fertility, and this is why, when the Philistines
defeated Saul, they deposited his armor in the Temple
of 'Ashtaroth, undoubtedly as a token of gratitude.

In Chapter I we argued that the goddess whose
worship Solomon introduced into Jerusalem in honor
of his Sidonian wife was none other than Asherah,
the Elath of Sidon. As a result of a confusion between
Asherah and Astarte, which, as we have seen, began
with the 14th century B.C. Amarna letters and whose
sporadic traces can be found down to our present day,
the Hebrew historian of the Solomonic era repeatedly
refers to the goddess of whose worship Solomon was
guilty as " 'Ashtoreth, the goddess of the Sidonians." [32]
In a reference to the same goddess at a later time,
she is no longer accorded the title "goddess" but
instead is called " 'Ashtoreth, the detestation of the
Sidonians." [33] This is how she is spoken of by the
historian who records that King Joshiah of Judah
defiled the high places which Solomon had built for
'Ashtoreth.

3. THE ARCHAEOLOGICAL EVIDENCE

The Goddess Astarte is mentioned only nine times
in the Bible as against the forty times that Asherah
is referred to. The Bible thus fails to convey any idea
as to the prevalence of the worship of Astarte among

the Hebrews. A somewhat better idea can be gained from the archaeological evidence that has come to light in excavations conducted in the last few decades in many parts of Palestine. By the early 1940's, a total of no less than 300 terracotta figurines and plaques representing a nude female figure had been unearthed. These nudes fall into several distinct types, such as those with arms extended to the sides and holding stalks or serpents, or with hands holding the breasts, or with one hand placed over one breast and the other over the genital region, or with hands crossed before the breasts. Some are figures of pregnant women, other pillar figurines, etc. The persistence and ubiquity of these figurines is remarkable. They have been found in every major excavation in Palestine, and their prevalence extends from Middle Bronze (2000–1500 B.C.) to Early Iron II (900–600 B.C.), that is, to the end of the period of the divided Israelite monarchy, and even later. The so-called Qadesh-type is clearly associated by its symbolism with a goddess; the other types are assumed by most scholars to have been representations of the goddesses Asherah, Astarte, or Anath, although no direct or definite identification could be made so far. According to a very cautious view, it is still an open question whether the figurines represented "the goddess herself, a prostitute of the cult of the goddess," or were talismans "used in sympathetic magic to stimulate the reproductive processes of nature." [34] (See Plates 11–18.)

In the following remarks we shall concentrate on one single site which has been studied more thoroughly and systematically than probably any other in the country. This is Tell Beit Mirsim, to the southwest of Hebron, today on the Israeli-Jordanian border. The Tell (mound of ruins) was excavated in the course of several years by William F. Albright and identified as the Biblical town Devir.[35] The systematic archaeological study of this tell has shown that the site was first occupied by Canaanites in the Early Bronze Age, Period 4 (ca. 21st century B.C.), that it flourished

during the Middle and Late Bronze Ages (ca. 21st–
13th centuries B.C.), and that it was destroyed towards
the end of the 13th century, evidently by the Hebrews
who at that time conquered the area. In the beginning of the Early Iron Age (12th century B.C.) the
town was resettled by the Hebrews, and it flourished
until the end of the 6th century B.C., when it was
destroyed in the course of the general devastation of
Judaea at the time of the First Exile (586 B.C.). All
in all, there were in Devir some ten or eleven periods
of occupation. The town itself was larger than the
average Israelite towns of the First Temple period,
measuring about 7½ acres inside the walls.[36]

The old name of the town was Kiriath-Sepher,
meaning "Book City." At an undetermined date this
name was changed to Devir, which is the Biblical
term for the Holy of Holies of the Jerusalem Temple.[37]
The name seems to indicate that there was a temple
or sanctuary in Devir, which is reported to have been
given "unto the children of Aaron the priest," together
with eight other cities in the territories of Judah and
Simeon.[38]

Whether or not the town played a special role in
the religious life of the Canaanites prior to the Israelite
occupation, we do not know. It is, however, a patent
fact that the commonest religious objects found in the
Late Bronze levels (21st–13th centuries B.C.) of Tell
Beit Mirsim are the so-called Astarte plaques, made
of clay, generally oval in shape, bearing the impress
(from a pottery or metal mold) of the nude figure
of the goddess Astarte. In many cases she holds her
arms upraised, grasping lily stalks or serpents or both.
The goddess' head is adorned with two long spiral
ringlets identical with the Egyptian Hathor ringlets,
or she wears a Philistine-type helmet. Other plaques
show the goddess with her arms hanging down, or
with her hands clasped together under her protruding
navel. These plaques go back to earlier prototypes
found in Mesopotamia, where they have a long prehistory in the Early Bronze. Other types of naked

goddesses, both plaques and figurines, also occur.[39] (See Plates 19–23.)

When we come to the Israelite layers (12th–6th centuries B.C.), the character of the finds changes. In Stratum A alone, stemming from the 8th and 7th centuries B.C., no less than 38 recognizable examples of female figurines were found, as well as many more fragments of such figures. These differ from the Astarte plaques, inasmuch as these Israelite naked female figures wear none of the insignia of the earlier or contemporary Canaanite goddesses. One must assume that these figures do not represent Astarte; they have a style and appearance of their own, with a broader face emphasized by the straight horizontal hairline across the forehead, with curly hair framing the face as well, and with no trace of the horns or "Hathor" ringlets characterizing the Canaanite Astarte. The breasts are usually strongly emphasized, but below them the body line becomes that of a pillar, with its base flaring outward, which indicates that these figurines were intended to stand up unsupported.[40] Because of the pillar-like appearance of these figurines, some scholars suggest that they may have been clay representations of Asherah, the goddess whose larger images were carved out of tree trunks.

However that may be, the archaeological evidence leaves no doubt that these figurines were very popular among the Hebrews in the period of the divided Kingdom. "The clay molds were doubtless made by a few potters who were good sculptors, and these men [non-Israelites] would sell their molds to ordinary Israelite potters scattered throughout the land." [41] One type of these nude fertility figurines, representing women in the process of parturition, was probably used as a charm to bring fruitfulness to women or to ensure an easy delivery. Seals with Hebrew names, such as Elyaqim, Yoyakhin, etc., found in the same Stratum A, prove beyond a doubt that these female figurines were made and bought by Israelites who used them for religious purposes.[42]

4. THE UGARITIC MYTH OF ANATH

As mentioned above, the Canaanite mythical material about Anath is abundant. This is due to the discovery and decipherment of the alphabetic cuneiform tablets of Ugarit, written in a language closely resembling Hebrew and dating from the 14th century B.C. In Ugaritic mythology, Anath is the by far most important female figure, the goddess of love and war, virginal and yet wanton, amorous and yet given to uncontrollable outbursts of rage and appalling acts of cruelty. She is the daughter of El, the god of heaven, and of his wife the Lady Asherah of the Sea. She has so many features in common with the Sumerian Inanna and the Akkadian Ishtar that one must regard her as heir and kin of those great Mesopotamian goddesses.[43]

However, instead of being concerned primarily with finding ever new divine, human, and animal bedfellows, as Ishtar was reputed to have been, Anath spent most of her energies on the battlefield. She too, to be sure, was a typical goddess of love, both chaste and promiscuous. Her character is aptly epitomized in a 13th-century B.C. Egyptian text in which she and Astarte are called "the goddesses who conceive but do not bear," meaning that they are perennially fruitful without ever losing their virginity. In the Ugaritic myths her constant epithet is "the maiden Anath" or "the Virgin Anath." And, as late an author as Philo Byblius, who flourished in the early 2nd century A.D., still refers to the virginity of Anath, whom he identifies with Athena, the famous virgin goddess of the Greeks. Like Ishtar, Anath was called "lady of heaven, mistress of all the gods," and, again like Ishtar, she loved gods, men, and animals. (See Plate 24.)

Her foremost lover was her brother Baal. When she approached, Baal dismissed his other wives, and she, in preparation for the union with him, bathed in sky-dew and rubbed herself with ambergris from a

sperm whale. The actual intercourse between Anath
and Baal is described with a graphic explicitness
which is unique even among the unrestrained accounts
of love-making usual in ancient Near Eastern texts.
In a place called Dubr, Baal lay seventy-seven times
with Anath, who assumed the shape of a heifer for
the occasion, and, it appears, that the wild bull born
to Baal was the issue of this union. A mortal lover
of Anath was Aqhat, whom, after what must have
been an intimate tête-à-tête (description unfortunately
missing), Anath addressed as "My darling great big
he-man!" On the motherly side, Anath was said to
have been one of the two wetnurses of the gods, to
have given suck to a son of King Keret, and one of
her appellations was "Progenitress of the Peoples." In
Egypt, Anath came to be regarded as the wife of the
god Seth, and an Egyptian magical text from the 13th
century B.C. describes in surprisingly sadistic terms
how Seth deflowers Anath on the seashore.

Yet all these adventures in the fields of love pale
to insignificance next to Anath's great exploits in war
and strife. In fact, no ancient Near Eastern goddess
was more bloodthirsty than she. She was easily provoked to violence and, once she began to fight, would
go berserk, smiting and killing right and left. One
sees her plunge into fighting with real pleasure: she
smites the peoples of both East and West, so that
their heads fly like sheaves and their hands like
locusts. Not satisfied with this, she binds the severed
heads to her back and the cut-off hands to her girdle,
and plunges knee-deep in the blood of troops and
hip-deep in the gore of heroes. Now she is in her
element: her liver swells with laughter, her heart fills
up with joy.

It was this bloodthirsty and warlike Anath whose
worship penetrated Egypt sometime prior to the 13th
century B.C. She was, for the Egyptians as well,
"Anath, Lady of Heaven, Mistress of All the Gods,"
a war-goddess who was associated with horses and
chariots and who, equipped with shield and spear,

protected the Pharaoh. Indeed, because of her warlike nature, Anath in Egypt was called "the goddess, the victorious, a woman acting as a man, clad as a male and girt as a female." [44]

5. ANATH IN THE BIBLE

It is a remarkable fact that the name Anath is never mentioned in the Bible as that of a foreign goddess. The explanation seems to be that the Biblical authors referred to her by her epithet 'Ashtoreth rather than by her proper name, just as they referred to her Canaanite-Phoenician brother and lover by his epithet Baal ("Lord") rather than by his proper name, Hadd.

This, however, does not mean that the proper name Anath is entirely absent from the Bible. Mention is made of a Canaanite town in the territory of Naphtali called Beth Anath ("House of Anath"),[45] whose inhabitants were subjugated but not dispossessed by the Hebrews. Better-known is the priestly town of Anathoth, north of Jerusalem (today Anatha) which was located in the territory of Benjamin and was the birthplace of Jeremiah and other Biblical figures.[46] Place names such as these point to some connection with the goddess Anath; most probably, their founders named them after the goddess and in her honor, in accordance with the custom prevalent all over pre-Biblical and Biblical Palestine to name localities after deities.

Anathoth is the plural of Anath (as 'Ashtaroth is of Ashtoreth, or Baalim is of Baal), and it indicates generalization of the concept; the town was not named after any local Anath in particular, but after the Anaths in general who manifested themselves in many places. The same form, Anathoth, appears also as the name of two men: one of them, a grandson of Benjamin, lived in the early days of the Israelite judges; the other, a contemporary of Nehemiah, after the

return from the Babylonian exile.[47] From the days of
the Judges the name of another individual survived,
in the singular: one of the Judges themselves, we
read, was a son of Anath. One single heroic deed is
reported of this Judge, Shamgar son of Anath: he
"smote of the Philistines six hundred men with an ox-
goad" and thus saved Israel.[48] It is tempting to conjecture that Anath was the name of the mother (and
not of the father) of Shamgar, and that in the brief
notice there is a residue of an old myth about a son of
the goddess Anath who inherited his mother's warlike
qualities. The ox-goad Shamgar used as a weapon reminds us of the two bludgeons, Ayamur ("Driver")
and Yagrush ("Chaser"), which Baal, Anath's brother
and lover, used to defeat his arch-enemy Yamm.[49]

The last Biblical reference to Astarte-Anath does
not contain either of these names but refers to the
goddess as "Queen of Heaven." As we shall recall,
the title "Lady of Heaven" was given to Anath and
Astarte by their Egyptian worshipers,[50] which makes
it more likely that the "Queen of Heaven" who formed
the subject of a heated argument between Jeremiah
and his Judaean fellow-refugees in Egypt was none
other than the "virgin Anath," the "maid" Astarte.
Jeremiah was convinced, and tried to convince also
the remnant of Judah in Egypt, that the great national
catastrophe that had befallen them had come about
as a punishment by Yahweh for the people's sin of
idolatry. Unless they would repent, the prophet
warned them, they would all perish in Egypt as the
others had in Judaea.

But the people's interpretation of the downfall of
Judaea was diametrically opposed to that of Jeremiah.
They too recognized that the calamity that had overtaken them was a divine punishment for a religious
sin, but a sin which, they felt, they had committed
against the Queen of Heaven and not against Yahweh.
The answer given to Jeremiah by "all the people that
dwelt in the Land of Egypt, in Pathros" [51] therefore
was:

As for the word that you have spoken to us in
the name of Yahweh—we shall not listen to you.
But we shall without fail do everything as we
said: we shall burn incense to the Queen of
Heaven, and shall pour her libations as we used
to do, we, our fathers, our kings and our princes,
in the cities of Judah and in the streets of Jerusalem. For then we had plenty of food, and we all
were well and saw no evil. But since we ceased
burning incense to the Queen of Heaven and to
pour her libations, we have wanted everything
and have been consumed by sword and famine.

To these words the women added:

Is it that we alone burn incense to the Queen
of Heaven and pour her libations? Is it without
our husbands that we make her cakes in her
image and that we pour her libations?" [52]

This unique passage allows us a glimpse of the
actual ritual of the Hebrew Astarte worship. The rites
were led by kings of Judah and her princes; its participants were the men, women, and children of the
people; the locale was Jerusalem and the other cities
of the realm. About the ritual itself we learn more
details from another passage in Jeremiah in which the
prophet is addressed by God as follows:

Do you not see what they do in the cities of
Judah and in the streets of Jerusalem? The children gather wood and the fathers kindle the fire,
and the women knead the dough to make cakes
to the Queen of Heaven and to pour out libations
to other gods, in order to anger Me! [53]

The two passages together contain the following
features of the ritual performed in honor of the Queen
of Heaven:

1. The children were sent to gather wood.
2. The fathers lit the fire.

3. The women kneaded dough and made cakes.

4. The cakes were baked over fire.

5. The women, assisted by the men, burnt incense; and

6. Poured out libations.

7. They poured libations to other gods as well.

8. In return for this veneration, the Queen of Heaven was believed to provide the people with plenty of food and to secure their well-being in general.

9. It can be asumed that the Kings of Judah led the ritual in Jerusalem, and the princes in the other cities.

10. The burning of incense, the offering up of cakes, and the pouring of libations presuppose altars, which, in turn, may have stood either in sanctuaries in the cities or on "high places" in the countryside.

The lighting of fire on altars, the burning of incense, and the pouring of libations are all rites well known from both the Jerusalem Temple and the other ancient Near Eastern rituals. Only the baking of cakes requires a word of explanation.

In Athens, Artemis was honored with round cakes called *selenai*, which represented the moon. A Babylonian hymn on Ishtar mentions the *kamanu*, sacrificial cakes, offered her. If Hebrew *kawwan* ("cake") is, in fact, derived from Babylonian-Assyrian *kamanu*, then it is likely that the Queen of Heaven worshiped in Jerusalem corresponded to the Babylonian-Assyrian Ishtar, who is referred to as *Sharrat Shame*, Queen of Heaven, and similar titles.[54]

A recent archaeological find enables us to think of another explanation. In the course of excavations conducted at Nahariah (in Israel, north of Acre), on a *bamah* ("high place"), a stone mold was found dating from the 17th century B.C. The mold was used for casting small figures of the goddess Astarte—her identity is clearly indicated by the two horns which protrude to the left and right over her ears. She is "Astarte of the Horns," standing naked, except for her tall, conical headdress, looking down at her protruding navel, with an enigmatic smile on her lips.[55] (See Plate 9.) Could it be that such molds were used to bake cakes in the shape of Astarte, either to be eaten by the celebrants (perhaps as a precursor of the Holy Communion in which the Host, which is supposed actually to turn into the body of Christ, is eaten) or to be burnt on the altar? More data will be needed before this question can be answered, but the possibility that this is what was meant by the cakes in the image of the Queen of Heaven is an intriguing one.[56]

If the equation of the Queen of Heaven with Anath-Astarte is correct, as we believe it to be, then we can determine the period recalled by the Judaean exiles in Egypt as the time of their devoted Astarte worship. As we have seen above, the service of Astarte was forcibly terminated by King Joshiah.[57] Joshiah's reforms were carried out beginning with the 18th year of his reign,[58] that is, after the year 621 B.C. The controversy between Jeremiah and the people about the Queen of Heaven must have taken place within a year or two after the arrival of the Judaean refugees in Egypt, say, in 585 B.C. The Astarte ritual, forbidden by Joshiah only 36 years previously, could therefore have been quite well remembered by the older Judaean exiles in Egypt. Since Jeremiah began his prophetic activities in the 13th year of King Joshiah's reign,[59] that is, in 626 B.C., his description of the worship of the Queen of Heaven in Jerusalem and the other cities of Judah must date from the five years that elapsed between 626 B.C. and the reforms of Joshiah in 621.

That the Judaean exiles meant what they said to Jeremiah is proved by their history in the subsequent two centuries. In the Jewish military colony at Hermopolis in Egypt, the worship of the Queen of Heaven was pursued in the 5th century B.C. Her temple is mentioned in an Aramaic papyrus from that community, side by side with those of other deities.[60]

The last mention of the name of the old goddess in a Jewish environment comes some 175 years after

the determined vow of the Judaeans in Egypt to return
to the worship of the Queen of Heaven. In one of the
letters written by a member of the Upper Egyptian
Jewish military colony on the island of Elephantine,
dating from 419 or 400 B.C., it is stated that Yedoniah,
the son of Gemariah, who was the priest and head
of the Jewish community, had collected the following
donations: for Yaho (i.e., Yahweh) 12 karash and 6
shekels; for Ishumbethel 7 karash; and for Anathbethel
12 karash.[61] Since each contributor gave 2 shekels,
and 20 shekels made 1 karash, one can easily calculate
that, in addition to the 123 contributors who "gave
money to the God Yaho" and whose names are
enumerated in the Aramaic document, there were 70
who gave their two shekels each to Ishumbethel and
120 who gave the same amount each to Anathbethel.
Ishumbethel was a male, and Anathbethel a female,
Aramaean deity. In the name Anathbethel the two
elements Anath and Bethel are unmistakable. It has
been argued that these two deities were worshiped by
non-Jewish Aramaeans who lived in Elephantine and
for whom Jedoniah acted as treasurer or banker.[62]
This is unlikely for two reasons. Firstly, it is not
probable that members of competing rival religious
sects should entrust their cultic donations to the hands
of a man who was the leader of another religious
group. The keen religious rivalries which are known
to have been a feature of life in Elephantine would
have prevented this.[63] Secondly, in at least one letter
written by an Elephantinian Jew to another, blessings
are invoked of Yaho and another deity,[64] which proves
that the Jews of the island could and did worship,
along with Yahweh, other deities as well.

Chapter III

THE CHERUBIM

Whenever and wherever images were worshiped by the Hebrews, as it frequently happened in the period which ended with the Babylonian captivity of 586 B.C., such practices were always and uncompromisingly condemned in the Biblical and later sources as idolatrous abominations. The legal crystallization of this attitude was the commandment which ruled out the making and worshiping of "graven images or any manner of likeness." Biblical and subsequent Jewish religion has, therefore, justly been called "aniconic."

However, it is the exception that proves the rule. In the case of aniconic Judaism the exception was represented by the Cherubim, those winged human figures which were an integral part, and according to at least one Rabbinic opinion, the most important part, of all the Hebrew and Jewish sanctuaries and temples. The Cherubim were, by any criteria, "graven images," and yet they continued to figure prominently in the Temple ritual down to the very end of the Second Jewish Commonwealth (70 A.D.). Moreover, in their last version the Cherubim depicted a man and a woman in sexual embrace—an erotic representation which was considered obscene by the pagans when they at last had a chance to glimpse it. And nevertheless, the entire contemporary and subsequent Hebrew-Jewish literature contains not a word that could in the remotest be construed as a condemnation of the Cherubim. On the contrary, their presence in the Holy of Holies, the innermost sanctuary of the Temple, and the ritual significance attributed to them, are invariably referred to as a most sacred mystery. Only the Hellenistic Jewish authors, such as the philosopher Philo of Alexandria and the ex-priest Josephus Flavius, speak about the Cherubim with an embarrassment obviously created by the apprehension lest the pagan Greek readers for whom they wrote consider the Cherubim as but the Jewish equivalent of the statues of their own gods and goddesses and thus find a basis to refute and reject the claim that the Jews worshiped only the one invisible God.

Since one of the two Cherubim was a female figure, we find that, in addition to the Canaanite goddesses whose worship was condemned by the Hebrew prophets and Jewish sages, the Temple of Jerusalem contained a representation of the female principle which was considered legitimate at all times. It is to an examination of the Cherubim, their history, their changing appearance and their evolving symbolism that the present chapter is devoted.

1. THE IVORY CHERUBIM

Excavations in Samaria in the palace of King Ahab of Israel (873–852 B.C.) have brought to light a number of small ivory plaques whose presence in that royal residence earned it the name "Ivory House." [1] Among them is one which shows two crouching female figures facing each other. The women are shown in profile, with both arms stretched forward, and underneath each arm is a wing whose upper edge seems to adhere to the lower contours of the arm. In each hand the figures hold an object which seems to be a large flower, probably a lotus. The upper body of the figures is upright; their legs are bent so that their knees protrude forward toward each other and their buttocks rest on their upturned heels. The arms and legs are naked, but around the shoulders they wear

wide, fringed collars, and breast-plates hang down
from their necks. Their heads, covered by Egyptian-
type head-cloths which bind their foreheads tightly
and flow freely down over the shoulders behind the
ears, are crowned by a hollow, ring-like ornament
rising vertically upward. Between the two figures is a
vertical ritual object, with the same kind of ring on
top, and under it a four-tiered structure supported
by slender, out-turned legs. This object engages the
attention of the two figures who seem to shield or
fan it with their wings.[2] (See Plate 26.)

Whatever the actual purpose of this ivory plaque,
it is the closest illustration found to date of the
Cherubim, which in the Solomonic Temple shielded
the Ark in the Holy of Holies—closest not only in
general arrangement and detail, but also in time of
provenance and place of discovery, as well as origin
since both Solomon's and Ahab's Cherubim point to
Phoenician workmanship. Of all this we shall have
more to say later, but one detail should be stressed
already here: the two genii from Ahab's ivory palace
are *female* figures.

A very similar pair of winged protective female
genii is shown on an Egyptian relief from Karnak,
from the time of Thutmoses II (ca. 1500 B.C.). The
two genii are seated, face each other, their upraised
wings touch at the tips, and in each of their hands
they hold an *ankh*, the Egyptian key of life.[3]

We cannot go into a discussion of the numerous
variations of winged beings, human, animal or com-
posite, which have been unearthed in excavations in
Palestine, Egypt, Mesopotamia and other places in
the Near East. Let us only mention in passing that
the representation of such imaginary hybrid forms was
a favorite theme all over the area for several thousands of years, and that the winged female genii of
the Cherub type were merely one of the many sub-
varieties of these ubiquitous creatures of fantasy.

That the Cherubim in Solomon's Temple were
human and not animal figures has been convincingly
argued by Biblical scholars.[4] Others opinioned that

they were animal figures, shaped like winged oxen, or winged lions. The Samarian ivory plaque suggests that they were, indeed, winged women.

Before reviewing the Biblical evidence, a word should be said about the meaning and derivation of the term Cherub (Hebrew, *K'rubh*). Many attempts have been made to explain this Biblical Hebrew noun, none of them completely satisfactory. It has, however, become accepted that it is related to Akkadian *karibu*, which designates an intermediary between men and the gods, a being who presents the prayers of men to the gods.[5]

2. THE CHERUBIM OF THE DESERT TABERNACLE

Let us leave aside the complicated question of the historicity of the Book of Exodus in general and of the passage describing the Cherubim of the desert Tabernacle in particular. For our present purposes it makes little difference whether Exodus truly portrays the conditions of the tribes of Israel during their wanderings in the desert in the 13th century B.C., or whether, to take the other extreme view, it represents the ideas of the post-exilic Judaeans about the early history of their ancestors after their liberation from Egypt. In any case, as far as the Cherubim in Solomon's Temple are concerned, it must be taken for granted that they were patterned after earlier prototypes, which, through the Shiloh Tent which was called "the House of Yahweh," [6] may well have derived from an ancient period reaching as far back as the age of Moses. This must be considered a distinct possibility even if the actual execution of the Solomonic Cherubim was entrusted to Phoenician artists and craftsmen.

According to the Biblical tradition, in both the desert Tabernacle and the Jerusalem Temple the only supernatural beings represented were the Cherubim.

These, however, were shown so often that they must be regarded as the architectural and decorative, and consequently also the religious, *leitmotif* of both sanctuaries.

In the Tabernacle, two figures of Cherubim stood on both sides of the ark-cover, separated by its width of one and one-half cubits (or 2¼ feet). They were made of beaten gold, and, together with the ark-cover, formed a single piece. Their faces were turned to each other, and downwards toward the ark-cover, which was shielded by their outspread wings. It was upon the ark-cover, from between the two Cherubim, that God was believed to speak to Moses.[7]

Cherubim-figures appeared also on each of the ten curtains which formed part of the sides of the Tabernacle.[8] In addition, Cherubim were depicted on the Veil, which separated the Holy from the Most Holy of the Tabernacle. This Veil hid the Ark and its two Cherubim from all eyes, but it carried a picture of the Cherubim, reproducing on the outside what it concealed within. Like the ten curtains mentioned above, the Veil was made of fine twined linen, blue, purple and scarlet, and was "the work of the skilful workmen."[9]

By simple count we thus find that there were twelve pairs of Cherubim represented in the desert Tabernacle: one over the Ark in the round, and one embroidered on the Veil and ten on the ten curtains.

3. THE CHERUBIM OF SOLOMON'S TEMPLE

In the Solomonic Temple the Cherubim motive was even more in evidence. There were, first of all, the two Cherubim over the Ark. These were made of olive wood and overlaid with gold. Their height was ten cubits (15 feet), and their wing-span measured the same. Both Cherubim were of equal size and form; their inner wings touched each other, while their outer wings reached the two opposite walls of the Holy of Holies in which they stood: the total span of the two pairs of wings was 20 cubits (or 30 feet), stretching across the entire width of the Holy of Holies.[10] Beneath the inner wings of the Cherubim stood the Ark.[11] The pattern, we are told, for the Cherubim, as for the entire Temple and all its holy vessels, was handed down by David to his son Solomon.[12]

The ten curtains of the Tabernacle embroidered with Cherubim were replaced in the Solomonic Temple by solidly built walls, and these, in turn, were decorated with the Cherubim-motive: "And he [Solomon] carved all the walls of the House round about with carved figures of Cherubim and palm-trees and open flowers, both within and without." Also on the two wings of the main entrance door to the innermost Sanctuary (*devir*) "he carved carvings of Cherubim and palm-trees and open flowers, and overlaid them with gold," and, similarly, on the outer door of the Temple (*hekhal*), which was made of cypress wood, "he carved Cherubim and palm-trees and open flowers, and he overlaid them with gold fitted upon the graven work." [13]

According to Chronicles, there was no door between the Holy and the Holy of Holies, but a veil separated them, as had been the case in the desert Tabernacle. The manner in which it was made and decorated was also the same as in the old Tent of Meeting: blue purple, crimson and fine linen, with Cherubim wrought thereupon.[14]

In addition to the above, Cherubim figured among the decorating of the wheeled bases of the ten lavers. On the frames of these bases "there were lions, oxen and Cherubim," while on the sides of the bases there were engraved "Cherubim, lions and palm-trees according to the space of each, and wreaths round about." All these bases were cast in one mold, and they were placed five to the right and five to the left of the House.[15]

Ezekiel, in his vision of the Temple, singles out the

walls and the doors only as being decorated with figures of Cherubim:

> It was made with Cherubim and palm-trees, a palm-tree was between Cherub and Cherub, and every Cherub had two faces: there was a man's face towards the palm-tree on the one side, and a young lion's face towards the palm-tree on the other side, thus was it made through all the house round about. From the ground unto above the door were the Cherubim and the palm-trees made, and so on the wall of the Temple. . . . And the Temple and the sanctuary had two doors: each door had two wings, two turning leaves were there to each door. And on the door-wings of the Temple there were made Cherubim and palm-trees like as were made upon the walls. . . .[16]

While it may be difficult to establish the precise meaning of each detail of this visionary description of the Cherub-decorated walls and doors of the Temple, it largely corresponds to the Solomonic Temple, with a few added details: in the description of the Temple of Solomon we are not told how the Cherubim and palm-trees were arranged; from Ezekiel we learn that these two decorative motives alternated: one Cherub, one palm tree. We also learn that the Cherubim and palm-trees were quite large: they reached from the floor to above the height of the door. And finally we are told that the Cherubim had two faces each, one human face and one lion's face, turned Janus-like in opposite directions.

As we see, in all the above references to the Cherubim in the Solomonic Temple they are consistently associated with palm-trees. Cherubim and palm-trees appear side by side on numerous ivory plaques, such as those that decorated the bed of Hazael, King of Damascus, in the late 9th century B.C., or those found in Arslan Tash, northern Syria, and dating from the 9th–8th century B.C. (See Plates 27 and 28.)

From all this it becomes evident that the Solomonic Temple contained a surfeit of Cherubim. From the moment one entered the Temple court from where the House itself was visible, nowhere could one's glance escape the impact of this ubiquitous, endlessly repeated decorative motive. The outer walls of the Temple were full of carved Cherubim, and so were the doors and the inner walls. On the right and left sides of the Temple stood five huge lavers, each supported on bases decorated lavishly with Cherubim. The Veil which one faced upon entering the Temple, displayed figures of Cherubim embroidered in white, blue, purple and crimson. And those to whom it was granted to glance behind the Veil into the Holy of Holies, saw there again two huge, sparkling, golden statues of Cherubim, fifteen feet tall and filling with their outstretched wings the entire thirty-feet width of the adytum.

4. THE CHERUBIM AS YAHWEH'S MOUNTS

No less interesting than the question of the Cherubim's shape is that of their symbolic import, or, to be more precise, of the successive reinterpretations of their symbolism.

The earliest symbolic meaning attributed by the Hebrews to the Cherubim was that they represented, in a tangible, plastic form, the clouds of the stormy winter sky upon which God was supposed to ride across the face of the earth. That gods ride on clouds is an old mythologem, traces of which can be found among many peoples.[17] Among the Canaanites it is attested in the 14th century B.C. Ugaritic myths, in which "Rider of the Clouds" is one of Baal's epithets.[18] The same epithet, "Rider in the clouds," refers to Yahweh in one of the Psalms, while in another, Yahweh is addressed thus:

Who makest the clouds Thy chariot
Who walkest upon the wings of the wind,
Who makest winds Thy messengers,
The flaming fire Thy ministers.[19]

Isaiah, in an eschatological vision, sees Yahweh "riding on a swift cloud" on His way to Egypt.[20] The cloud as the mount of God is personified as a Cherub: "He rode upon a Cherub, and did fly; yea, He did swoop down upon the wings of the wind." [21] Yahweh's epithet, "Rider in the clouds," was paralleled by another which referred to him as "the Sitter on the Cherubim." [22]

In a magnificent prophetic epiphany Habakkuk sees Yahweh appearing in an earth-shaking storm, riding on his horses and chariots, treading the sea with his stallions, and making Cushan and Midian tremble.[23] Clouds—winds—Cherubim—horses and chariots, all these, then, appear as interchangeable concepts in the poetic and prophetic imagery of the Bible in speaking of the vehicle or mount on which Yahweh appears. Of them, only the clouds, 'arabhoth in Hebrew, have the feminine form. Yahweh's horses have the masculine gender, although mares were known to the Bible as Egyptian chariot horses.[24] However, there seems to have existed an old tradition which held, possibly under the influence of the She-Cherubs, that God's mount, when in animal shape, was a mare. A late trace of this view is found in the midrash which tells of God riding a mare—and, in a more daring version, of taking himself the shape of a mare —and being pursued by the ruttish Egyptian stallions into the Sea of Reeds.[25]

A more personified concept of the Cherubim is expressed in the myth of Genesis, acording to which God placed at the east of the Garden of Eden Cherubim with "the revolving sword of flame" to watch over the way leading to the Tree of Life.[26] Related to these angel-like Cherubim is the jewel-bedecked Cherub who was set by God into the Garden of Eden until he became overweening and rebelled.[27]

In connection with the desert Tabernacle there was an explicit mythical tradition according to which God descended onto and into it in a cloud. In fact, the desert Sanctuary was called Tabernacle (Hebrew, *mishkan*; literally, "dwelling place") because of the divine cloud that abode (*shakhan*) over it and in it. When Moses finished the construction of the Tabernacle,

the cloud covered the Tent of Meeting and the glory of Yahweh filled the Tabernacle. And Moses was not able to enter into the Tent of Meeting because the cloud abode thereon, and the glory of Yahweh filled the Tabernacle. And whenever the cloud rose up from over the Tabernacle, the Children of Israel set out on their journeyings. But when the cloud did not rise up, then they journeyed not till the day that it did rise up. For the cloud of Yahweh was upon the Tabernacle by day, and there was fire therein by night, in the sight of all the house of Israel, throughout all their journeys.[28]

This passage must not be subjected to logical scrutiny (because the latter would, e.g., lead to the conclusion that Moses was able to enter the Tent only when Yahweh raised the cloud which, however, was the signal for breaking camp and setting out on the day's journey), but instead be treated as a myth. It says that God's presence in the Tabernacle was indicated by a cloud which both seemed to hover over the tent and to fill it, and which at night glowed like fire. This conception of the manifest presence of God on and in the Tabernacle closely parallels that of God's presence on Mount Sinai: there too, cloud covered the mount, and in that cloud was God: "He called unto Moses out of the midst of the cloud"; and at the same time, "the appearance of the glory of Yahweh was like devouring fire on the top of the mount in the eyes of the Children of Israel."[29] The cloud that filled the House was the palpable sign of God's presence in Solomon's Temple as well: after the priests deposited the Ark in the Sanctuary, under the wings of the Cherubim, "when the priests were come out of the holy place, the cloud filled the house of Yahweh, so that the priests could not stand to minister because of the cloud, for the glory of Yahweh filled the house of Yahweh." [30]

The connection between clouds and Cherubim as the vehicle of God is emphasized in the visions of Ezekiel. Once the prophet sees "the glory of the God of Israel rising above the Cherub"; another time he sees four Cherubim, each standing upon a wheel and, in turn, supporting the divine throne. As the glory of Yahweh "mounts up from the Cherub to the threshold of the Temple" the latter fills with a cloud, and "the sound of the wings of the Cherubim is heard even to the outer courts as the voice of God Almighty [El Shaddai] when He speaks." These Cherubim, moreover, had four faces each: a Cherub face, a human face, a lion's face, and an eagle's face. Their bodies, even their backs, hands and wings, were full of eyes. Each Cherub had four wings, and when they spread them to fly, the whole apparition, the Cherubim, the wheels, the throne and the glory of God, rose up from the earth as one unit. [31]

This then was the myth: in both the desert Tabernacle and the Temple of Solomon, Yahweh's presence was manifested by a cloud, personified in the Cherubim-figures, which made it impossible for Moses, and later the priests, to enter the holy place. That the Cherubim were the translation of this myth into ritual reality is shown by the statement in Exodus that Yahweh was believed to have spoken to Moses "from between the two Cherubim which were upon the Ark of Testimony." [32] As far as the Biblical period is concerned, the Cherubim were thus unmistakably the symbolic representation of the clouds "out of the midst of which" God spoke and which served also as His mount or chariot.

5. PHILO'S CHERUBIM

A different view of the Cherubim appears in the earliest post-Biblical Jewish source in which references to them are found. Philo, the early-1st-century A.D. Alexandrian Hellenistic Jewish philosopher,[33] gives no less than three interpretations of the Cherubim, ranging from cosmological to theosophic. Philo did visit Jerusalem, and may have seen the Cherubim in the Temple, although he does not mention that he saw them. In general, in describing the Temple he exhibits a remarkable reticence. As long as he speaks of the courtyards and the exterior of the Temple, his description is detailed and even verbose. But when he comes to talk of the Holy of Holies, he manages to say nothing definite about it without, however, stating that there was nothing in it:

> All inside is unseen, except by the High Priest alone, and indeed, he, though charged with the duty of entering once a year, gets no view of anything. For he takes with him a brazier full of lighted coals and incense, and the great quantity of vapor which this naturally gives forth covers everything around it, beclouds the sight and prevents it from being able to penetrate to any distance.[34]

Could Philo have had any reason to refrain from stating categorically that there was nothing in the Holy of Holies? Could it be that he, indeed, knew, either because he was told, or because he himself saw it, that the adytum contained the Cherubim? The manner in which Philo treats the Cherubim of the desert Tabernacle seems to indicate that the question must be answered in the affirmative. When describing that portable sanctuary whose existence, according to tradition, lay in a period preceding his own by more than a thousand years, Philo talks of the ten curtains which were in it, but does not mention that they were decorated by figures of Cherubim. And as to the Cherubim over the Ark, all he has to say is: "The mercy-seat serves to support the two winged creatures which in the Hebrew are called Cherubim, but as we should term them, recognition and full knowledge." [35] After which he launches into his symbolic explanations of the Cherubim of which more anon.

Philo's tendency to gloss over the tangible form of the Cherubim even in the archaic desert Tabernacle and to direct all attention to their symbolic significance is quite evident. That he was nevertheless greatly preoccupied with the physical appearance of the Cherubim, as he himself may have seen them in Herod's Temple, is shown in his treatise *On the Cherubim*. In that book, soon after setting out to explain the significance of the Cherubim whom God placed "at the East of the garden of Eden," he inadvertently slips over into a discussion of the Cherubim figures of the Sanctuary. The passage in which this occurs contains Philo's three interpretations of the Cherubim:

> The Cherubim and the sword of flame which turns every way . . . are an allegorical figure of the revolution of the whole heaven. . . . One of the Cherubim then symbolizes the outermost sphere of the fixed stars . . . the other of the Cherubim is the inner contained sphere. . . .

This is one interpretation. The second is:

> But perhaps, on another interpretation, the two Cherubim represent the two hemispheres [of heaven], for we read that the Cherubim stand face to face with the wings inclining to the mercy-seat; and so, too, the hemispheres are opposite to each other. . . .

The Cherubim which "incline their wings to the mercy-seat" are, of course, no longer the living Cherubim who with their flaming sword bar the way to the tree of life, but the sculptured ones which, according to Biblical tradition, were placed into the desert Tabernacle over the Ark.

In propounding his third interpretation, Philo ostensibly speaks again of the Cherubim of Paradise, but here, too, he cannot rid himself of the image of the two Cherubim with the Ark between them:

> But there is a higher thought than these. . . . While God is indeed one, His highest and chiefest powers are two, even goodness and sovereignty. Through His goodness He begot all that is, through His sovereignty He rules what He has begotten. And in the midst between the two is a third which united them, Reason, for it is through reason that God is both ruler and good. Of these two potencies, sovereignty and goodness, the Cherubim are symbols, as the fiery sword is the symbol of reason . . . these unmixed potencies are mingled and united . . . where God is good, yet the glory of His Sovereignty is seen amid the beneficence . . . where He is sovereign, through the sovereignty the beneficence still appears.[36]

In the Genesis narrative there is not the slightest hint as to the position occupied by the fiery sword in relation to the Cherubim. To say that "the flaming sword which turned every way" was "in the midst between the two" Cherubim and "united them" is, to say the least, forced. It is quite clear that Philo here is thinking again of the Cherubim which stood in the Holy of Holies, with the Ark cover (or "mercy seat") between them and actually uniting them into one single piece of statuary, as explicitly stated in Exodus: "on one piece with the ark-cover shall ye make the Cherubim."[37] The uncertainty in Philo's mind concerning this "third which united" the Cherubim is also indicated by his inconsistency with regard to the symbol that stood for Reason. In the above passage he says that Reason was symbolized by the fiery sword; elsewhere, however, he states that God the father is Reason, while Knowledge is God the mother, and these two aspects of the godhead are symbolized by the two Cherubim.

Before turning to the passages in which Philo expresses these ideas, let us note that while in his interpretations of the Cherubim just quoted the idea of bisexual symbolism is hinted at or implied, he stops short especially of saying anything about a female aspect of God. God's goodness is the begetter, i.e., the male principle, this he states; but he does not make God's other aspect, His sovereignty, the female principle; instead, all he says is that 'through His sovereignty He rules what He has begotten."

In speaking of the creation of the world, however, Philo does take this highly significant step when he says:

> . . . the Architect who made this universe was at the same time the father of what was thus born, whilst its mother was the Knowledge possessed by its Maker. With His Knowledge God had union, not as men have it, and begot created things. And Knowledge, having received the divine seed, when her travail was consummated, bore the only beloved son who is apprehended by the senses, the world which we see. Thus in the pages of one of the inspired company, wisdom is represented as speaking of herself after this manner: 'God obtained me first of all his works and founded me before the ages.' [38] True, for it was necessary that all that came to the birth of creation should be younger than the mother and nurse of the All . . . I suggest, then, that the father is reason, masculine, perfect, right reason, and the mother the lower learning of the schools, with its regular course or round of instruction. . . . [39]

The process of *creation* is represented in this passage in symbolic terms, but quite unequivocally, as *procreation*: God, the Father, who is Reason, had union with the Mother, who is God's Knowledge (also called by Philo Wisdom, Lower Learning and Education, and "the Nurse of All"); the Mother "received the divine seed," and, "when her travail was consummated, bore the only beloved son," the visible world. Elsewhere Philo calls God "the husband of Wisdom," who "drops the seed of happiness for the race of mortals into good and virgin soil." [40]

Philo employs a varied terminology in expressing the same idea in different contexts. In two other passages, speaking of the Cherubim of the Sanctuary, he says that they symbolized "the two most ancient and supreme powers (or 'virtues') of the divine God": his creative power, called "God" which is a "peaceable, gentle, and beneficent virtue," and his kingly power, called Lord, which is "a legislative, chastising and correcting virtue." [41]

It is clear that in all these explanations Philo had in mind one and the same dichotomy which can be subsumed as follows:

God (Elohim)	*Lord* (Yahweh)
Father	Mother
Husband	Wife
Begetter	Bearer
Creator	Nurturer
Reason	Wisdom (Knowledge, Learning, Education)
Goodness	Sovereignty (Kingly Power)
Peaceable	Legislative
Gentle	Chastising
Beneficent	Correcting
Symbolized by Cherub A	Symbolized by Cherub B

Each of these two series of divine attributes is symbolized, acording to Philo, by one of the two Cherubim. Here, then, is the earliest indication of the idea that one of the Cherubim in the Temple represented a male, the other a female figure. This is consonant with the Talmudic tradition, to be discussed anon, according to which the Cherubim couple was shown in marital embrace in a sculpture which stood in the Holy of Holies of the Second Temple. This statuary, we read in Talmudic sources, was shown to the pilgrims who flocked to the Temple on the three pilgrimage-festivals. It is thus probable, or at least possible, that when Philo made his pilgrimage to the Temple, he saw the Cherubim "entwined" like man and wife, as the Talmudic phrase has it. Thus when Philo says that the two divine potencies of goodness (male) and sovereignty (female), represented by the two Cherubim, were "mingled and united," he may be influenced by the Cherubim as he had seen them in the Temple of Jerusalem.

We shall see below that the two divine "virtues" or "powers," formulated by Philo, became subsequently a part of Talmudic theology and were systematically developed in the theosophy of the Kabbala. What is surprising, at first glance, in Philo's dichotomy of the deity is that he attributes the "legislative, chastising and correcting" activities, as well as the kingly power, to the female, maternal aspect of the deity, and the "peaceable, gentle, and beneficent" virtues, as well as goodness, to God's male, paternal aspect. However, there is a logical consistency in thus assigning these two sets of attributes. The mother is the bearer, nurturer, educator, that is, the establisher and maintainer of order; she, therefore, must be the one who wields the legislative, chastising, and correcting powers which are the attributes of sovereignty. The father, who is, of course, the begetter and creator, is, by contrast to the mother, representative of gentleness, beneficence, goodness. In thus assigning "soft" qualities to the father, Philo may also have had in mind Biblical passages such as "Like as a father has compassion upon his children, so has Yahweh compassion upon them that fear Him," [42] and many others which speak of God's compassion; while in characterizing the mother as the maintainer of order, he may have relied on verses which talk of her as the parent who has to be obeyed, or as a fierce lioness.[43] However this may be, there can be no doubt that it is in this Philonic doctrine that we have to look for the earliest roots of medieval Kabbalistic symbolism in which, as Scholem has pointed out, "women represent not, as one might be tempted to expect, the quality of tenderness, but that of stern judgement," a concept which "was unknown to the old mystics of the Merkabah period, and even to the Hassidim in Germany, but . . . dominates Kabbalistic literature from the very beginning and undoubtedly represents a constituent element of Kabbalistic theology."[44] In the Kabbala, as in Philo, "Kingdom" is the female aspect of the deity (in the Kabbala "Kingdom" is the tenth Sephira and identical with the Shekhina, the personified, female "Presence" of God), is associated with the stern, uncompromising, divine principle of justice, while the male aspect is manifested in the qualities of compassion and mercy.

6. JOSEPHUS ON THE CHERUBIM

Should we hope to obtain additional information about the Cherubim from the writings of Flavius Josephus (ca. 37–100 A.D.), the only eyewitness who left us a detailed description of the Jerusalem Temple as it appeared in the last years prior to its destruction by Titus (70 A.D.), we shall be sorely disappointed. Josephus, like Philo half a century before him, shows extreme reticence even when describing the earlier Cherubim, those that formed part of the desert Tabernacle and the Temple of Solomon. About the former he says:

> Upon its [the Ark's] cover were two images which the Hebrews called Cherubim; they are flying creatures, but their form is not like that of any of the creatures which men have seen, though

Moses said he had seen such beings near the throne of God.[45]

There seems to be an intention here to deny all similarity between the Cherubim and any living creature, and to assert that they were supposed to represent *divine* beings, stationed near the throne of God. Incidentally, instead of "Moses" one should read "Ezekiel"; it is in the latter's prophecies, and not in the Pentateuch, that the Cherubim surrounding the throne of God are described.[46]

Even more remarkable is the omission by Josephus of any reference to the Cherubim which adorned the curtains and the Veil in the desert Tabernacle. He describes the curtain as "composed of purple and scarlet and blue and fine linen, and embroidered with diverse kinds of figures, excepting the figures of animals," and the Veil which separated the Holy from the Holy of Holies as "very ornamental, and embroidered with all sorts of flowers which the earth produces; and they were interwoven into all sorts of variety that might be an ornament, excepting the form of animals." [47] His account, as we see, follows closely the one contained in Exodus, except that where Exodus mentions the Cherubim, Josephus substitutes the words "excepting the figures of animals."

In describing Solomon's Temple, Josephus proceeds in a similar manner: he says nothing about the Cherubim on the Veil, on the walls of the Temple, or in any other place, and purposely emphasizes that there is general ignorance as to the shape of the Cherubim over the Ark. The passage in question reads:

He [Solomon] also had veils of blues and purple and scarlet and the brightest and softest of linen, with the most curious flowers wrought upon them, which were to be drawn before those doors [leading from the Holy into the Holy of Holies]. He also dedicated for the most secret place, whose breadth was 20 cubits and the length the same, two Cherubim of solid gold; the height of each of them was five cubits; they had each of them two wings stretched out as far as five cubits; wherefore Solomon set them up not far from each other, that with one wing they might touch the southern wall of the secret place, and with another the ´northern; their other wings, which joined to each other, were a covering to the Ark which was set between them: but nobody can tell or even conjecture what was the shape of these Cherubim.[48]

Let us interject one single comment here. All the measurements contained in this passage are identical with those in Kings, except that of the Cherubim's height which is given as ten cubits (15 feet) in Kings and as five (7½ feet) by Josephus. It seems that by reducing the height of the Cherubim to one-half of the Biblical figure, Josephus hoped to reduce their importance as well.

Preceding the above-quoted sentences, Josephus describes the walls of the Temple which, as we shall recall, were decorated by alternating figures of Cherubim and palm trees as well as by flowers. All that Josephus has to say, however, is that Solomon, "as he enclosed the walls with boards of cedar so he fixed upon them plates of gold, which had sculptures upon them. . . ."[49] Again, not a word as to what these sculptures represented.[50]

When reading these descriptions of Josephus in which he flatly contradicts Biblical texts, one begins to suspect that he must have had a definite purpose in mind in omitting to mention the Cherubim so ubiquitous in the Solomonic Temple. It is not difficult to surmise his reasons for so doing. By underplaying the Cherubim in both the desert Tabernacle and the Solomonic Temple, he leads up to the total omission of any reference to them in his description of the Temple of Herod with which, as a priest, he had a thorough, firsthand familiarity. As we shall see below, there can be little doubt that there were Cherubim in the Holy of Holies of the Second Temple; they

even played an important role in the ritual of the
pilgrimage festivals. If Josephus passes over them in
silence, his reason, as that of Philo before him, must
have been that as an interpreter of Judaism to the
Hellenistic world in general and to Rome in particular
he was loath to admit that aniconic Judaism did, in
fact, tolerate the representation of human or semi-
human and semi-divine figures within the sacred pre-
cincts of the Temple. Writing as he did after the
destruction of the Temple, he wished to portray it
as a place of pure spiritual worship, unmarred by any
figure of living creatures, whether human, animal or
divine. To be able to do so, he had to obliterate the
memory of the Cherubim, and he tried to do this by
the simple expedient of silence.

It is, however, not easy to deny something one
knows, and especially when that knowledge is of considerable weight. Josephus *knew* that the Holy of
Holies contained the statues of the Cherubim pair,
but he wanted to assert that there was nothing at all
in that most holy place of the Temple. The result
was that he got involved in a peculiar series of self-
contradictions which bear looking into. In one passage
he writes:

> The innermost part of the temple of all was
> of 20 cubits. This was also separated from the
> outer part by a Veil. *In this there was nothing at
> all*. It was inaccessible and inviolable and not to
> be seen by any; and was called the Holy of
> Holies.[51]

Contrast with this what Josephus says in another
passage:

> . . . although Theos [Epiphanes], and Pompey
> the Great, and Licinius Crassus, and last of all
> Titus Caesar, have conquered us in war, and
> gotten possession of our Temple, yet has none
> of them found any such thing [i.e., an ass's head

made of gold] there, nor indeed anything but what was agreeable to the strictest piety; *although what they found we are not at liberty to reveal to other nations.* . . .

But for Antiochus [Epiphanes], he had no just cause for that ravage in our temple that he made . . . *nor did he find anything there that was ridiculous.* . . .

This is again contradicted in the very next section where Josephus says:

. . . nor is there anything [in the Temple], but the altar [of incense], the table [of showbread], the censer, and the candlestick, which are all written in the law: *for there is nothing further there*, nor are there any mysteries performed that may not be spoken of; nor is there any feasting within the place.[52]

This curious vacillation between the categorical assertion that there was nothing at all in the Holy of Holies, and the admission that something indeed was there but that it was not anything ridiculous, and that "we," i.e., the Jews or the priests, were not at liberty to reveal to other nations what it was, seems to stem from two mutually contradictory impulses. On the one hand, Josephus felt constrained to deny the existence of any image or object in the Holy of Holies in accordance with his tendency to represent Judaism as a purely aniconic religion in both doctrine and ritual. On the other, he felt impelled to impress upon his readers, and especially so in his polemical treatise *Against Apion*, his own thorough familiarity with even the most secret aspects of Jewish religion: hence the sentence on the imperative of secrecy which slipped into his argument.

What was there in the Holy of Holies of which Josephus knew but of which he did not want to speak, we could surmise, even without the evidence of the

Talmudic sources, on the basis of his omission of any reference to the Cherubim reliefs on the walls of the Temple: it could have been nothing else but the figures of the two Cherubim. These figures, as we know from the earlier evidence of Philo as well as the later one of the Talmud, had assumed, by the beginning of the 1st century A.D., the character of sacred mystical symbols. Yet Jewish apologists familiar with Hellenistic culture and religion, as both Philo and Josephus were, feared that the idolatrous Hellenistic world, if it knew about the Cherubim, could not but regard them as analogous in purport and intent to its own images of gods and goddesses housed in Greco-Roman temples all over the Mediterranean area. To explain that the Cherubim were sacred symbols and not idols, that they tangibly expressed certain attributes of God, without in any manner representing or depicting God himself, would have been a well-nigh impossible task. The impression, therefore, both Philo and Josephus wished to create among their Hellenistic readers was that although in an archaic period of Jewish history, it is true, the Sanctuary contained symbolic figures called Cherubim, of unknown shape and appearance, all that was a thing of the distant past, while in the present Temple (or, from the point of view of Josephus, in the recently destroyed Temple) there was no image at all. In the first part of this statement Philo and Josephus are unanimous. In the second, Philo, who wrote while the Temple still stood, avoids the possibility of being caught in a lie by the simple expedient of saying that only the High Priest was allowed to enter the Holy of Holies once a year, and even then he could see nothing because of the incense smoke. Josephus, writing after the destruction of the Temple, is bolder: he asserts that there was nothing in the Holy of Holies of the Herodian Temple; then he invalidates this denial by asserting that there was nothing shameful in it and that he was not at liberty to divulge what the most holy chamber actually contained.

7. THE CHERUBIM IN EMBRACE

An echo of Philo's Cherubim symbolism is found
in a midrashic passage attributed to Rabbi Pinhas
ben Yair, a 2nd-century A.D. Palestinian teacher who
seems to have been an Essene and certainly was a man
of extreme piety. The passage, which is quite lengthy
and contains a symbolic interpretation of each and
every part of the Tabernacle, begins as follows:

> The Tabernacle was made so as to correspond
> to the creation of the world. The two Cherubs
> over the Ark of the Covenant were made so as to
> correspond to the two Holy Names. . . .[53]

The "Two Holy Names" are, of course, those of
God: Yahweh ("Lord") and Elohim ("God"), which
is precisely the idea expressed by Philo as we have
seen above.

The midrashic source containing the above passage
subsequently discourses about the symbolism of the
Tabernacle's successor, the Solomonic Temple, and,
in returning to the Cherubim, becomes guilty of a
curious confusion between the Cherubim statuary that
stood in the Temple's Holy of Holies and the cosmic
or elemental Cherubim which, as we have seen, were
the personification of the world-embracing winds:
"The wings of the Cherubim [in Solomon's Temple]
reached from one end of the world to the other. . . ."

This is followed by a remarkable statement which
indicates that, at least according to one school of
thought, the Cherubim were the most important
feature in the entire Temple:

> It was due to them [i.e., the Cherubim], and
> due to their maker [or: makers] that the Temple
> stood. They were the head of everything that was
> in the Temple, for the Shekhina rested on them

and on the Ark, and from there He spoke to Moses.[54]

From a Talmudic tradition [55] we learn that the Cherubim, although they were golden statues, were held to have possessed a certain amount of life and mobility: As long as Israel fulfilled the will of God, the faces of the Cherubim were turned toward each other: however, when Israel sinned, they turned their faces away from each other.[56]

As late as the 3rd and 4th centuries A.D., the memory of the original function and the significance of the Cherubim in the Sanctuary survived among the Babylonian Talmudic masters. According to one of them, a certain Rab Qetina, who flourished in the late 3rd and early 4th century,

> When Israel used to make the pilgrimage, they [i.e., the priests] would roll up for them the *Parokhet* [the Veil separating the Holy from the Holy of Holies], and show them the Cherubim which were intertwined with one another, and say to them: 'Behold! your love before God is like the love of male and female!' [57]

Rashi, the 11th-century commentator, explains the passage: "The Cherubim were joined together, and were clinging to, and embracing, each other, like a male who embraces the female."

Whether the above tradition referred to the First or the Second Temple, was no longer clear to the Babylonian teachers. Some held that it must have referred to the First Temple, because in the Second there were no Cherubim; others, like Rab Aha, son of Jacob (a contemporary of Hana bar Qetina), argued that it referred to the Second Temple and that the Cherubim discussed in it were those painted or engraved on the wall.

Yet another detail concerning the Cherubim is given by Rabbi Shimeon ben Laqish (ca. 200–275 A.D.), an outstanding Palestinian teacher:

When strangers entered the Sanctuary, they saw the Cherubim intertwined with each other; they took them out into the marketplace and said: 'Israel, whose blessing is [reputedly] a blessing and whose curse is a curse, should occupy themselves with such things!' And they despised them, as it is written, 'All that honored her, despise her, because they have seen her [shameful] nakedness' [58]

The same tradition is contained in several Midrashim with a few added details:

When the sins caused that the gentiles should enter Jerusalem, Ammonites and Moabites came together with them, and they entered the House of the Holy of Holies, and found there the two Cherubim, and they took them and put them in a cage and went around with them in all the streets of Jerusalem and said 'You used to say that this nation was not serving idols. Now you see what we found and what they were worshiping!' [59]

As to the time when the Cherubim were shown to the people filling the courts of the Jerusalem Temple, the only statement we have is that of Rab Qetina: the exhibition, and the accompanying explanation, were made "when Israel made the pilgrimage" to the Temple. According to Biblical command, every male Israelite was duty-bound to make the pilgrimage to the Temple three times a year: on Passover in the spring; on the Feast of Weeks, seven weeks later; and on the Feast of Booths (Sukkoth) which fell in autumn, two weeks after New Year.[60] Of the three, the greatest and most enthusiastically celebrated was the last one, on which, more than on any other Hebrew holiday, the populace was commanded to rejoice.[61] From descriptions contained in the Mishna and in Talmudic sources we know not only the ritual details of this joyous feast,[62] but also the fact that both men and women participated in it, and that on the seventh day of the festival the two sexes used to mingle and commit what is euphemistically referred to as "lightheadedness." We can only surmise that the showing of the Cherubim representing a male and a female figure in marital embrace, may have preceded, and, indeed, incited the crowds to, the commission of this "lightheadedness," which could have been nothing but an orgiastic outburst of sexual license.

Such ritual license was in accordance with both old Hebrew practice and the religious customs of other ancient Near Eastern peoples. As to its Hebrew antecedents, we happen to know from the incident of the Golden Calf that sexual rioting was the traditional response to the exhibition of statuary symbolizing or representing the deity. When Aaron made the Golden Calf (as a representation of Yahweh) and showed it to the people, they "offered burnt-offerings and brought peace-offerings and . . . sat down to eat and to drink," and then engaged in sexual intercourse.[63]

Ritual license as a regularly (in many places annually) recurring feature of temple worship is well attested from all over the ancient Near East. It was, one might say, standard practice of the cultic veneration of the divine powers of life and fertility. As Nelson Glueck recently observed: "The excitement of pagan worship and participation in feasts of sacrificial offerings apparently often led male and female worshipers to join together in feverish consummation of fertility rites."[64]

The mythical counterpart of this orgiastic ritual was, in ancient Israel as well as among the other ancient Near Eastern peoples, the great cosmogonical and cosmological myth cycle, according to which the annual period of vegetative fertility was preceded by a union of the male and female elements of nature. To ensure that this great cosmological copulation take place in the proper measure and with the requisite intensity, man himself, it was felt, had to perform the sacred sex act, thereby both indicating to the elements of nature what was expected of them and inducing them to do the same through the compulsive force of a religio-magical act.[65]

However, what was considered in earlier days as a proper manifestation of popular enthusiasm at the sight of divine statuary, became intolerable in the eyes of the sages, probably in the last century of the existence of the Second Temple of Jerusalem. They felt they had to put an end to the festive "lightheadedness," and where originally the women used to gather in the Great Courtyard of the Temple, the so-called Women's Court, while the men stood without, they ordered that the two sexes should change places, in the hope that this would prevent the repetition of the mass orgy. However, next year, they had to witness the futility of their measure, proving to them once again that in the hour of joy the "evil inclination," that is, the sexual drive, is apt to overpower both men and women. Thereupon they had special galleries built on three sides of the courtyard, leaving open only the side which faced the Sanctuary, and confined the women to them.[66]

When this important reform took place, we do not know. But we can understand, to some extent, the stubborn popular resistance to it if we assume that the exhibition of the Cherubim in embrace was continued at the three annual feasts of pilgrimage, while at the same time the populace was prevented by the reform from indulging in its old traditional practice of *imitatio dei* called for by the momentary glimpse of divine mystery.

8. THE PROVENANCE OF THE CHERUBIM-IN-EMBRACE

When these Cherubim-in-embrace replaced the earlier two Cherubim figures which were equal in shape and touched each other only with the tips of their inner wings, is an intriguing question. The incident remembered by Shimeon ben Laqish, when the foreigners broke into the Temple and exposed the holy figures to the sacrilegious glances of the mob, can serve as *terminus ad quem*. Can the date of this incident be fixed with any degree of certainty or at least likelihood?

In the year 170 B.C., Antiochus Epiphanes, the Seleucid King of Syria (175–164 B.C.), on his return from an Egyptian campaign, took Jerusalem, massacred its inhabitants, and looted the Temple. He removed all the Temple treasures, including the three large sacred gold objects, the incense altar, the seven-armed candelabrum, and the table of the showbread, and, as Josephus indignantly remarks, "he did not abstain even from the Veils, which were made of fine linen and scarlet, but took everything along with him to Antiochia." [67] Two years later, Antiochus sent his henchmen to Jerusalem to Hellenize the city; those of the Jewish population who were recalcitrant were exterminated: the men murdered, the women and children sold into slavery. Whoever could, fled from the city, and in their places foreigners were settled.[68] This was a sequence of events into which an incident such as that of the Cherubim would have fitted well. In contrast to Nebuchadnezzar, who was not interested in combating the religious beliefs and practices of the Judaeans, Antiochus Epiphanes was passionately intent on eradicating Judaism. He may have seized upon the opportunity of publicly humiliating the Jews by parading the Cherubim in the streets.

Another consideration which points to the same conclusion is that it is much more likely that the sages of the Talmud, in whose names the Cherubim incident is recorded, would retain an oral tradition concerning an event that had occurred four centuries earlier, in the days of Antiochus Epiphanes, rather than one that had taken place almost nine centuries before their time. Legends concerning the cruelties of Antiochus and his henchmen, which provoked the Maccabees to their revolt, circulated in Rabbinic circles throughout the Talmudic period and even following it.[69]

If the Cherubim incident took place in 170 B.C.,
their male and female figures in embrace must have
been introduced into the Holy of Holies sometime
prior to that date, that is, between 170 B.C. and 515
B.C., when the Second Temple was rebuilt. It is, however, unlikely that this was done at the time of the
rebuilding of the Second Temple. We know that the
Cherubim in the Solomonic Temple had a completely
different appearance: they were two identical human
figures, flanking the Ark on both sides and touching
each other only with their wings, which met over the
Ark. It is not known whether, when Ezra rebuilt the
Temple, he had new Cherubim placed into the Holy
of Holies; but if he had, it is most probable that his
new statuary was a copy of the old one, since his
purpose was to *restore* the Temple in the shape it had
when it was destroyed a few decades earlier. A change
in the shape of the Cherubim could have been made
only at a time when there was a tendency to improve
upon existing forms, to embellish the building, to
refurbish the sacred vessels, to increase the splendor
of the appurtenances. By a mere chance, we happen
to know of such a period.

Among the scanty documents relating to the second
Jewish commonwealth, there is a little book about
whose historicity there has been much scholarly controversy. It is the so-called *Letter of Aristeas*, which
was written in Greek, in Alexandria, in all probability
shortly after 132 B.C.[70] This treatise has the pseude-
pigraphic form of a letter written by Aristeas, a gentile,
to his brother Philocrates during the reign of Ptolemy
II Philadelphus (285–247 B.C.), and it discusses three
major subjects: the golden vessels Ptolemy had made
for the Jerusalem Temple; the translation of the Pentateuch prepared at his instance; and a series of questions concerning kingship he put to the Jewish sages,
together with the latter's philosophical-moralistic
answers. The overriding aim of the treatise was to
demonstrate the excellence of Jewish religion and the
folly of idolatry.[71]

In spite of the late date of its composition—at least

120 years after the events described in it—and its ample legendary embellishments, *Aristeas* seems to contain a solid kernel of historical truth. As to the translation of the Pentateuch into Greek, for instance, scholarly opinion is that, whether the story told in *Aristeas* of the 72 elders sent by the Jerusalem High Priest Eleazar to Alexandria to do the translation is true or not, it seems to be a historical fact that the Pentateuch was translated in the time of Ptolemy II, for it fitted in with his general policy of Hellenization.[72] It seems to me that precisely the same argument supports also the historicity of the presents of exquisite Alexandrian workmanship which, according to *Aristeas,* were sent by Ptolemy II to the Jerusalem Temple. It is in this event that we can find a clue as to the installation of the Cherubim-in-embrace into the Holy of Holies.

The presents were ritual objects, mostly made of gold, to whose description *Aristeas,* and, following him, Josephus [73] devote an inordinate amount of space. They consisted of a table of pure gold (of which, more anon); two large golden bowls set with stones, of a capacity of 20 gallons each; several highly polished silver bowls; golden flagons with inlaid stones; etc.[74] The longest description, quite out of proportion with the rest of the treatise, is accorded to the table which was sent to Jerusalem to replace the old table of the showbread, one of the most sacred objects in the Temple.[75] The instructions the king gave to the goldsmiths in making this table are described in detail in *Aristeas*: "Where there was no prescription in Scripture, he ordered the construction to follow principles of beauty; where there were written prescriptions, their measurements were to be adhered to." [76]

The table and all the other vessels were duly delivered to the hands of the High Priest Eleazar who "devoted them to God," [77] in other words, put them to use in the Temple. Thus far the semi-legendary account of Ptolemy II Philadelphus' bountiful gifts to the Temple. Does the historical background of the period render it likely that such an event actually took place?

The religious atmosphere in Palestine in the first few decades following the penetration of Hellenism was a relatively liberal one. Many Jewish leaders felt no qualms about paying lipservice to Greek polytheism, as attested, for instance, by the use of the phrase "many thanks to the gods," in a letter written to Appollonius, the head of the finances in the Ptolemaean empire, by the Jewish merchant-prince Tobias in the middle of the 3rd century B.C.[78] In these circumstances there was no objection raised on the part of the Temple authorities to the introduction of ritual vessels and other objects donated by foreigners.[79] Even as late as the early 1st century A.D., King Monobaz and Queen Helena of Adiabene (a kingdom on the left bank of the Upper Tigris) had the handles of all the Temple vessels used on the Day of Atonement overlaid with gold, and donated a golden lamp which was placed over the door of the Holy House; Nikanor presented the Temple with bronze door panels; Alexander Lysimachus had all the door-panels covered with gold.[80] Especially close was the relationship between the Temple and the Jewish craft-guilds in Alexandria, headed by those of the gold and silver smiths who are several times mentioned in Tannaitic sources as having carried out repairs on Temple equipment. Thus when the old cymbals and copper mortar, which, according to tradition, dated "from the days of Moses," became damaged, they were repaired by Alexandrian craftsmen; when the family of Garmu refused to divulge the trade-secrets of the preparation of the showbread, and again, when the members of the Eutimos family did the same with regard to the preparation of the incense, the sages tried to break the monopolies of these artisan families by sending for Alexandrian Jewish experts. While all this took place about the middle of the 1st century A.D.,[81] the practice of importing Alexandrian artifacts to Jerusalem must have begun with the spread of Hellenism to Palestine and Egypt.

The first half of the 3rd century B.C., described in *Aristeas* as a period of what today would be called "interfaith cooperation" between Jerusalem and Alexandria, seems to be the most likely time for the introduction of a new Cherubim statuary into the Temple. At a time when the High Priest replaced the old table of the showbread with a new one, of identical size but executed in a completely different style with the utilization of the latest achievements of the Alexandrian goldsmiths' art, he may have accepted from the same source a new Cherubim group, also conforming in size to the traditional one, but representing the current artistic and symbolic understanding of the ancient figures described in Exodus and Kings.

We cannot know the details of the work or the process of its execution. Was it Ptolemy who entrusted the Alexandrian Jewish goldsmiths with the task, so sensitive from both the artistic and the religious point of view? Did it precede or follow the translation of the Pentateuch into Greek, which made the description of the Cherubim in the desert Tabernacle available to the Hellenized Jewish artisans ignorant of Hebrew? Were they, in giving their Cherubim the shape of a male and a female figure in marital embrace, influenced by Egyptian or Hellenistic mysteries in which they may have participated at that early date as did their descendants several generations later, arousing the ire of Philo?[82] Or did they rather emulate early prototypes of that type of Indian temple sculpture which we know from such late examples as the Konarak façade, showing divine pairs in various positions of ecstatic embrace, and which may have been known to them following the onset of cultural contact between Hellenistic India and Egypt? [83] Did the Cherubim-in-embrace, once installed in the Holy of Holies of the Jerusalem Temple inspire the idea of the male and female aspects of the one God first expressed by Philo? Or did the idea precede the representation, and the golden statue of the Cherubim merely express in tangible form notions that had jelled either in Jerusalem or in Alexandria? There are no answers to these questions, nor will there be unless completely new and unsuspected evidence comes to the surface. The argument of this section must, therefore, remain conjectural, based on circumstancial evidence and a few, more or less equivocal, passages.

One counter-argument may be disposed of before closing this section. If, it may be asked, a Cherubim statuary was installed in the Temple at or about the time when the new table and other vessels were, why is there no mention made of this in *Aristeas*? The answer, I believe, lies in the same considerations which explained above the reticence of Philo and Josephus when speaking of the decorations of the Tabernacle and the First Temple. Like Philo and Josephus, so their predecessor who wrote *Aristeas,* endeavored to represent Judaism as a pure, aniconic faith. No mention could, therefore, be made in his treatise of the Cherubim who, in the eyes of the pagans, would have appeared as idolatrous symbols. In fact, *Aristeas* goes even further in this respect than either Philo or Josephus: in his description of the Temple, which he maintains to have seen on a visit to Jerusalem, the only object inside the Temple he mentions is the curtain.[84]

One last question remains to be answered before we can go on to the Kabbalistic reflection of the Cherubim-in-embrace. This is whether, following the removal and public exhibition of the Cherubim by Antiochus Epiphanes, a new statuary of the Cherubim was set up in the Temple to replace the old one. Such a step could have been taken by the Maccabees when they cleansed and rededicated the Temple in 165 B.C. No mention of the Cherubim is found in the Book of Maccabees, but then that book tells only in most general terms of the restoration of the Temple, so that one could not expect to find in it a reference to the Cherubim in particular. However, on the general principle that *restoration* meant the re-establishment of the status quo, one is inclined to assume that every sacred vessel and object contained in the Temple when it was desecrated by the Syrians was restored in it five years later by the Maccabees. The words of Philo and Josephus quoted above also point in this direction. Nor does the recollection of Rab Qetina about the showing of the Cherubim to the Temple pilgrims read as if it would refer to a period which came to an end more than four centuries prior to his time, but rather sounds like a tradition handed down from eyewitness a few generations previously.

However that may be, the Cherubim-in-embrace were regarded as a fitting symbolic expression of the relationship between God and Israel. Rab Qetina was, of course, far from being the first to speak of this relationship as one like that between man and wife. God as the husband and Israel as His wife had become a prophetic commonplace, from Hosea to Ezekiel, that is for the last two centuries of the First Temple period. It was this relationship that the Cherubim visually depicted, according to the Talmudic sages quoted above.

While the female Cherub thus symbolized Israel, she also became closely attached to God, due to her position in the Temple. Once the idea of a female Cherub emerged, it was further developed in Rabbinic literature. A midrash, e.g., says that the Cherubim whom God placed to the east of Eden to watch over the way to the tree of life constantly changed their shapes: at times they were men, at others women, then again spirits, or angels.[85] The angels likewise change their sex according to the will of God: at times He makes them appear in the shape of women, and at others in that of men, while occasionally he makes them assume the appearance of wind or fire.[86]

9. THE CHERUBIM IN THE MIDDLE AGES

For many centuries after the destruction of the Jerusalem Temple by Titus (in 70 A.D.), and the consequent disappearance of the Cherubim statuary, the problem of the symbolic significance of those winged male and female figures continued to pre-occupy some of the most outstanding teachers and thinkers to Judaism. Those among them who were rationalistically inclined, tended to disregard the Talmudic tradition according to which the Cherubim were represented in marital embrace, and concentrated on attributing new symbolic meanings to them. The mystics, on the other hand, seized precisely upon this aspect of the Cherubim and utilized it for the reinforcement of their basic doctrine about the sanctity and cosmic necessity of cohabitation between man and wife.

Maimonides, the greatest of medieval Jewish philosophers (born in 1135 in Cordoba, Spain; died in 1204 in Cairo, Egypt), can be quoted as an example of the former group. In describing the furnishings and sacred vessels of the Sanctuary, he has the following to say about the Cherubim:

God, may He be exalted, has commanded that the image of two angels [i.e., the Cherubim] be made over the ark, so that the belief of the multitude in the existence of angels be consolidated, this correct opinion, coming in the second place after the belief in the existence of the deity, constituting the originative principle of belief in prophecy and the Law and refuting idolatry, as we have explained. If there had been one image, I mean the image of one Cherub, this might have been misleading. For it might have been thought that this was the image of the deity who was to be worshipped—such things being done by the idolaters—or that there was only one individual angel, a belief that would have led to a certain dualism [i.e., belief in one God and one angel]. As, however, two cherubim were made and the explicit statement enounced: 'The Lord is our God, the Lord is one,' [87] the validity of the opinion affirming the existence of angels was established and also the fact that they are many. Thus measures were taken against the error that they are the deity—the deity being one and having created this multiplicity.[88]

Maimonides' view is reechoed in the *Midrash Ha-Gadol*, a midrashic compilation only slightly later than the renowned *Guide of the Perplexed*, and which was made in Yemen. In it we find also a unique description of the Cherubim:

'And thou shalt make two Cherubim,' [89] These Cherubim, what was their purpose? To make known that there are Cherubim on high. . . . If so, would one not have sufficed? No, lest people err and say, 'It is God [*Eloah*].' What was their appearance? Their faces, backs, hands and breasts looked like those of human beings, and they had wings like the wings of the fowl, like the Cherubim of the *Merkaba* [the divine chariot] on high. . . .[90]

As to the Kabbala, it found in the Cherubim-in-embrace a most welcome basis for two of its central doctrines: one, that only the togetherness of male and female is a state of blessedness; and two, that when a man sins he thereby causes a separation between the male and female aspects of the deity (of which more in the next two chapters), which, in turn, leads to a transcendental and universal disaster. In the Zohar, the *magnum opus* of 13th-century Spanish Kabbala, these two ideas are expressed as follows:

Three times a day a miracle took place with the wings of the Cherubim. When the holiness of the king [i.e., God] revealed itself over them, the Cherubim, of themselves, stretched out their wings and covered their bodies with them. . . . A cloud descended, and when it settled upon the Lid, the wings of the Cherubim intertwined and they beat them and sang a song. . . . And the Priest in the Temple heard their voices as he was putting the incense in its place. . . . The two

Cherubim, one male and one female, both sang. . . . 'And he heard the Voice speaking unto him . . . from between the two Cherubim, and He spoke unto him.' Rabbi Yitzhak said: From this we learn that God is 'just and right,' [91] that is, male and female, and likewise the Cherubim were male and female.[92]

We shall easily recognize in this passage a late variant of the theme we first found adumbrated by Philo twelve hundred years earlier: the male and female Cherubim representing the male and female elements in God. The Talmudic view quoted above to the effect that the position of the heads of the Cherubim changed, reflecting the moral behavior of Israel, is also elaborated in the Zohar:

Rabbi Yose said: Woe to the world when one Cherub turns his face away from the other, for the verse 'with their faces one to another' [93] [refers only to times] when there is peace in the world. Rabbi Yitzhak said: This is meant by 'The nakedness of thy father and the nakedness of thy mother shalt thou not uncover' [94]—woe to him who uncovers their nakedness.' [95]

What this Zoharic passage means is that woe to him who creates strife in the world, because thereby he causes the two Cherubim to turn their faces away from each other, which in turn is but the visible manifestation of the separation of the divine Father (the King) and the divine Mother (the Matronit). Such a sundering of the Father and the Mother is spoken of repeatedly in the Zohar as an uncovering of their nakedness, because the disruption of their union denudes them of each other, weakens them and dishonors them.

A little younger than the Zohar is the Kabbalistic Bible commentary of Bahya ben Asher, the distinguished Spanish exegete who lived in Saragossa and died in 1340. Bahya refers repeatedly to the Cherubim in the Temple, whom he considers as having been male and female, in embrace, and representing symbolically a number of important things.

The two Cherubim corresponded to the brain and the heart in man, Bahya says, or the human soul and the human reason.

> Of the two Cherubim, one was male and the other female, because the human soul and reason are like male and female, one acts, is active, and the other receives, is passive.
>
> The two Cherubim were different in their substance, one being male and the other female. . . . in order to make manifest how greatly Israel was loved by God, like the love of male and female. . . . The Cherubim in this form were a powerful symbol testifying to the uttermost attachment between God and Israel with nothing intervening between them. . . .[96]

10. CONCLUSION

In conclusion, let us return for a moment to the earliest period of Hebrew history from which unequivocal data are so scant that they invite conjectures and hypotheses. Hugo Gressmann, in a study about the Ark expressed the view that originally there must have been two images in it, that of Yahweh and that of his wife Anathyahu, or Astarte.[97] Twenty years later, more cautiously, yet along the same lines, Julian Morgenstern conjectured that the two sacred stones in the Ark originally "represented Yahweh and, in all likelihood, His female companion."[98] The findings of the present study tend to agree with these conjectures. In the beginning, the story can be recapitulated, two images, or slabs of stone, were contained in the Ark, representing Yahweh and his consort. At a later stage, when this anthropomorphic view of the deity was overcome, Yahweh was conceived of as the male, patriarchal, and only God, whom it was forbidden to represent in visual form. His erstwhile female companion now was reduced to the position of a female guardian, represented in the two female Cherubim, who covered the Ark with their wings, which at the same time also served as the seat of Yahweh. Following the destruction of the First Temple, the idea slowly gained ground that the one and only God comprised two aspects, a male and a female one, and that the Cherubim in the Holy of Holies of the Second Temple were the symbolic representation of these two divine virtues or powers. This was followed by a new development, in Talmudic times, when the male Cherub was considered as a symbol of God, while the female Cherub, held in embrace by him, stood for the personified Community of Israel. When, finally, the Kabbala developed its mystical theory of the Sephirot, and especially of the two most important divine entities of the King and the Matronit, and endowed each of them with a mythical, independent existence, it considered the Cherubim pair as the fitting visual representation of these two divine concepts.

Chapter IV

THE SHEKHINA

Shekhina is the frequently used Talmudic term denoting the visible and audible manifestation of God's presence on earth. In its ultimate development as it appears in the late Midrash literature, the Shekhina concept stood for an independent, feminine divine entity prompted by her compassionate nature to argue with God in defense of man. She is thus, if not by character, then by function and position, a direct heir to such ancient Hebrew goddesses of Canaanite origin as Asherah and Anath. How did the Shekhina originate and develop, and what did she mean for Talmudic Judaism? These are the questions that we shall attempt to answer in this chapter.

1. THE "DWELLING" OF GOD

In Biblical times, when God was imagined to dwell in or ride upon clouds, as Baal had done in the older Canaanite mythology,[1] the mythological validation of the sanctity of the desert Tabernacle and the Solomonic Temple was the myth of Yahweh descending in a cloud into the sanctuary.[2] The presence of God in this "cloud of Yahweh" was regarded as something more tangible than its visual aspect: because of the cloud, "Moses was not able to enter into the Tent of Meeting." [4] Similarly, after the completion of

99

Solomon's Temple, "the cloud filled the House of Yahweh so that the priests could not stand to minister by reason of the cloud, for the glory of Yahweh filled the House of Yahweh." [5] The archaic nature of this mythologem of the deity's physical presence in his temple is attested by the poetic passage following the above statement: Then spoke Solomon:

> Yahweh meant to dwell in darkness,
> But I built a house for Thee
> A seat to abide in forever.[6]

A careful perusal of the passages referring to the manifestation of God in the sanctuary shows that the nouns "cloud" and "glory" are used interchangeably, and that the "cloud" was undoubtedly regarded as the visible form taken by the "glory" of Yahweh when He wished to indicate His presence in His earthly abode, the sanctuary.[7]

Since Yahweh was believed to have "dwelt" in the desert Tabernacle, one of the names of that tent-sanctuary was *mishkan*, "dwelling" or "abode." [8] According to the older Elohistic tradition, Yahweh merely put in temporary appearances in the Tent of Meeting; he was a visiting deity whose appearance in, or departure from, the Tent was used for oracular purposes.[9] In contrast, the younger Priestly tradition makes Yahweh a permanent inhabitant of this sacred Abode,[10] thus retrojecting into the mythical past a belief that was an integral part of the Jerusalem-centered theology of the later monarchy, i.e., that God's permanent abode was on Mount Zion, in His holy Temple.

2. HOKHMA—WISDOM

While the quasi-physical manifestation of God's "dwelling" in His sanctuary is thus an integral feature of Biblical theology, the term Shekhina does not occur in the Bible. However, in the late Biblical period a theological tendency made its appearance which prepared the ground for the emergence of the Talmudic Shekhina. The trend referred to is that of interposing personified mediating entities between God and man. These entities, originally conceived of either as having been created by God or as being His attributes or emanations, gradually developed into angel-like beings who act upon man and the world under instruction by God. The most frequently appearing of these intermediaries, or *hypostases* (as they are called), is *Hokhma,* or Wisdom. In the Book of Job,[12] Wisdom is described as a personage whose way is understood and place known only by God himself, while the Book of Proverbs[13] asserts that Wisdom was the earliest creation of God, and that ever since those primeval days she (Wisdom) has been God's playmate.

In the Apocrypha, this role of Wisdom is even more emphasized.[14] A passage in the *Wisdom of Solomon* states that "she [Wisdom] proclaims her noble birth in that it is given to her to live with God, and the Sovereign Lord of all loved her. . . ."[15] It was observed by Gershom Scholem that the term "symbiosis" used in this passage appears again in the same chapter in the sense of marital connubium, and that it is therefore clear that Wisdom here was regarded as God's wife.[16] Philo states quite unequivocally that God is the husband of Wisdom.[17]

Wisdom played a particularly important role among the Jewish Gnostics. References to the role of Wisdom in the primordial days of the world seem to indicate the existence of a Gnostic Hokhma-myth which originated in Jewish circles and was hypothetically reconstructed as follows:

Out of the primeval Chaos God created the seven archons through the intermediacy of his Wisdom, which was identical with the "dew of light." Wisdom now cast her eidolon, or shadow-image, upon the primeval waters of the Tohu wa-Bohu, whereupon the archons formed the world and the body of man. Man crawled about upon the earth like a worm, until Wisdom endowed him with spirit. Satan, in the shape

of the serpent, had intercourse with Eve who thereupon bore Cain and Abel. Thus sexuality became the
original sin. After the Fall, the sons of Seth fought
the sons of Cain. When the daughters of Cain seduced
the sons of Seth, Wisdom brought the flood upon the
earth. Later, in her efforts to help mankind, Wisdom
sent seven prophets, from Moses to Ezra, corresponding to the seven planets. In this myth Wisdom, acting
like a female deity, clearly resembles the Gnostic
concept of the *anima mundi*, the "world soul." [18]

Whether this myth reconstruction is or is not correct
in all details could be decided only on the basis of
a thorough study of Jewish, Early Christian, and
Gnostic sources. However, there can be little doubt
as to the importance of Wisdom in Jewish Gnosticism,
which built its speculations on the role assigned to
Hokhma in the late books of the Bible itself.

While Wisdom thus had all the prerequisites for
developing into a veritable female deity, no such development took place within Judaism. Instead, post-
Biblical Judaism created for itself a new concept of
feminine divinity in the figure of the Shekhina, who
first appears in the Aramaic translation-paraphrase of
the Bible, the so-called *Targum Onkelos*. While the
exact date of this work is still in doubt (some scholars
hold that it was written as early as the 1st century
A.D., while others think that it had not attained its
final form until the 4th century), it is generally agreed
that its author used an older version as the basis of
his translation.

3. THE EARLY SHEKHINA

Shekhina (*sh'khinah*) is a Hebrew abstract noun
derived from the Biblical verb *shakhan* discussed
above and means literally "the act of dwelling."
These abstract nouns, constructed from the verbal
root-letters with the added -*ah* suffix, have the feminine
gender. In actual usage, the term Shekhina, when it

first appears, means that aspect of the deity which can be apprehended by the senses. Whenever the original Hebrew Biblical text speaks of a manifestation of God through which He was perceived by man, the *Targum Onkelos* interpolates the term Shekhina. For instance, the verse "Let them make Me a Sanctuary that I may dwell [*w'shakhanti*] among them," [19] is rendered by the Targum Onkelos as follows: "Let them make before Me a Sanctuary that I may let My Shekhina dwell among them." The original "I will dwell [*w'shakhanti*] among the Children of Israel . . . that I may dwell [*l'shokhni*] among them," [20] becomes in the Targum "I will let My Shekhina dwell among the Children of Israel . . . that I may let My Shekhina dwell among them." The Biblical "that they defile not their camp in whose midst I dwell" [21] becomes "that they defile not their camp in whose midst My Shekhina dwells." [22] The Targum, evidently, could not tolerate a direct reference to God even in a poetic text, and thus it paraphrases the original "He [God] found him [Israel] in a desert land . . . He compassed him about . . ." [23] as follows: "He filled their needs in a desert land . . . He let them dwell around His Shekhina. . ."

From these examples, to which many more could be added, [24] it appears that the earliest use of the term Shekhina was in the sense of an abstract hypostasis, interpolated wherever a Biblical statement appeared to be too anthropomorphic to the greater sensitivity of a later age. The fact that the noun Shekhina had the feminine gender (*shekhinta* in Aramaic) had no significance at all in these early references.

In the Talmudic literature, the term continued to be used in the same sense. E.g., Rabbi Yehoshua, a 1st–2nd century Palestinian teacher, states that the following features were enjoyed by Israel in the desert: the manna, the quails, the well, the Tabernacle, the Shekhina, the priesthood, the kingship, and the Clouds of Glory. [25] A Talmudic discussion flatly equates God with the Shekhina: "Rabbi Yose (2nd century) said: 'Never did the Shekhina descend to earth, nor Moses and Elijah ascend to heaven. . . . It is correct that the Shekhina never descended to earth? Is it not written, 'And Yahweh came down upon Mount Sinai . . .'?" [26]

At the same time, however, there is a tendency to endow the Shekhina with more physical attributes than those associated with God, and thus to distinguish between the deity Himself who is beyond all sense-perception and His tangible manifestation as the Shekhina. One passage in which this physical view of the Shekhina is expressed with great clarity is the following:

> All those years that Israel was in the desert, these two caskets, one of a corpse [of Joseph] and the other of the Shekhina [containing the two stone tablets of the Law] were carried [by the Israelites] side by side. When the passersby would say: 'What is the nature of these two caskets?' they would answer: 'One is the casket of a corpse, and the other of the Shekhina.' 'Is it the custom that a corpse should be carried with the Shekhina?' They would answer: 'This one [i.e., Joseph], observed what is written in the other one.' [27]

It is evident that the presence of the Shekhina in the casket is imagined in this passage in a manner corresponding to that of Joseph's body in the other casket—both are actual, physical presences.

Similarly, the Biblical notion that the Tabernacle was built in order to serve as a dwelling place for Yahweh is transformed in Talmudic literature into the idea that both the desert sanctuary and the Solomonic Temple were the earthly abode of the Shekhina. It was the Shekhina who, according to Rabbi Azaria in the name of Rabbi Yehuda bar Simon, the 4th-century Palestinian Amora, dwelt in the Temple, lining it, as it were, with love.[28]

The notion is made tangible by Rabbi Yehoshua of Sikhnin in the name of Rabbi Levi, a 3rd–4th century Palestinian Amora:

A simile: Like unto a cave on the seashore:
when the waves rise, it fills with water, yet the
sea is in no way diminished. Thus it was with the
Tent of Meeting: it became filled with the glory
of the Shekhina, but the world was in no way
diminished.[29]

According to Rabbi Yehoshua (end of 1st century
A.D.),

. . . while the Children of Israel were still in
Egypt, the Holy One, blessed be He, stipulated
that He would liberate them from Egypt only in
order that they build him a Sanctuary so that He
can let His Shekhina dwell among them. . . . As
soon as the Tabernacle was erected, the Shekhina
descended and dwelt among them.

To this Rab (the early-3rd-century Babylonian
Amora) added:

On that day a thing came about which had never
existed since the creation of the world. From
the creation of the world and up to that hour the
Shekhina had never dwelt among the lower beings.
But from the time that the Tabernacle was
erected, she did dwell among them.[30]

According to another opinion however, the Shekhina originally did well here below, on earth. However, when Adam sinned, she removed herself to the
first heaven. When the generation of Enosh sinned,
she moved up from the first to the second heaven.
The sins of the generation of the Deluge caused her
to withdraw to the third heaven; those of the generation of the Tower of Babel—to the fourth. When the
Egyptians sinned in the days of Abraham, she withdrew to the fifth heaven. The sins of the Sodomites
impelled her to seek refuge in the seventh heaven.
But when the seven righteous men (Abraham, Isaac,

Jacob, Levi, Kehat, Amram, and Moses) arose, they
brought her back down to earth step by step.[31]

Since the Shekhina dwelt in the Temple, any desecration of that holy place affronted her directly. When
King Manasseh set up a graven image in the house of
God, he did this purposely so that the Shekhina
should see it and be angered.[32]

It was a Talmudic tenet that the physical presence
of the Shekhina in the Temple, or in any other place
on earth, was of such a nature that it could be local-
ized, and her movements from place to place followed.
The classical expression of this view is the statement
of Rabbi Yehuda ben Idi in the name of Rabbi
Yohanan bar Nappaha (a teacher in Tiberias who
died in 279 A.D.), according to which the Shekhina
went through the following ten stages of wandering:

> From the ark-cover she moved onto the Cherub;
> from the Cherub onto the other Cherub;
> from the second Cherub onto the threshold of the
>   Temple;
> from the threshold into the court of the Priests;
> from the court onto the altar in the court;
> from the altar onto the roof of the Temple;
> from the roof onto the wall;
> from the wall into the city of Jerusalem;
> from the city onto the Mount of Olives;
> from the mount into the desert.[33]

The idea is that each of these stations in the wanderings of the Shekhina took her to a place more remote
than the previous one from her original dwelling place
over the ark-cover. It was, of course, the sins of
Israel which caused the Shekhina thus to go into exile.
In the desert, the Shekhina waited six months for
Israel to repent. When they failed to do so, she said
in desperation, "Let them perish!" [34]

According to another version, the Shekhina dwelt
for three and a half years on the nearby Mount of
Olives, and cried out from there three times a day:
"Return, you backsliding children!" [35] When all this

proved futile, she began to fly around and say, "I shall go and return to my place till they acknowledge their guilt," [36] that is to say, she withdrew to heaven to wait there for repentance to bring redemption.

4. PERSONIFICATION

As to the presence of the Shekhina in the Second Temple, opinions were divided. Some said that while in the First Temple the Shekhina dwelt continuously, in the Second Temple she was present only intermittently.[37] Some sages, however, like the 4th-century A.D. Palestinian Amora, Shemuel ben Inya, asserted that the Shekhina never graced the Second Temple with her presence, and that this circumstance constituted one of the seven features marking the inferiority of this sanctuary in comparison with the First Temple.[38] Rabbi Yohanan, too, was of the opinion that the Shekhina never dwelt in the Second Temple, the reason being that it was built with the aid of the Sons of Japheth, i.e., the Persians, and, as stated in Genesis 9:27, God dwells only in the tents of Shem, that is in a Temple built by the Children of Israel themselves.[39]

Again others held not only that the Shekhina was present in the Second Temple,[40] but that, following its destruction, she transferred her seat to several important synagogues in Babylonia, where her presence was both visible and audible. Especially two synagogues, those of Huzal and Shaf Weyatibh, had the reputation of serving as alternate dwelling places for the Shekhina. The Shaf Weyatibh synagogue in Nehardea was built, according to tradition, by King Yechonia and his men, of stones and dust they had brought along from Jerusalem.[41] At times the Shekhina would dwell in this synagogue, at others in that of Huzal. Once, so the story goes, the fathers of Shemuel and Levi were sitting in the Shaf Weyatibh synagogue in Nehardea when the Shekhina appeared making a noise, whereupon they got up and left. On another occasion, blind Rab Sheshet sat in the same synagogue when the Shekhina again came, but he made no move to leave. Thereupon ministering angels came to frighten him away, but he said: "Master of the World! If one is afflicted and the other is not, who is to yield?" Whereupon He (i.e., the deity) spoke to them: "Let him be!" [42]

As to the precise nature of the noise made by the Shekhina, another Talmudic passage describes it as follows: "The Shekhina rang before him [Samson] like a bell." [43] As we shall see in another context, God's approach, too, was said to have been accompanied by the tinkling of bells.

In general, it was an accepted article of faith that wherever their exile took the people of Israel, whether to Egypt, to Babylonia, or to Edom (Rome), the Shekhina went along with them, and that she would remain with them until the time of their redemption.[44]

In addition to her appearance in places of primary or secondary sanctity, the Shekhina would also show herself to individuals and even to animals. According to a Palestinian view, transmitted to Babylonia by Rab Dimi (early 4th century A.D.), the Shekhina spoke to Adam, to the Serpent, and to the fishes, and, as a consequence of this distinction, members of these three species copulate in a face-to-face position, while all the other animals perform the sexual act face-to-back.[45]

That the Shekhina can be seen is almost a commonplace in the Midrash. The sign of the Abrahamic covenant which the Children of Israel carried on their flesh enabled them to gaze at the Shekhina; had it not been for the circumcision, they would have fallen flat on their faces at her appearance.[46] Even Nadab and Abihu, the two rebellious contemporaries of Moses, "feasted their eyes on the Shekhina, but had no enjoyment from her; Moses, on the other hand, did not feast his eyes on her, but enjoyed her." [47] Already as a babe, Moses was joined by the Shekhina. When the daughter of Pharaoh found the ark of bulrushes into which he had been placed by his mother, and opened it, she saw the Shekhina in it.[48] Of all men, Moses was the only one to whom the Shekhina spoke "every hour, without setting a time in advance." Therefore, in order to be always in a state of ritual purity and readiness to receive a communication from the Shekhina, Moses separated himself completely from his wife.[49]

The Shekhina joins the sick to comfort them,[50] and helps those who are in need.[51] Moreover, she has special concern for the repentant sinners of Israel:

> [These] are accepted by the Shekhina as if they were righteous and pious persons who never sinned. They are carried aloft and seated next to the Shekhina. . . . He whose heart is broken and whose spirit is low, and whose mouth rarely utters a word, the Shekhina walks with him every day. . . .[52]

Good deeds, even if performed by idolaters, attract the Shekhina: when the prophets of the Baal practiced hospitality, the Shekhina descended and rested upon them.[53]

If husband and wife are worthy and deserving, the Shekhina rests between them.[54] On the other hand, Rab Abin bar Ada, a Babylonian Amora of the 3rd–4th centuries, said in the name of Rab: "He who marries a woman not suitable for him, when God lets his Shekhina rest, he will give testimony concerning all the tribes, but him." [55]

A different view of the Shekhina shows her as being attracted by aesthetic and aristocratic qualities. "The Shekhina rests only on him who is wise, heroic, rich and tall of stature." [56] Rabbi Yohanan bar Nappaha (died 279 A.D.) enumerated a very similar list of excellences as attracting the Shekhina: "God lets His Shekhina rest only on him who is heroic, rich, wise and modest." [57] Rabbi Hama bar Hanina, a Palestinian Amora of the 3rd century, said: "When God lets His Shekhina rest, He will let her rest only on the noble families in Israel." [58] According to another view, "the Shekhina rests only where there is no sadness, no sloth, no laughter, no levity, no merriment, and no senseless chatter, but where there is rejoicing over the fulfillment of a commandment." [59]

Lest one think that the Shekhina was thought of as ranking merely with the angels, we adduce a few passages which emphasize her superiority to them: The splendor of the Shekhina feeds the ministering angels. Her radiance, however, is so great that the angels must cover their faces with their wings so as not to see her.[60] The ministering angels are removed from the Shekhina by myriads of parasangs, and the body of the Shekhina herself measures millions of miles.[61]

These ideas are complementary without being contradictory: on the one hand, the Shekhina can be so small as to find place in the Tabernacle or even in the small ark of bulrushes next to the child Moses; on the other, her size overshadows the world. A midrash neatly reconciles the two ideas:

> The emperor said to Rabban Gamaliel: 'You say that wherever ten men are assembled, the Shekhina dwells among them. How many Shekhinas are there?' Thereupon Rabban Gamaliel beckoned the servant and began to beat him [saying]: 'Why did you let the sun enter the emperor's house?' ['Nonsense'] said the emperor, 'the sun shines all over the world!' 'If the sun,' answered Gamaliel, 'which is only one of a thousand myriad servants of God, shines all over the world, how much more so the Shekhina of God!" [62]

The problem of how to reconcile the omnipresence of the Shekhina with her "dwelling" in the sanctuary was solved in a different manner by Rabbi Yohanan bar Nappaha by the introduction of the concept of "contraction" of which the Kabbala was later to make extensive use in its cosmogony. Yohanan explained

that when Moses heard God say "Let them make Me
a Sanctuary," [63] he was frightened by what he assumed would be a task of immense magnitude, because
he knew that even the "heaven and the heaven of
heavens cannot contain" God.[64] But God reassured
him that a small Tabernacle would, indeed, be sufficient for Him: "I shall descend and contract my
Shekhina between [the planks of the Tabernacle] down
below." [65]

5. THE SHEKHINA CONFRONTS GOD

These, and many other similar passages clearly
demonstrate a pronounced tendency to personify the
Shekhina and to conceive of her as a manifestation
of the deity in a lower form, capable of being perceived by the human senses. This Shekhina was the
direct heir of the Biblical Cloud of Glory which had
dwelt in the sanctuary and had been the visible
manifestation of Yahweh's presence in His House.
There is as yet no indication in any of these passages
that the Shekhina was considered a divine entity
separate from God to the extent of being able to
confront him. However, in view of the mystical dual-
istic theosophy of Philo and the Cherubim-symbolism
of the Second Temple,[66] it was inevitable that the
step from regarding the Shekhina as the manifestation
of God to seeing in her a discrete divine entity should
be taken. The earliest evidence that it was, dates
from the end of the 3rd century A.D.

Before presenting the passage in question, a word
must be said about the relationship of the two Talmudic concepts of the Shekhina and of the "Holy
Spirit." As A. Marmorstein has convincingly shown,
these two concepts were used synonymously in the
Talmudic period.[67] When, therefore, a Talmudic
teacher speaks of the Holy Spirit, he may as well have
used the term Shekhina. With this in mind, let us
quote a saying of Rabbi Aha, a Galilean teacher who
lived ca. 300 A.D.

The Holy Spirit comes to the defense [of sinful Israel by] saying first to Israel: 'Be not a witness against they neighbor without a cause,' [68] and thereafter saying to God: 'Say not: I will do to him as he hath done to me.' [69]

This passage has great significance in the historical development of the Jewish God concept. We have here a very early testimony as to the idea that the "Holy One, blessed be He" or God, and the Shekhina or Holy Spirit, are two separate and discrete divine entities. The Holy Sipirt is said here to have admonished God not to practice retribution and to refrain from punishing Israel. She (she, because the "Holy Spirit," like the Shekhina, is feminine) was, therefore, considered to have an opinion, a mind, a will, and a personality of her own. She is opposed to God and tries to influence him.[70]

The Shekhina plays a similar role in another passage which is of considerably later provenance. It is found in Midrash Mishle, whose late age is indicated by the fact that the first to quote it was Rabbi Hananel (died 1050 A.D.). In it we read:

When the Sanhedrin wanted to add King Solomon to the three kings and four commoners who had no share in the World to Come, Shekhina rose up before the Holy One, blessed be He, and said: 'Master of the World! Seest Thou a man diligent [i.e., Solomon] . . . ?! They want to count him among mean men.' In that hour, a divine voice was heard saying to them: 'Let him stand before Kings, let him not stand before mean men!' [71] [i.e., do not include Solomon together with those mean men who are excluded from the heavenly Paradise.]

A clear-cut differentiation between God and the Shekhina is made by Moshe Hadarshan, the early-11th-century Midrashist of Narbonne, in his book entitled *Bereshit Rabbati*. He says, in the name of Rabbi Akiba (the 2nd century A.D. Tanna), that

> when the Holy One, blessed be He, considered the deeds of the generation of Enoch and that they were spoiled and evil, He removed Himself and His Shekhina from their midst and ascended into the heights with blasts of trumpets. . . .[72]

Although three passages may be considered rather meager evidence, they are sufficient to establish that the idea of two separate divine entities did exist in Talmudic times and that there were at least some teachers who saw nothing exceptionable in it. Others, however, took a different view, and opposed any implication of such a plurality, thereby adding indirect evidence to the existence of such beliefs. Rabbi Eliezer, the Palestinian Amora of the 3rd century, warned that one must carefully refrain from implying a divine plurality even inadvertently in translating Biblical passages which contain references to the physical appearance of God:

> Rabbi Eliezer said: 'He who translates a Biblical verse literally is a liar, and he who adds to it is a blasphemer. For instance, if he translates the [Hebrew] verse "And they saw the God of Israel" [73] [into Aramaic]: "And they saw the God of Israel," he is a liar, for the Holy One, blessed be He, sees but cannot be seen. If, however, he translates "And they saw the glory of the Shekhina of the God of Israel," he blasphemes because he makes three [i.e., instead of one God, he refers to three deities], namely, Glory, and Shekhina, and God. What "And they saw the God of Israel" means is that they feasted their eyes on the splendor of the Shekhina.' [74]

Rabbi Eliezer here objects to both the literal translation of a Biblical anthropomorphic expression and its paraphrase by the interpolation of such terms as

Glory and Shekhina. The basis of his objection to the first method is that it makes it appear as if God could directly be apprehended by human sense organs, which, of course, is untrue with reference to a purely spiritual deity. His objection to the second method must stem from the experience or knowledge that his contemporaries tended to regard such expressions as Glory and Shekhina as designations for discrete deities. While Rabbi Eliezer considered such a view as blasphemous, others, as we have seen above, saw nothing exceptionable in it, at least as far as the Shekhina was concerned.

6. THE FEMININE SHEKHINA

The passages which establish the Shekhina as a separate divine personality, indicate her feminity in no way except by the grammatical gender of her name. It should be emphasized, however, that both in Hebrew and Aramaic, the gender of the subject plays a much greater role in the sentence structure than in Indo-European languages. In English, for instance, one can say, as in the last quoted passage, "The Shekhina rose up . . . and said," without becoming aware at all of the gender of "the Shekhina." In Semitic languages, the verb as well as the adjective have separate male and female forms; in the sentence "the Shekhina rose up . . . and said," therefore, both verbs impress the reader (or hearer) with the feminity of the Shekhina by taking themselves the feminine forms. Thus, even without any explicit pronouncement to the effect that the Shekhina was a female divine entity, her sex was kept in the forefront of consciousness by every statement made about her.

In Midrashic homilies, the Talmudic sages allowed themselves considerable latitude in throwing light on the mystery of the deity by comparing him to human beings of both sexes. The following passage, transmitted in the name of Shemuel bar Nahman, a

Palestinian teacher of the 3rd and 4th centuries, can serve as an example:

> It is the wont of the father to have mercy, 'Like as a father has compassion upon his children, so has the Lord compassion upon them that fear Him'; [75] and it is the wont of the mother to comfort, 'as one whom his mother comforts, so will I comfort you.' [76] God said: 'I shall do as both father and mother.' [77]

It is, of course, a far cry from saying that God acts like a father and a mother to asserting, as Philo did,[78] that he has two components, a fatherly and a motherly. Yet the Shekhina, with her feminine gender, comes quite close in the Talmudic sources to being regarded as a feminine manifestation of the deity. The following statement by Rabbi Aha, a Palestinian Amora of the early 4th century, definitely points in that direction:

> When the Shekhina left the Sanctuary, she returned to caress and kiss its walls and columns, and cried and said: 'Be in peace, O my Sanctuary, be in peace, O my royal palace, be in peace, O my precious house, be in peace from now on, be in peace!' [79]

In another passage it is the Community of Israel (Knesseth Yisrael, also of feminine gender and subsequently identified with the Shekhina or symbolized by her), lamenting the destruction of the Temple:

> The Community of Israel said before the Holy One, blessed be He: 'Master of the World! I remember the safety, the security and the peace which I used to enjoy, and now it is all departed from me. And I cry and lament and say: O, if I could return to former years when the Sanctuary stood, and when you used to come down into it from the high heavens, and let your Shekhina

rest on me, and the nations of the world would praise me! And when I would seek forgiveness for my sins, you would answer me. But now I am covered with shame and disgrace.'

And she also said before Him: 'Master of the World! My heart breaks in me when I pass by your house and it is destroyed, and the voice of silence is in it and says: The place in which Abraham's seed presented sacrifices before you, and the priests stood on their platform, and the Levites intoned praise on their harps, how can it be that now foxes dance in it?! . . . But what can I do, since my sins brought this about, and the false prophets who arose in me led me astray from the way of life to the way of death. . . .

When the Temple was destroyed by fire, the Holy One, blessed be He, said: 'Now that I have no seat on earth, I shall remove my Shekhina from her [the earth] and shall ascend to my first abode.' . . . In that hour the Holy One, blessed be He, cried and said: 'Woe to me, what did I do, I let my Shekhina dwell below for the sake of Israel, and now that they sinned, I returned to my first place . . . I became a laughter unto the nations and a derision to the creatures.' In that hour Metatron [God's chief ministering angel] came, fell upon his face, and addressed God: 'Master of the World! Let me cry in Your place!' But God answered him: 'If you do not let me cry now, I shall retire to a place into which you have no permission to enter, and shall cry there.' . . . [Thereafter] God said to the ministering angels. 'Come, let us descend, I and you, and see what the enemy did to my house.' . . . When God saw the Sanctuary, He said: 'Verily, this is my house, and this is my resting place, into which the enemy entered and did what he wanted.' And God cried and said: 'Woe to me because of my House! My sons, where are you? My lovers, where are You? What shall I do to you? I warned you, but you did not repent.' [80]

That the Shekhina is the love aspect of God is clearly stated in a parable which compares the Temple to Solomon's palanquin: just as the latter was inlaid with love, so did the Shekhina fill the sanctuary.[81] But she also represents the divine punitive power. This is most succinctly expressed in a Tannaitic passage which states that on ten occasions did the Shekhina descend from on High: after the Fall, when she entered the Garden of Eden to punish Adam, Eve, and the Serpent; when she confused the builders of the Tower of Babel; when she destroyed Sodom and Gomorrah; when she saved the Children of Israel from Egyptian slavery; when she drowned the Egyptians in the Sea of Reeds; when she appeared on Mount Sinai; when she led the Children of Israel in the pillar of cloud; when she entered the Sanctuary; and once more will she descend in the future in the days of the battle of Gog and Magog.[82] We note that in the above list, which actually enumerates only nine descents—one evidently got lost while the tradition still circulated orally—five descents of the Shekhina are punitive expeditions. As we shall see in a subsequent chapter, the punitive aspect of the Shekhina, closely paralleled by the cruel aspect of the ancient Near Eastern love-goddesses, plays an important role in the Kabbalistic figure of the Shekhina-Matronit.

A mixture of the punitive and the merciful aspects of the Shekhina appears in the legends which attribute to her the function of taking the souls of exceptionally meritorious men. There were six individuals, we read in the Talmud, whom the Angel of Death could not overcome, and who died only through a kiss of the Shekhina; they were Abraham, Isaac, Jacob, Moses, Aaron, and Miriam.[83] According to another passage, it was God who took the soul of one of them, Moses, by kissing him on the mouth.[84] But after Moses died, it was the Shekhina who carried him on her wings a distance of four miles to the place where he was to be buried.[85]

Since Moses is said to have to given up all carnal contact with his wife in order to be always ready to

receive communication from the Shekhina, it seems
probable that a notion clearly stated in the Zohar
was already present in rudimentary form in Talmudic
times: the idea that the relationship between Moses
and the Shekhina was like that of husband and wife.[86]
If so, there is an interesting parallel between the Shekhina carrying her dead husband, Moses, to his burial
place, and the Ugaritic myth about Anath carrying
the body of her husband-brother, Baal, to his burial
place.[87]

7. CONCLUSION

We have followed, in this chapter, the development
of the Shekhina concept from its Biblical antecedents,
through its early Targumic beginnings in the 1st or
2nd century B.C., to the stage it reached a thousand
years later, just prior to being taken up by Kabbalism
and made into one of the cornerstones of its mystical
theosophy. At first, it seems, the Shekhina served
merely as a convenient means of solving the problem
presented by Biblical anthropomorphisms in the eyes
of a later, more sensitive, theology. By interpolating
the Shekhina, it was no longer God himself who was
said to have acted in a human manner, but his
"presence" which, evidently, was conceived as something akin to a "presence" manifesting itself at a
spiritualists' seance, a barely visible indication of what
is acknowledged to be pure spirit and therefore not
apprehensible by the senses.

Before long, however, this spiritual "presence" began to take on substance. Her movements from place
to place could now be discerned, and, having acquired
a physical aspect, she became subject to historical
events: more and more closely joined to the fate of
Israel, she suffered its vicissitudes, accompanied the
people into their exiles, and experienced the hopes
and despairs with which Israel reacted to the blows
dealt her by fate or, as the Sages of the Talmud

would have put it, shared in the punishments meted out by God to his sinful people. In this capacity, the Shekhina came very close to being identified with the Knesseth Yisrael, the personified, female "Community of Israel."

Next, almost inadvertently, as the distance between God and the Shekhina grew, the latter took on increasingly pronounced physical attributes. The more impossible it became to think of God himself in anthropomorphic terms, the more the Shekhina became humanized. Now she could be heard as well as seen, and, having found her voice, it was inevitable that she would speak not only to man but to God. Once she was allowed to do this, there was no longer any doubt that the deity was considered as comprised of two persons: God and the Shekhina.

In Biblical times, there was nothing strange, let alone heretical, about a plural concept of the godhead. Most of the nations in whose midst Israel dwelt recognized divine pluralities, and the old Hebrew myth saw nothing remarkable in the fact that Yahweh appeared to Abraham in the shape of three men who, however, were unhesitatingly recognized by Abraham as one person. The narrative is masterly in conveying the mystery of this three-in-one deity by changing back and forth between plural and singular,[88] to which has to be added the further mystery of the unexplained changeover of the "three men" into "two angels" by the time they reached Sodom, and their contradictory identification as Yahweh's messengers.[89] Thus, Philo's theosophic discernment of the two aspects of the deity[90] is, in fact, not too far removed from this old Biblical indeterminacy as to the number of persons in the deity, nor is the Talmudic postulation of God and the Shekhina as two divine entities.

Philo assigned masculinity to one, and femininity to the other, aspect of the godhead. Such a step was never taken by Talmudic Judaism, or at least such a thought was never clearly formulated or expressed, until the days of the Kabbala. Yet the very fact that all the names of God (Yahweh; Elohim; the Holy One, blessed be He; etc.) were masculine, while the name Shekhina was feminine (as were other manifestations of the deity, such as the Holy Spirit, the Word, Wisdom, etc.), inevitably pointed in the direction of such a sexual differentiation, which came about, as it was bound to, with the great medieval mystical movement of the Kabbala.

The latency of the feminine elements in the Jewish God concept for one millennium and a half is a psychologically remarkable phenomenon. From about 400 B.C. to 1100 A.D. the God of Judaism was a lone and lofty father-figure, and whatever female divinity was allowed to exist in his shadow was either relegated to a lower plane, or her femininity was masked and reduced to a grammatical gender, as in the case of the Shekhina. Yet in spite of the masculine predominance on the highest level of the Talmudic God concept, popular belief and imagination dwelt in a world peopled and haunted by feminine numina, ranging from lowly and loathsome she-demons to exalted personifications. It is to an examination of these ideas that we next turn.

Chapter V

THE KABBALISTIC TETRAD

Let us now turn to the development of the Hebrew goddess myth in the Middle Ages, when the mythical-mystical figure of a feminine divinity occupied a central place in Jewish religious consciousness.

There are some puzzling factors about this medieval Jewish religious development. One is that it took place in an entirely religion-bound community, whose official doctrines could never have tolerated deviation from strict monotheism. Another, that, on the surface at least, it appears as if the primary factor in the emergence of the goddess figure and her divine family had been mystical speculation about the nature of the deity, which in turn led to the creation of mythical narratives about the relationship among the four members of the supernal Tetrad.

There is, of course, no hard and fast dividing line between mystical symbolism and mythical narrative. On the contrary, these two areas of religious expression imperceptibly merge, and those whose religious inclinations impel them to approach the border region from either side, may suddenly find that they have crossed over to the other. Historical examples show that at times such crossings-over were effected purposely: old polytheistic myths were, in this manner, transformed into mystical theological ideas and thereby fitted into the framework of a narrower, more rigidly monotheistic religion. The best known, though not always readily acknowledged, example of this type of transformation is the re-emergence of the ancient

Near Eastern mythological feature of divine triads (a group of three gods) in the Christian doctrine of the Holy Trinity.

At other times, the searching mind, striking out along unexplored paths of religious discovery, finds itself on the other side, having crossed the invisible border unintentionally and inadvertently. Such an accidental slippage from the realm of mystical speculation into that of mythical narrative occurred in connection with the Kabbalistic interpretation of the mystical meaning of the Tetragrammaton, the secret and most holy four-letter name of God, which to pronounce was considered a mortal sin. An examination of the psychological and traditional channels along which this slippage took place will occupy us in this chapter, together with the attempt to reconstruct the myths of the four divinities constituting the Kabbalistic tetrad. First, however, let us look at the world of the Kabbala in which this tetrad occupied a pivotal position.

1. THE KABBALA

The Kabbala was a great Jewish religious movement which reached its literary zenith in the 13th century, and its greatest popularity in the 16th and 17th centuries. Its roots go back to Talmudic notions and ideas, and even beyond them, to doctrines first adumbrated by Philo of Alexandria, the 1st century Hellenistic Jewish philosopher, whose teachings about the Cherubim were examined in Chapter Three. Central to the Kabbala is a secret and esoteric doctrine about the nature of the deity and the relationship between God, World, and Man. While the Kabbala as a whole is deeply mystical, it is speculative rather than ecstatic. It emphasizes the intuitive grasp of ultimate truths, but at the same time demands the most exacting observance of all the laws and rules of traditional Judaism. It stresses the personal religious experience, yet, paradoxically, it considers itself as a body of old, transmitted wisdom, as indicated by the meaning of its very name, Kabbala, literally "Reception," that is, something "received" from ancient masters. In fact, the chain of Kabbalistic tradition is believed to lead back to Adam himself, whose knowledge of all the ultimate secrets was derived directly from divine communication.[1]

The foundations of medieval Kabbalism were laid in Babylonia and Byzantium in the 7th and 8th centuries, when a number of Midrashim with marked Kabbalistic tendencies made their appearance. Several of these (e.g., the *Alpha Beta of Rabbi Akiba* and the *Midrash Konen*) deal with the mysteries of Creation and the structure of the universe. Other writings of the same period describe the heavens, represented as seven celestial palaces (the so-called *Hekhalot*), and the divine chariot (*Merkaba*) which served as the throne of God. These early ventures into mystical cosmogony, cosmology, and theosophy were transmitted in the 9th century to Italy and Germany, and, soon thereafter, also to Spain, which in the 13th century became the chief center of the Kabbala.

The most important work of the entire Kabbalistic movement, the Zohar, or "Book of Splendor," was written ca. 1286 by Moses de Leon (ca. 1240–1305) in Castile, Spain, but was attributed by him to Shimeon ben Yohai, the 2nd-century Palestinian teacher and mystic. With this voluminous book (it contains close to a million words), written in the forms of a mystical commentary to the Five Books of Moses, in a somewhat artificial Aramaic, Spanish Kabbala reached its culmination. For the subsequent two centuries, however, Kabbalism remained the esoteric preoccupation of a few select individuals. An important new development took place following the expulsion of the Jews from Spain in 1492, which brought about a powerful upsurge of Messianic longings for a redemption, and resulted in the migration of several leading Spanish Kabbalists to the town of Safed in the Galilee. Within a few years thereafter, Safed became the new center of the Kabbala and held this position for a short but remarkable period in the 16th century.

From Safed, the Kabbala spread rapidly to all the Asian, African, and European centers of the Jewish diaspora. It soon became a veritable mass religion, and as such prepared the ground for the Messianic movement led by Shabbatai Zevi (1626–1676) and, a century later, for East European Hassidism, the pietistic-mystical sectarianism which nearly caused a schism in Judaism in the 19th century. Thus Kabbalistic mysticism became one of the most powerful forces to lead the Jewish people forward on its historic course, until Enlightenment and Emancipation, and then Nationalism and Zionism, took over to serve as vital propellants.

In the Kabbalistic doctrine of God, fully developed in the Zohar, the feminine element plays an extremely important role. As Gershom Scholem, the foremost authority on the subject, put it, the introduction of the idea that the Shekhina was the feminine element in God, opposed to "the Holy One, blessed be He," as the masculine element in Him,

> was one of the most important and lasting innovations of Kabbalism. The fact that it obtained recognition in spite of the obvious difficulty of reconciling it with the conception of the absolute unity of God, and that no other element of Kabbalism won such a degree of popular approval, is proof that it responded to a deep-seated religious need. . . . It says something for its vitality that despite the opposition of such powerful forces [as the philosophers and the Talmudists] this idea became part and parcel of the creed of wide circles among the communities of Europe and the East.[2]

The Zohar and the later Kabbalistic works are replete with references to the Shekhina, the female divine entity already familiar to us from her appearances in the earlier Talmudic and Midrashic literatures.

In the next chapter we shall discuss in detail this feminine divinity whose favorite Kabbalistic name is "the Matronit," i.e., the Matron. What we wish to consider here is the question of the relationship of the Shekhina to God, and the issue of polytheism versus monotheism represented by it. The learned among the Kabbalists were undoubtedly aware of the problem, grappled with it, and succeeded in solving it in a manner satisfactory to them. One can imagine that by extraordinary mental effort they were able to remain unfailingly aware of the absolute oneness of God even while their imagination was assaulted by the most outspoken descriptions of passionate embraces between the male and female "elements" of the deity.

But the learned were always few, while the ignorant and near-ignorant were many. The strength of Kabbalism lay not in what it meant for the select few who were able to devote a lifetime to its study, even as the intellectual elite of the anti-Kabbalists did to the study of the Talmud. The Kabbala's significance lay precisely in the great influence it exerted, from the 16th century on, upon the many, the masses, for whom intensive study was out of the question. If the most conspicuous ideas and teachings of Kabbalism nevertheless reached them, it was by word of mouth and in greatly simplified form. To put it differently, a simpler idea had a greater chance of popular acceptance than a more difficult one. The belief in the Shekhina (or Matronit), the matronly, divine figure, who, in a way, functioned as an intermediary between the People of Israel and God, was a simple, easily comprehended idea. Since it "responded to a deep-seated religious need," it won ready acceptance among wide circles in the Jewish communities everywhere. Much more difficult to understand was the complementary doctrine which maintained that God and the Shekhina were one. Lip-service, to be sure, was paid by all to the time-honored orthodox Jewish concept of the Oneness of God. On the logical level, many were even able to assert that the Shekhina and the other elements (of which more below) discerned in

God were merely symbols which helped in comprehending the mystery of His nature, or emanations issuing forth from Him, but in no way affecting His fundamental Oneness.

Yet on the deeper level of emotion and imagination, the image of the wifely and motherly, passionate and compassionate female divinity met with immediate, spontaneous and positive response. Especially to popular imagination, the Shekhina was no mere symbol or emanation, but a great heavenly reality whose shining countenance shoved the theoretical doctrine of the Oneness of God into the background. The deep emotional attachment of the simple, unsophisticated followers of the Kabbala to the Shekhina was comparable to the relationship of the Italian or Spanish villagers to their Madonna. In both cases it cannot be denied that one is faced with the veneration of a goddess, and it is impossible to dispute that she means more for the satisfaction of deep-seated religious-emotional needs than God Himself.

Numerous passages in the Zohar, whatever their possible interpretation as mystical speculations about God, struck a responsive chord in hearts yearning for a divine mother-image. Some of these passages deal with the tragic figure of the Matronit which we shall analyze in the next chapter. Others discuss the divine tetrad, the four major persons of the Zoharic godhead, and several of these passages make it appear that the name Yahweh, composed of four letters, was the basis from which the concept of the divine family of four was derived. We shall, therefore, turn next to that most ancient, most holy and forbidden name of God, the Tetragrammaton.

2. THE TETRAGRAMMATON

In the Bible, God is referred to by several names, such as El, Elohim, Shaddai, Yahweh, or a combination of these. In the Talmudic period, the most frequently used name of God was "the Holy One, blessed be He." In the Zohar and Kabbalistic literature in general, God is still called "the Holy One, blessed be He," but, in addition, several other mystical divine names appear, which refer to God in relation to various stages in the history of the universe, or designate certain aspects of His being.

The ancient Biblical Tetragrammaton, Yahweh (YHWH), is regarded in the Kabbala as an abbreviated symbol of four divine elements which form part of the deity. The four elements are *Hokhma* (Wisdom), *Bina* (Understanding), *Tif'eret* (Beauty), and *Malkhut* (Kingship). Moreover, Wisdom is identified with the Father, Understanding with the Mother, Beauty with the Son, and Kingship with the Daughter. These four divine concepts form the Kabbalistic tetrad.

One passage in the Zohar, for instance, states that "the letter Y in the name YHWH is called Father and stands for Wisdom; the first H is the Supernal Mother, called Understanding; and the W and the second H are the two children, a son and a daughter, who were crowned by their Mother." [3]

A related passage explains:

Wisdom spread out and brought forth Understanding, and they were found to be male and female, Wisdom the Father, and Understanding the Mother. . . . Then these two united, and lighted up each other, and the H [i.e., the Mother] conceived and gave birth to a Son. Through the birth of the Son the Father and the Mother found their perfection [*tiqqun*], and this led to the completion of everything, the inclusion of everything: Father, Mother, Son and Daughter.[4]

In yet another Zoharic passage more details are given about the origin of this divine family:

The Y brought forth a river which issued from the Garden of Eden and was identical with the Mother. The Mother became pregnant with the two children, the W who was the Son, and the second

H who was the daughter, and she brought them forth and suckled them. . . . These two children are under the tutelage of the Father and the Mother. . . . After the Mother gave birth to the Son, she placed him before her, and this is why the first H in the name YHWH must be written close together with the W. The Son received a double share of inheritance from his Father and Mother, and he, in turn, nourished the Daughter. This is why when writing the Tetragrammaton in sacred texts, one must bring the W and the second H close together.[5]

In spite of the explicitness of these passages, which is matched and even surpassed by many others to be dealt with further on, all the modern students of the Kabbala interpret them as nothing more than mystical symbolism.[6] They argue that it is in the nature of the Kabbalistic style to speak of aspects or emanations of the One God as if they were independent entities. Since God is known to be wise, they speak of His Wisdom; since He is possessed of understanding, they speak of His Understanding, etc., and to further clarify these attributes, they designate them as Father, Mother, Son, and Daughter.

Two considerations render this interpretation unsatisfactory. One is the "slippage" phenomenon referred to above, which can be observed in many Kabbalistic elaborations of the four "elements" in the deity, dealing with their affairs and vicissitudes, the relationships between them and their reactions to one another. Even if the Kabbalistic tetrad had actually and demonstrably originated in purely mystical speculation, somewhere on the way such a slippage occurred, with the result that the colorful details supplied about the four persons of the deity clearly belong to the realm of myth.

The other consideration which vitiates the mystical-symbolic interpretation of the Kabbalistic tetrad is the existence of numerous divine tetrads in other religions with occasional surprising similarities between the myths told about them and the statements made about the four "elements" of God in Kabbalistic literature.

This not only renders it unlikely that what the Kabbala has to say about the tetrad was engendered merely by mystical symbolism, but makes us suspect that the Kabbalistic myths about the tetrad reflect outside, non-Jewish influences. A rapid survey of polytheistic tetrad myths is here called for to substantiate this assumption.

3. ANCIENT TETRADS

Tetrads, although not as common as triads, are found in several religious cultures of antiquity. The earliest known group of four related gods is that of ancient Egyptian religion. The father-god, Shu, we read in early Egyptian mythological texts, was the air that carried the sky. His female counterpart was Tefnut, goddess of moisture. Their union produced a son Geb, or Earth, and a daughter Nut, or Sky. Geb and Nut were united in tight marital embrace, until Father Shu separated them by raising the sky up from the bosom of the earth.[7] (See Plate 29.)

Only somewhat younger is the tetrad myth of the Sumerians, the old, non-Semitic inhabitants of Mesopotamia. The precise family relationships of the gods of the Sumerian pantheon is obscure, and in most cases little is known about which god was whose son, husband, father or brother, and which goddess was whose daughter, wife, mother or sister. Nevertheless, it has become clear, primarily thanks to the indefatigable studies of Samuel N. Kramer, that there was a close, first-degree relationship between a group of four gods who were in control of heaven, earth, sea, and air, and who, among them, created all the other cosmic entities.[8] The four were the god of Heaven, An; the great mother goddess Ninhursag; the god of water, Enki; and the god of air, Enlil. That they were a clearly defined tetrad is evident not only from their position of primary creator gods, but also from their continued importance after the emergence of the other gods. It is they who "usually head the god lists, and are often listed as performing significant acts together as a group." Moreover, "at divine meetings and banquets they were given the seats of honor." [9]

An, the heaven-god, was once the supreme ruler of the Sumerian pantheon, but as early as the 3rd millennium B.C. his place was taken by Enlil, the air-god, who is also titled "father of the gods," and "king of all lands." He was also the god of Wisdom, and the ruler of the abyss (*absu*)—an early indication of the oft-recurring connection between wisdom and water.

Ninhursag was also called Ninmah, Nintu, and Aruru, although her original name seems to have been Ki, meaning "[mother] Earth." She was probably taken to be the wife of An (Heaven), and the two, An and Ki, may have been conceived as the parents of all the gods.[10] In her capacity as the great mother and the earth goddess, Ninhursag was also "the lady who gave birth," the mother of all living things, and especially the mother of the earthly kings. The early Sumerian kings liked to describe themselves as "constantly nourished with milk by Ninhursag." [11]

Enki, king of the watery abyss, calls himself in a paean of self-glorification "the first-born of An," [12] which would make Ninhursag his mother. However, in another passage of the same long poem, Ninhursag is called "Enlil's sister," [13] and she calls Enki, "my brother." [14] This apparently reflects another version of the early Sumerian tetrad, according to which An (Heaven) had three children, Ninhursag, Enki and Enlil. The contradiction in the position of Ninhursag, who appears as both mother and sister of Enki and Enlil, can possibly be resolved by referring to the Zoharic explanation of the Tetragrammaton discussed above. The Father ("Wisdom" there too), we shall recall, brought forth the Mother, that is, the Mother was originally the Father's daughter. But then Father and Mother had union, and the Mother gave birth to the Son and the Daughter. Thus the Mother was, at one and the same time, also the sister of her Son and Daughter. It can be conjectured that a lost Sumerian myth may likewise have told how Father An brought forth Ki (Ninhursag) by spontaneous generation (or by masturbation, as Atum was said to have engendered Shu and Tefnut in Egyptian mythology).[15] If so, then Ninhursag, like the Mother in Kabbalism, was both the mother and the sister of her two children.

The tetrad of the Hittites, whose ancient empire centered on the Anatolian plateau and who spoke several unrelated languages, can be mentioned only in passing. The Hittites absorbed so much foreign mythological material that the isolation of original Hittite myths would be a major scholarly task which lies far beyond the present author's competence. However, even a cursory perusal of the readily accessible Hittite myths shows that groups of four gods appear repeatedly. One text-fragment enumerates the four gods Kashku (the Moon-god), Taru (the Storm-god), Hapantalli, and Katakhziwuri. Another appeals to "the mighty gods" Naras, Napsaras, Minkins, and Ammunkis.[16] A Hittite myth of unquestionably Canaanite origin is the one in which the tetrad of Elkunirsa (that is, the Canaanite *El qone eretz,* "El, Creator of the Earth"), his wife Ashertu (Asherah), their son Baal-Hadad, the Storm-god, and their daughter Ishtar (Astarte or Anath) figures prominently.[17]

An ancient Near Eastern bronze figure of unknown provenance shows a divine tetrad in the form of four human figures rising out of a common stem and held together at their lower legs by a ring. (See Plate 30.)

In the ancient Canaanite pantheon itself the four gods El, Asherah, Baal, and Anath stand out among all the other gods as a clearly recognizable divine family. Thanks to the major archaeological discovery of the Ugaritic tablets at Ras Shamra, near the northeastern corner of the Mediterranean, we have an exceptionally complete picture of the mythological world of the northern Canaanites in the 14th century B.C.

The chief of all gods was El, the father god, often called "bull of his father." His wife Asherah, also referred to as "Lady Asherah of the Sea," was the mother of all other gods whom she suckled at her breasts. Their son Baal, also called Aliyan, Prince, King, and Rider of Clouds, was the god of rain, and fertility, who periodically died and again came to life. Their daughter Anath, usually referred to as the Virgin or the Maiden Anath, or simply as The Girl, was the goddess of love and female fecundity, as well as of the war and the hunt, who enjoyed fighting as much as she did love-making, was bloodthirsty, tempestuous and unrestrained.[18]

In Greek mythology, Cronus, Rhea, Zeus and Hera seem to have formed the original divine tetrad. Cronus and Rhea were brother and sister as well as husband and wife. After castrating his father Uranus ("Sky"), Cronus ruled in his stead, until he, in turn, was castrated and dethroned by his own son, Zeus, who then became King of the gods, and god of the sky and of thunder. The wife of Zeus was Hera, his sister, goddess of the earth, fecundity, marriage, and women, and worshiped as Maid, Wife, and Widow.

The Roman equivalent of this tetrad was that of Saturn, Ops, Jupiter (Jove), and Juno. Juno's eldest and most common name was Juno Lucina, or Lucetia, referring to her original light-nature. In her capacity as the goddess of marriage, she was also known as Matrona, a name which, of course, reminds us of the Kabbalistic name of the daughter-goddess, the Matronit, who will be the subject of the next chapter. Juno Matrona's principal festival was the Matronalia or Matronales, celebrated on May 1, when husbands and wives would pray to her and offer sacrifices for marital happiness. The priest of Jupiter, the *flamen dialis*, had to be married; his wife was the *flaminica dialis*, priestess of Juno.[19]

Turning now to the great Asian world east of Mesopotamia, and first of all to Iran, we find again the by now familiar tetrad, although in a modified form. The mythical history of the world in Iran begins with

Zurvan ("Time"), a hermaphrodite, who existed prior to heaven, earth, and everything else. For a thousand years Zurvan sacrificed in order to have a son, and finally Ohrmazd and Ahriman were conceived in the womb of his female half. Overjoyed, Zurvan vowed that whichever of his children should emerge first would receive the kingdom from him. It was evil Ahriman who ripped the womb open, and presented himself to Zurvan, saying: "I am your son Ohrmazd." Zurvan, however, rejected him, and while he was still talking to Ahriman, the true Ohrmazd was born, whom Zurvan thereupon instructed to rule and order all things.[20]

A divine tetrad figures importantly in Hindu mythology. Shiva is the generative principle, the four-armed and four-legged great lord of procreation, the gigantic Phallus, identical with the Vedic storm-god Rudra, "the Roarer." His home is in the Himalayas where he lives in perfect marital happiness with his wife, Parvati, the Great Mother, symbolized by the female generative organ, and known also by many other names, among them especially Devi (goddess), i.e., *the* goddess par excellence. Parvati assumes terrifying forms also, such as that of Kali; as such she carries in her many arms a great array of weapons, and demands bloody animal and human sacrifices. She is also known as Shakti ("Power"), and, as a medieval ode puts it, "If Shiva is united with Shakti, he is able to exert his powers as lord; if not, the god is not able to stir." Anyone who truly grasps the goddess's complete nature can master the whole universe, because he becomes one with her. In her resides all love. Her devotees call upon her as children addressing their mother, and she cherishes them, taking them to herself, so that they at last become one with her, experiencing a flood of supreme joy, and tasting boundless, intense bliss.

This divine couple had two children: Ganesha, god of wisdom and remover of obstacles, and Kartikeya, god of war and patron of thieves. Shiva's vehicle is the bull Nandi, and Parvati's is a lion.

Shiva, incidentally, is also Nataraja, "Lord of the Dance," who, when attacked by the demon Muyalaka, pressed his toe upon Muyalaka's back, until he broke it, and then, with him underfoot, danced the cosmic dance of creation, maintenance, and destruction.[21]

The last tetrad we shall refer to here is central to Japanese mythology. Izanagi ("The Male Who Invites") and Izanami ("The Female Who Invites") were brother and sister who had union and procreated a great variety of divinities in many different ways. From the left eye of Izanagi, also called the August Male (his sister-wife is also the August Female), was born Amaterasu, the "Heaven Shining," the sun goddess, and from his nose, Susanowo, the "Impetuous Male." These two couples occupy the central place in Japanese cosmology. Amaterasu is resplendent and shining, and receives from Izanagi the Plain of High Heaven as her dominion. Susanowo is dark, and the rule over the Sea Plain is given to him. He becomes desirous of visiting his mother Izanami, who in the meantime had died of burns suffered in her genitals when she gave birth to the god of Fire and now inhabits the Land of Darkness. Izanagi is furious at this impertinence of his son and banishes him from the land. Susanowo thereupon resolves to take leave of his sister, who, however, mistakes his approach for an attack and meets him fully armed with bow and arrows. Susanowo assures her of his peaceful intentions and suggests that they take an oath together and produce children, which they do.

A number of common features can be distilled from these tetrad myths: the divine tetrad consists of parents and two children, usually a son and a daughter, but occasionally two sons. The four deities making up the tetrad stand for, or are in control of, the major component parts of the world, such as air, moisture, earth, and sky (Egypt); heaven, air, water, and earth (Sumer); or they represent a combination of such major components of nature and of cosmic principles, such as earth, vegetation(?), storm (i.e., rain), and fertility (Hittites); heaven, sea, rain, and fertility (Canaan); time(?), earth, sky, and female fecundity (Greece); sowing (or agriculture), abundance, sky, and marriage (Rome); male principle, female principle, heaven (or sun), and sea (Japan); or else they stand for cosmic principles and concepts, such as time (a hermaphrodite, pointing both backward to the past and forward to the future), light, and darkness (Iran); procreative principle, fertility principle, wisdom, and war (India).

Another recurrent characteristic is that the daughter in several tetrads is a goddess of both love (the fertility principle) and war (the destructive principle); thus in Hittite, Canaanite, and Japanese mythologies; in Hindu mythology, the same double role falls to the mother goddess. In several tetrads the mother goddess is conceived of as clasping her children, both gods and men, to her breast and suckling them (in Sumerian, Canaanite, and Hindu mythologies).

In at least one mythology (Hindu) one of the gods forming the tetrad is Wisdom, and the power of the Father is said to depend on his union with the Mother.

Mention can also be made of the separation of the Son and the Daughter, which in Egyptian mythology (as well as in many others in which no tetrads can be discovered) [23] figures as a precondition for the establishment of the existing cosmic order, and of the representation of creation as a victory of the creator-god over opposing forces (in Iranian and Hindu mythologies).

4. THE FATHER AND THE MOTHER

We are now ready to turn to the testimony of the Kabbalistic literature itself, and to review those passages which give evidence of "slippage" from the symbolic into the mythological realm. These passages contain numerous accounts of episodes in the life of the divine Father, Mother, Son, and Daughter, which in their sum total amount to veritable biographies. As we shall see, so many of these episodes are clearly mythological that in the face of their cumulative evidence the contention that all this is merely mystical symbolism and speculation about the "aspects," or "emanations," or even "elements" of a one and only God, must appear as pious fiction. The four entities of the godhead in these passages function as independent persons who address, converse with, act upon and react to, each other. Moreover, the deeds they perform, the experiences they undergo, and the feelings they display are all well couched in unmistakably mythological terms, strikingly similar to the tetrad myths sketched above.

To begin with, let us refer again to the fact that the explanation of the four consonants of the Tetragrammaton is given in sexual-familial terms. The four letters, as we have seen, are not only stated to symbolize (or stand for) Wisdom, Understanding, Beauty, and Kingship (which in themselves could be understood as purely conceptual attributes of God), but are also identified with Father, Mother, Son, and Daughter, respectively. In addition, as we have likewise seen, reference is made to the manner, purely sexual, in which these divine components (or may we already be permitted to call them "persons"?) originated: the Father brought forth the Mother, then copulated with her, and thus the Son and the Daughter were born.

The relationship between the Father and the Mother is discussed in numerous other passages as well, of which a few are presented here:

"Never does the inclination of the Father and the Mother toward each other cease. They always go out together and dwell together. They never separate and never leave each other. They are together in complete union." [24] We have seen above that this mythological motif (or "mythologem") is contained in the Egyptian myth of Geb and Nut, and the Hindu myth of Shiva and Parvati. Here we may add that the mythologem of the World Parents, of the Sky-father and Earth-mother as the progenitors of the universe, of their clinging together in a permanent embrace, of the timeless bliss they enjoy in their complete and ceaseless union, is quite common all over the world,[25] which

in itself renders it most unlikely that the author of
the Zohar happened by coincidence to hit upon the
same idea simply on the basis of his mystical speculations about the meaning of the first two consonants
of the Tetragrammaton.

In another Zoharic passage, the sexual union of the
Father and the Mother (here referred to as "Zaddik,"
i.e., Righteous One, and his "Female") is described
in unflinching physiological detail:

> When the seed of the Righteous is about to be
> ejaculated, he does not have to seek the Female,
> for she abides with him, never leaves him, and is
> always in readiness for him. His seed flows not
> save when the Female is ready, and when they
> both as one desire each other; and they unite in
> a single embrace, and never separate. . . . Thus
> the Righteous is never foresaken.[26]

The unceasing love between the Father and the
Mother, and its tangible expression, their permanent
union, earned them the name "Companions" (re'im):

> The Father and the Mother, since they are
> found in union all the time and are never hidden
> or separated from each other, are called 'Com-
> panions'. . . . And they find satisfaction in per-
> manent union. . . .[27]

The Supreme Mother is called "Companion" (ra'aya),
because the love of the Father never departs from
her.[28]

The marital embrace of the father-god and the
mother-goddess is so tight and so permanent that the
two give the impression of one body, androgynous in
nature, like Zurvan in ancient Iranian mythology. The
emergence of this idea in Jewish mysticism can be
traced back to Joseph ben Abraham Gikatilla (1248–
1305), whose writings influenced the author of the
Zohar and who, reciprocally, was influenced by the
Zohar.[29] In fact, Gikatilla warned against the belief,

held by contemporary or earlier Kabbalists, that the deity actually had the physical form of an androgyne:

> He who understands this mystery will understand all the *Merkaboth* [30] and all the Grades of Emanation which take the shape of receiver and influencer. And this is the mystery of the androgyne.[31] Not as if there was there the actual shape of an androgyne, God forbid that one should believe such a thing and broadcast such a calumny. . . . [But] each Grade of all the Grades of YHWH, blessed be He, has two faces. One face which receives from the one above it, and a second face which emits good to the one beneath it, until it reaches the navel of the earth. Thus, each Grade has two aspects, a [feminine] power of receiving . . . and a [masculine] power of emanating . . . and in this manner the *Merkaboth* are called androgyne. . . . This is a great mystery among the mysteries of the Cherubim, and the mystery of the shape of the *Merkaba*. . . .[32]

In the sequel the author makes it clear that, when speaking of the androgynous character of the godhead, he has in mind a double body joined back to back, with two front sides looking in opposite directions—the classical, Midrashic concept of the androgyne.[33]

In spite of Gikatilla's warning, however, the Kabbalistic tendency to discern a male and female element in the deity could not be suppressed. In fact, it remained an established doctrine that God consisted of male and female components. Thus we read in the Zohar:

> The Female [component of the godhead] spread out from her place and adhered to the Male side, until he moved away from his side, and she came to unite with him face to face. And when they united, they appeared as veritably one body. From this we learn that the male alone appears as half

a body . . . and the female likewise, but when
they join in union they seem as veritably one
body. . . . [On the Sabbath] all is found in one
body, complete, for the Matronit clings to the
King and they become one body, and this is
why blessings are found on that day.[34]

Moses Cordovero (1522–1570), the influential
Safed (Palestine) Kabbalist, expatiates on the subject
repeatedly in his *Pardes Rimmonim* ("The Pome-
granate Orchard"), which he completed in 1549. Typical of his approach is the following comment on the
highest of the ten Divine Emanations, or Sephirot,
called Crown: "The Crown itself is comprised of Male
and Female, for one part of it is Male, the other Female. . . ."[35]

The view that the deity is androgynous or hermaphroditic in nature, if not in form, must have existed
several centuries prior to its first explicit mention by
Gikatilla. For we read in an early Midrash that "When
the Holy One, blessed be He, created man, He created
him as an androgyne."[36] Since it was a pivotal doctrine
in Hebrew religion that God created man in His own
image,[37] the statement that man was first created in
an androgynous shape must have meant that the deity
too was imagined as hermaphroditic. This, however,
is merely our inference; in no Midrash is there even
as much as a reference or an allusion to the hermaphroditic nature of God. In Kabbalistic literature,
beginning with the Zohar, on the other hand, with its
penchant for sexualizing the entire spiritual world, the
doctrine of the male and the female aspects of the
godhead had become commonplace, and almost inevitably crystallized into the concept of the androgynous deity.

But to return to the mythical biography of the divine
parents, as a result of the enduring marital embrace,
the Supernal Mother became pregnant (again like
Zurvan in Iranian mythology) and gave birth to a
Son and a Daughter:

The Supernal H [i.e., the Mother] became pregnant as a result of all the love and fondling—since the Y never leaves her—and she brought forth the W [the Son], whereupon she stood up and suckled him. And when the W emerged, his female mate [the Daughter, represented by the second H in the Tetragrammaton] emerged together with him.[38]

The twin birth of the Son and the Daughter took place, according to another version, in the form of the birth of a single but androgynous being. In other words, the second generation of the godhead duplicated in its original shape that of the first. The passage containing this idea combines theogony with cosmogony by referring to the Son as "Heaven" and to the Daughter as "Earth": "Understanding [i.e., the Supernal Mother] brought forth Earth [i.e, the Daughter], but the latter was contained in Heaven [i.e., the Son], and they emerged together, joined together back to back. . . ." Then Heaven took Earth and set her in her proper place,

and when Earth turned to dwell in her place and became separated from the back of Heaven, she was confused and wished to adhere again to Heaven as in the beginning, because she saw that Heaven was bright while she was dark. But then Supernal Light poured forth, illuminating her, and she returned to her place to gaze at Heaven face to face, whereupon Earth was established and became joyful.[39]

This passage is significant not only mythologically but also cosmogonically. It states, as do the mythical cosmogonies of so many peoples, that the sexual union between the Father-god and the Mother-goddess resulted in the birth of Heaven and Earth. At first, Heaven carried Earth upon his back; then he separated from her and placed her beneath and opposite himself. Earth, dark and desolate, tried to reunite with

Heaven in the former position. But Heaven turned his radiance upon her, and, basking in the light reflected from Heaven, Earth was content with her place below, which she has occupied ever since. The basic similarities between this cosmogonic myth and those of other ancient cultures are obvious.

Let us now look at the relationship of the parental couple of the tetrad to their children. The Father and the Mother loved their children exceedingly, adorned their heads with many crowns, and showered them with a flood of blessings and riches. However, the Father loved the Daughter more, while the Mother's favorite was the Son. In fact, the Father's love for his Daughter knew no bounds. He called her not only Daughter, but also Sister, and even Mother, and he constantly kissed and fondled her. For the Mother, this was too much; she suffered pangs of jealousy and reproached the Daughter, demanding that she cease beguiling her husband.[40]

The wifely jealousy of a goddess is a feature frequently encountered in ancient mythologies.[40a] It is a true mythological motif, anchored in an oft-recurring human situation whence it is projected out into the divine realm. To maintain, in the face of the above passage, that the Father, Mother, and Daughter figuring in it are but mystical symbols of the different aspects of the One God requires, to say the least, a tour de force. Apart from the intrinsic evidence of the passage itself, its derivation, too, shows that it considered its protagonists as separate personalities. For, it so happens that we know the classical example after which the passage was fashioned. It is contained in a Midrash on the Song of Songs in which the love of God for Israel is made tangible by comparing it to the overpowering love a King felt for his only daughter. In his boundless love, the King was not satisfied to call his daughter "my daughter," but addressed her as "my sister" and even "my mother." And, this is exactly how God addressed His beloved Israel, the Midrash states and proceeds to illustrate its proposition by citing Biblical passages.[41]

It is on this Midrash that the author of the Zohar based his myth of the exceeding love of God the Father for his daughter, the Matronit, using the identical terms of endearment. There can be little doubt that just as in the Midrash the king and his daughter, standing for God and Israel, are two separate persons, so in the Zoharic myth the two divine figures of the Father and the Daughter were also conceived as discrete and independent personages. The jealousy of the Mother was added by Moses de Leon to the Midrashic prototype of this myth, based probably on his familiarity with similar motifs in other mythologies.

As for the divine Mother's love for her Son, she expressed it by holding him against her breast and giving suck to him, and continuing to do so even after he grew up and was ready to marry:

> As long as Israel is found with the Holy One, blessed be He [i.e., the Son], He, so to speak, is in a state of completeness, and He nourishes himself aplenty by sucking the milk of the Supernal Mother. . . .[42]

Only when the Matronit (i.e., the Daughter) was separated from the King (i.e., the Son) did "the Supernal Mother, too, remove herself from the King and cease to suckle him. . . ." [43]

The Mother-goddess suckling her son (or sons) is, as we have seen, a mythologem frequently recurring in accounts of ancient tetrads.

5. THE SON AND THE DAUGHTER

In many mythologies, the older of the two couples which form the tetrad withdraws at an early juncture to a remote position and leaves most of the troublesome dealings with mankind to the younger divine pair. Because of this, most of the myths telling about the lives of the gods focus not on the parent deities, but on their children, the two younger gods. This is certainly the case in seven out of the nine tetrads sketched above, and this is what we find in the Zoharic mythology as well. The passages dealing with the Father and the Mother, or dwelling on the relationship between them and their Son and Daughter, are relatively short texts, reiterating or alluding to a very few events. In contrast, the passages concerning the Son and the Daughter stretch into lengthy narratives, describing in detail the relationship between them, and especially the tragic phase of their tempestuous love affair, their separation which came about with the destruction of the Temple of Jerusalem and the exile of the people of Israel. An analysis of this material will be contained in the next chapter. But a summary of those features which bear directly upon the Kabbalistic tetrad belongs to the present context.

The terminology itself is complex and confusing. The Son is called "the King," "the Holy One, blessed be He," Zoharariel (meaning "Splendor of Ariel," Ariel being a name of the altar, and itself meaning "Lion of El"), Adiryaron ("The Mighty One Sings"), Aktariel ("My Crown is El"), Tetrasia ("Four God," referring to the Tetragrammaton, or to God as the ruler of the four elements, air, earth, water, and fire),[44] as well as "Heaven," as we have seen above.

His sister-wife, the divine Daughter, has even more names: Malkhuth ("Kingship," the name of the tenth Sephira), Shekhina ("Dwelling"), Matronit (Matron or Lady), "Pearl" (or "Precious Stone"), "Discarded Cornerstone," [45] as well as the "Community of Israel," "Female," "Moon," "Hart," "Earth," "Night," "Garden," "Well," "Sea," "The Supernal Woman," "The Light Woman." According to Joseph Gikatilla, " in the days of Abraham the Shekhina was called Sarah; in the days of Isaac—Rebekah; and in the days of Jacob —Rachel." [45a]

The Son and Daughter, or, as we shall refer to them from now on, the King and the Matronit, were destined to marry, like many a brother and sister in divine families. When their marriage took place is not stated, but it seems that it could not be celebrated until Solomon had built the Temple in Jerusalem, which was to serve as their wedding chamber and thereafter as their bedroom.

The problem of incest involved in the marriage of the King and the Matronit arose but did not bother the Kabbalists. Their view was that under ideal circumstances, which, of course, prevail in heaven, all unions are permitted, because "Above on high there is neither incest, nor cutting off, nor separation, nor keeping apart; therefore, above on high there is union between brother and sister, and son and daughter." [46]

While the love between the King and the Matronit was thus licit, it was very different in character from that between their parents. Where the steady, solid love of the elder couple earned them the name "Companions," the love affair of the King and the Matronit was marked by quarrels, temporary separations, and tempestuous reunions, so that the pair was properly referred to as "lovers" (*dodim*).

The reason for many of the difficulties besetting the King and the Matronit was that she became closely associated with the People of Israel (this is why she was often referred to by the name "Community of Israel," Knesseth Yisrael). Hence, when the People of Israel sinned, this resulted in a separation between God, the King, and his wife, the Matronit.

The visible expression of their separation was the destruction of the Temple, their bedroom. Invisible, but no less painfully felt, was the consequent impairment of the King's power, an idea reminiscent of the notion of Hindu mythology that the male god (Shiva) is powerful only when united with the goddess (Shakti), but is unable even to stir without her. [47] As expressed repeatedly in Kabbalistic theosophy: "The King [i.e., God] without the Matronit is not a king, is not great, and is not praised. . . ." [48] Therefore, the separation of the King and the Matronit was a calamity for both the people of Israel and the godhead itself.

In other mythologies, as well as in the Zohar, it is

a commonplace that divine acts influence the fate of men. The reverse of this idea, that human deeds have a spontaneous, almost automatic effect on the fate of the gods, is not, as far as is known to me, a part of pagan mythologies. But precisely this idea plays an important role in Kabbalistic mythology. Two examples, expressing at the same time the close analogy between the marriage of man and woman and that of the King and the Matronit, will suffice:

> The groom and the bride, as soon as they receive the seven blessings under the wedding canopy, become united following the Supernal example. And therefore, he who commits adultery with another's wife damages the union and, as it were, causes a separation on high into two authorities. Because the union of the Community of Israel [i.e., the Matronit] is only with the Holy One, blessed be He [i.e., the King], such an adulterer 'Robs his father and his mother' [49]— 'his father,' this is the Holy One, blessed be He; 'his mother,' this is the Community of Israel.[50]

That is to say, an adulterer, who causes separation between a man and his wife, wreaks grave damage in heaven also, by causing separation between the divine couple.

The second example is a passage which expresses the idea that a man is supposed to practice *imitatio dei* by marrying and begetting a son and a daughter, thus reproducing, in flesh and blood, the divine tetrad; and that, by failing to do so, he "diminishes the image" of God, causing separation between members of the divine tetrad:

> When is a man called complete in his resemblance to the Supernal? When he couples with his spouse in oneness, joy, and pleasure, and a son and a daughter issue from him and his female. This is the complete man resembling the Above: he is complete below after the pattern

of the Supernal Holy Name, and the Supernal
Holy Name is applied to him. . . . A man who does
not want to complete the Holy Name below in
this manner, it were better for him that he were
not created, because he has no part at all in the
Holy Name. And when he dies and his soul
leaves him, it does not unite at all with him because he diminished the image of his Master.[51]

6. THE TETRAD AS MYTH

The above analecta will have to suffice at this stage
of our efforts to piece together a mythological biography of the divine tetrad of the Kabbala. That
we have to do here with polytheistic myths or, at
least, myth fragments cannot be doubted. But if so, it
remains now to give consideration to the question of
the meaning of these myth fragments for the author
of the Zohar (and of the other Kabbalistic treatises
quoted), and for the followers of the Kabbala, the
m'qubbalim, who believed in and were deeply influenced by these writings and doctrines. Two problems
at once become apparent.

One is that the Kabbala-believing Jews, no less than
their co-religionists who disapproved of the Kabbala,
were strict monotheists. The tenet that there is only
One God was equally axiomatic for both groups. Any
question as to the possible polytheistic meaning of the
passages quoted above would undoubtedly have met
with the most vehement and indignant denial on the
part of the Kabbalists, although their opponents were
wont to accuse them of precisely such pluralistic
heresies.[52] To the believers, however, the mystical
doctrines and the books expounding them simply
could not contain anything so blasphemous—indeed,
anything that was not in complete accord with the
teachings of pure faith first embodied in the Bible.
If it was pointed out to them that this or that
passage in the Zohar smacked of polytheistic heresy,

their answer was ready: what might seem heresy in a passage was not its *true* meaning, which could be understood only by immersing oneself in the "mysteries" (*razin*) of the hidden truths. To their thought processes, inured to and conditioned by turns of expression such as "this means," "as if," "as it were," and the like, with which every page of the Zohar is replete, any passage, even one speaking quite clearly of two or four deities, would appear to be referring to the One God in His various aspects, the very existence of which was one of the greatest "mysteries."

While such must have been the conscious and habitual mental processes which made the Zoharic doctrine of the tetrad unexceptionable to the Kabbalists, that doctrine struck a different chord in the subconscious realm of emotional response. Man everywhere fashions his gods in his own image, and familism was, and has remained until quite recently, a most important factor, if not the central one, in the socio-psychological image of the Jew. The Jew could not imagine a Jewish life without the family, nor one not centered around the family. The lone, aloof God, adored by the Jews up to the time of the Kabbalistic upsurge, could not satisfy the emotional craving which sought a reflection of earthly life in the heavenly realm. The lone, aloof God, even if cast in the image of the father, even if surrounded by all his heavenly hosts, the angels and archangels, functioning as the heavenly patrons of the elements of which nature and mankind were composed, could not be recognized as a reflection in God of the human condition. And vice versa, human existence, always appearing to Jewish consciousness in the multiple form of man, wife, and children, could not be recognized as the true reflection of God, in whose image man was said to have been created, as long as that God was alone.

The removal of this barrier of non-correspondence was a stroke of genius of Jewish mysticism. The divine tetrad, however successfully explained away on the conscious level, evoked an immediate response on the subconscious emotional level. Within it, the similarity of God and man was established down to small details. By marrying and procreating children, the Jewish man now fulfilled a great God-pleasing deed, not only because God commanded him to do so—that alone, one out of 613 commandments, would not explain the central importance of family life—but because in doing so he engaged in an *imitatio dei,* an emulation of God, of the most intrinsic and highest order. By uniting with his wife, begetting children, and maintaining his family, the Jew acted—now he knew—exactly as God did, because He too lived on high in a family circle of His own, with His Wife, His Son, and His Daughter. And more than that: by marrying and begetting children, man directly contributed to the well-being of the Divine Family, promoted the happiness and the completeness of the Supernal Couple and their children. The emotional satisfaction derived by the mystic from this belief, however much or little of it was allowed to rise over the threshold of conscious knowledge, contributed in no small measure to the popular appeal of the Zoharic doctrine.

The second problem centers around the authors of the Kabbalistic treatises—and, in particular, the author of the Zohar. Were they aware of injecting polytheistic ideas into Jewish faith and, if so, from where did they (or he) take the doctrine of the divine tetrad? If not, what train of thought led them to these concepts?

Let us begin by assuming, as all or most modern students of Jewish mysticism have, that Kabbalistic theosophy is nothing but the result of mystical speculation about the nature of God, and that the passages describing the Father, the Mother, the Son, and the Daughter and their interrelationships are free inventions created for the purpose of rendering various aspects of the One Divinity intelligible. In this case, we must also assume that the similarities between these inventions and the details contained in the mythologies of other religions about their respective tetrads were due to sheer coincidence. But this is highly unlikely, if not impossible, because the similarities are too numerous, too detailed, and too complex. It is impossible that, beginning with the name YHWH as the only point of departure, mystical speculation should develop a system of a divine tetrad which fits in as completely as the Zoharic one does with all the other ancient tetrads, from Rome in the West to Japan in the East.

We must, therefore, conclude that the author of the Zohar worked with a much greater supply of raw material than the Tetragrammaton alone. From where he drew his knowledge about other tetrads, and how much he knew about them, cannot at this stage be determined. Yet that Spanish Kabbalists were familiar with non-Jewish religious systems, and not only those that flourished around the Mediterranean Basin, is a fact that has been recognized by no less an authority on Jewish mysticism than Professor Scholem, who has pointed out that the teachings of Abraham Abulafia (a contemporary of Moses de Leon; born in Saragossa in 1240, died ca. 1291) "represent but a Judaized version of that ancient spiritual technique which has found its classical expression in the practices of the Indian mystics who followed the system known as *Yoga*," including such features as breathing, body postures, ecstatic visions, etc.[53] If Yoga could influence Abulafia, one is permitted to assume that Indian mythology may have been known to, and reflected in, the thinking of Moses de Leon. A knowledge of Indian theosophy could have reached 13th-century Spain, just as knowledge of Yoga practices, through the intermediacy of the Arabs. As we have seen, it so happens that the Zohar's tetrad shows greater similarity to the Indian than to any other tetrad. The idea that, if not united with the goddess, the God is powerless, found in almost identical phrasing in both the Zohar and Indian mythology, is an especially striking instance.

But if Moses de Leon knew of "pagan" divine tetrads, did he consciously include the idea in his Zohar? To answer in the affirmative would be tantamount to charging him with willful propagation of idolatrous heresies, and I do not believe this was the case. The idea that the Godhead was androgynous

by nature was a theosophic doctrine latent in Judaism
for many centuries. As we saw above, Philo of Alexandria discerned a male and a female element in the
deity as early as the 1st century A.D. Thus when Moses
de Leon came to explain the "hidden meaning" and
the "true significance" of the Tetragrammaton, he followed old, if indistinct, paths interpreting its first two
letters (YH, which in themselves are a short form of
the name of God) as referring to the male and female
elements in God, identified as Wisdom and Understanding. When speculating about the third and fourth
letters, his thinking was influenced by what he knew
and remembered of the "pagan" tetrads, and possibly
in the first place of the Indian one. The third and fourth
letters became identified in De Leon's mind with the
mystical offspring of the original divine couple. Had
he followed the Indian example, he would have made
both children males. But the fourth letter of the
Tetragrammaton was an H, like the second one; therefore it, too, had to stand for a female divinity. Thus a
son and a daughter were made to form parts of the
deity.

Once the four mystical aspects of the deity were
delineated, further speculation as to their nature and
interrelationships led to that inadvertent slippage referred to in the beginning of this chapter. Probably
without being aware of his mental processes, De Leon
referred again and again to the four aspects of the
godhead, briefly for the most part, but with decreasing
restraint, as if they were separate persons. Before
long, he felt no hesitation in attributing to the four
persons interrelationships and feelings which made
sense only if one regarded them as four separate gods,
very human in their behavior, emotions, and reactions.
In supplying details, De Leon again drew upon his
familiarity with other tetrads, whether consciously or
otherwise. His cognitive process must have been similar to that of the prophets and poets of the Hebrew
Bible who used phrases in praise of God and attributed
deeds to Him which had been applied, in exactly the
same terms, to the pagan gods Baal and Bull-El by

Asherah figurine (height 7⅛ inches), from Tell Duweir, Palestine, from the period of the Hebrew monarchy. COURTESY OF THE METROPOLITAN MUSEUM OF ART. GIFT OF HARRIS P. COLT AND H. DUNSCOMBE COLT, 1934.

Asherah head from Tell Erani ("Gat"), Israel, from Iron II
period. COURTESY OF THE ISRAEL DEPARTMENT OF ANTIQUITIES
AND MUSEUMS.

Asherah head from Tell Erani ("Gat"), Israel, from Iron II period. COURTESY OF THE ISRAEL DEPARTMENT OF ANTIQUITIES AND MUSEUMS.

Asherah head. COURTESY OF THE SEMITIC MUSEUM, HARVARD UNIVERSITY.

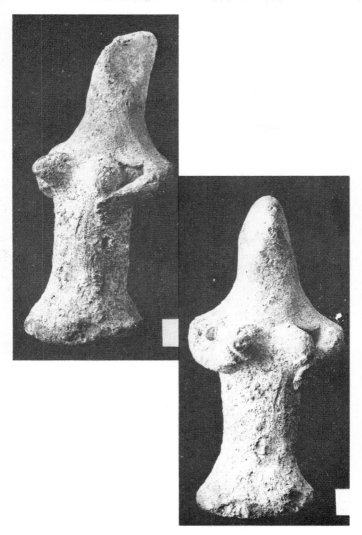

Primitive "bird-faced" Asherah figurine from Palestine. COURTESY OF THE REIFENBERG COLLECTION, JERUSALEM.

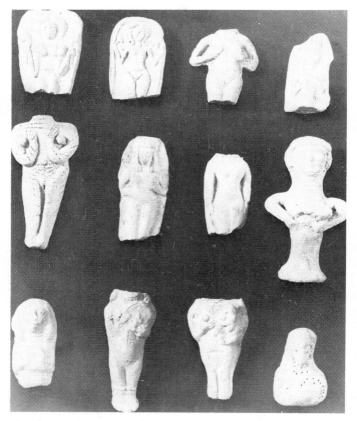

Figurines and plaques from Middle Bronze to Iron II periods.
The two plaques on the left and left-center of the first row are
clearly recognizable as Astartes by their horn-like ("Hathor")
hair style. The figurine on the right of the second row is an
Asherah. REPRINTED BY PERMISSION FROM JAMES B. PRITCHARD,
The Ancient Near East in Pictures, PRINCETON UNIVERSITY
PRESS, 1954.

Astarte of the Horns (height 8 inches). Left: the ancient mold (18th to 16th centuries B.C.) found in Nahariya, Israel; right: modern cast from it. COURTESY OF THE ISRAEL DEPARTMENT OF ANTIQUITIES AND MUSEUMS.

Facing page: Horned goddess from Sumer (height 4½ inches).
Ancient mold and modern cast. COURTESY OF THE BRITISH
MUSEUM.

Astarte (height 5¾ inches). Molded clay figurine from Megiddo, Israel, Middle to Late Bronze Age (2,000-1,200 B.C.).
COURTESY OF THE ORIENTAL INSTITUTE, UNIVERSITY OF CHICAGO.

Astarte plaque from Beth Shemesh, Israel. COURTESY OF THE
UNIVERSITY MUSEUM, PHILADELPHIA, PA.

Astarte holding sacred flowers. Plaque from Beth Shemesh, Israel. COURTESY OF THE UNIVERSITY MUSEUM, PHILADELPHIA, PA.

Astarte plaque from Beth Shemesh, Israel. COURTESY OF THE
UNIVERSITY MUSEUM, PHILADELPHIA, PA.

Gold pendant from Ras Shamra, Syria, with relief figure of Astarte standing on lion. 15th century B.C. COURTESY OF THE LOUVRE AND PROF. CLAUDE F. A. SCHAEFER.

Gold pendant from Ras Shamra, Syria, with relief figure of Astarte holding flowers. COURTESY OF THE SYRIAN DIRECTORATE OF ANTIQUITIES AND MUSEUMS, ALEPPO.

Astarte with lioness mask (height 4¾ inches). Pottery figurine from Beth Shean, Israel. COURTESY OF THE ISRAEL DEPARTMENT OF ANTIQUITIES AND MUSEUMS.

Goddess (Astarte?) holding flower. From Cyprus, 1st millennium B.C. COURTESY OF THE LOUVRE.

Queen of the Wild Beasts. Ivory from Minet el-Beida, Tomb III (ca. 13th century B.C.). COURTESY OF THE LOUVRE.

Silver figurine of a goddess with gold necklace and belt. From Ras Shamra, Syria. COURTESY OF THE LOUVRE.

Seated goddess. Hurrite art. Ivory from Ras Shamra, Syria, 19th-18th century B.C. COURTESY OF THE LOUVRE AND PROF. CLAUDE F. A. SCHAEFFER.

Silver figurine of goddess from the Canaanite temple at Nahariya, Israel, 18th-16th century B.C. COURTESY OF THE ISRAEL DEPARTMENT OF ANTIQUITIES AND MUSEUMS.

Bird-faced goddess with child. From Enkomi, Cyprus, 17th-15th century B.C. COURTESY OF THE LOUVRE.

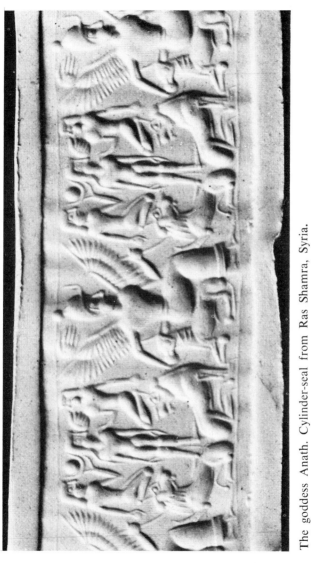

The goddess Anath. Cylinder-seal from Ras Shamra, Syria.
COURTESY OF THE LOUVRE AND PROF. CLAUDE F. A. SCHAEFFER.

The Canaanite goddess Qadesh standing on a lion and flanked by Min and Reshef. Egyptian relief. COURTESY OF THE BRITISH MUSEUM.

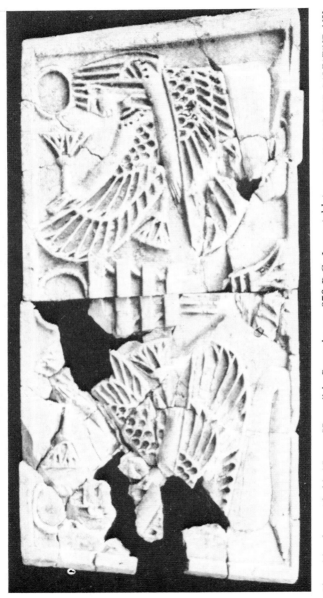

Cherubim from Ahab's "Ivory House" in Samaria, ca. 870 B.C. Ivory tablets. ORIGINAL IN THE PALESTINE MUSEUM OF ARCHAEOLOGY, JERUSALEM.

Female cherub with palm tree. Ivory plaque from the bed of Hazael, king of Damascus, late 9th century B.C. COURTESY OF THE LOUVRE.

Female Cherub with palm tree. Ivory plaque from Arslan Tash, North Syria. COURTESY OF DR. ELIE BOROWSKI AND THE ROYAL ONTARIO MUSEUM, TORONTO, CANADA.

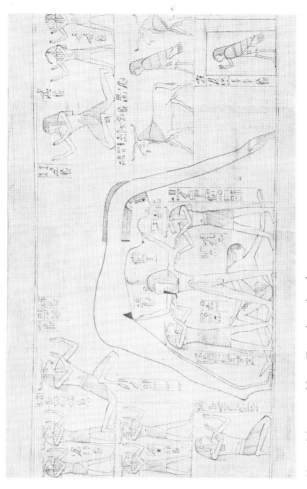

Shu raising up Nut. Egyptian drawing. COURTESY OF THE BRITISH MUSEUM.

Ancient Near Eastern bronze tetrad. Origin unknown.

Lilith. Sumerian terra-cotta relief, ca. 2000 B.C. Collection of
Colonel Norman Colville. REPRODUCED BY PERMISSION FROM
ERICH NEUMANN, *The Great Mother*, NEW YORK: PANTHEON
BOOKS, BOLLINGEN SERIES XLVII, 1955. COPYRIGHT © 1955 BY
PRINCETON UNIVERSITY PRESS.

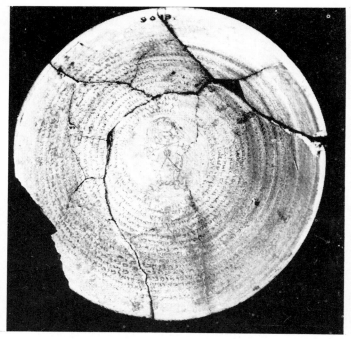

Aramaic incantation bowl with Lilith image in the center (6th century A.D.). COURTESY OF THE UNIVERSITY MUSEUM, PHILADELPHIA, PA.

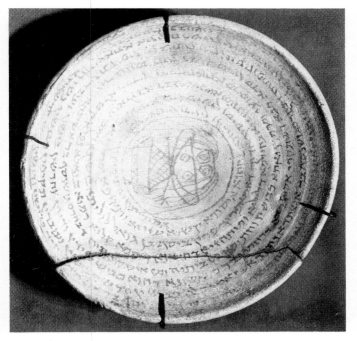

Aramaic incantation bowl, from Persia, with Lilith image in the center. COURTESY OF THE SEMITIC MUSEUM, HARVARD UNIVERSITY.

The Moses panel in the Dura Europos synagogue (3rd century A.D.), showing the Shekhina with the infant Moses in her arms. FROM ERWIN R. GOODENOUGH, <u>JEWISH SYMBOLS IN THE GRECO-ROMAN PERIOD</u>. BOLLINGEN SERIES XXXVII, VOL. 11. COPYRIGHT © 1964 BY PRINCETON UNIVERSITY PRESS. REPRODUCED BY PERMISSION.

their Canaanite predecessors.[54] As is well known, in the old days quite a few polytheistic references did in this manner slip into the Biblical image of God,[55] and this is presumably what happened again two millennia later, in the case of Moses de Leon.

To sum up: On the conscious level, De Leon spoke of four aspects of the Godhead, and this is what his theosophic teachings were taken to mean by the ever-widening circle of Kabbalists. But, in his endeavor to give emphatic, vivid expression to his ideas, he resorted to a rich array of mythological and sexual imagery. The features of this imagery grew out of De Leon's familiarity with Indian and other pagan tetrads. Without being aware of what he was doing, in speaking of the marriage of the Father and the Mother, the subsequent birth of their Son and Daughter, the emergence out of the Mother's womb of the androgynous Heaven-and-Earth, their separation, the love of the Father for the Daughter, the jealousy of the Mother, the suckling of the King (the Son) by the Mother, the marriage of the King (the Son) and the Matronit (the Daughter), etc., he composed a tetradic myth cycle. He set out to establish a doctrine of quatrinity, of the Divine condition of being fourfold, and ended up with the myth of a tetrad, a group of four separate and independent deities.

If the author, the master himself, was unaware of all this and knew only of the mystical symbolism of the Godhead's four aspects which his teachings purported to explore, one need little wonder that his followers felt no qualms in accepting his doctrines. They *knew* intellectually that whatever they read in the Zohar about the Father, Mother, Son, and Daughter referred, in its true meaning, to the four aspects of the one Godhead. Yet, at the same time, they responded emotionally not to the "true" meaning and purport of the statements, but to what the words actually said. Such simultaneous response on two levels is not an infrequent phenomenon. The Kabbalists not only gained insight into the mythical nature of the God-head from Zoharic accounts, but also derived a quasi-sensuous emotional satisfaction from learning about the sexual and familial life of the divine tetrad, which gave mythical sanction to the corresponding aspects of their own life on earth. And, although this second-level response remained subconscious, it was in large measure due to it that the Zohar, and with it Kabbalism, achieved such remarkable popularity in Judaism.

Chapter VI

MATRONIT—THE GODDESS OF THE KABBALA

Let us now turn our attention to the fourth person of the Kabbalistic tetrad, the Daughter, who, in addition to the old Talmudic name of Shekhina, is referred to in Jewish mystical literature by a profusion of names, epithets and appellatives, but most frequently by the Latin loan word *Matronita,* that is "the Matronit," or the Matron. Of the four persons of the Kabbalistic tetrad it is she who plays the greatest role as the central figure in both divine happenings and relationships, and the occurrences through which human fate, and in particular the fate of Israel, is propelled forward. She is the central link between the Above and the Below. She is the person through whom man can most easily grasp the ineffable mystery of the deity, and who most fully identifies herself with the interests, the joys, and the woes, of Israel. She is unquestionably the most poignant, and at the same time most Jewish, expression of the idea of a goddess.

Yet, and this is a striking example of perhaps the most fascinating facet of the history of religious and mythical ideas, there is a detailed similarity between the life history, character, deeds and feelings attributed by Jewish mysticism to the Matronit, and what ancient Near Eastern mythologies have to say about their goddesses who occupy central positions in their pantheons. In myths, epics, narratives, and visual representations these ancient Near Eastern goddesses are described and depicted in clear, realistic, down-to-earth colors,

without the veiling effect the mystical approach of the
Kabbala has on its goddess figure. A glance at them
will, therefore, materially aid our understanding and
characterization of the goddess of the Kabbala, the
Matronit.

1. THE GODDESS OF LOVE AND WAR

Three or four examples will have to suffice to introduce to us the goddess who played a central role
in the religious ritual as well as popular consciousness
of all Ancient Near Eastern people. Her name varied
from culture to culture—Inanna in Sumer, Ishtar in
Akkad, Anath in Canaan—yet her character remained
the same for centuries, even millennia. The life do-
mains in which she primarily manifested herself were
love and war, and her personality exhibited everywhere the same four basic traits of chastity and promiscuity, motherliness and bloodthirstiness.

The oldest of them was Inanna, the great Sumerian
goddess of love and war, the tutelary deity of Uruk
(the Biblical Erech), whose prominence in the Sumerian pantheon was well established by the 3rd
millennium B.C. That she was regarded a virgin is
evident from the two epithets which accompany her
name: in myths and other texts she is most frequently
called "the maid Inanna" and "the pure Inanna." Yet
throughout Sumerian history she was the goddess
primarily responsible for sexual love, procreation, and
fertility, who freely gave herself to Dumuzi (Tammuz), the earliest mythological ruler of Sumer, and
thereafter became the wife of all Sumerian kings. Nor
was she immune to the advances of ordinary mortals:
an old Sumerian story tells of a gardener who one
night managed to take advantage of Inanna's utter
weariness and had intercourse with her. Upon awaking
in the morning, Inanna was enraged over the indignity,
and the vengeance she wrought seems to us to have
surpassed all reason. But her behavior was in keeping

with her character, for she was a goddess of boundless rage and ruthless destruction, "the lady of battle and conflict," who had "great fury in her wrathful heart." It was she who armed King Hammurabi (ca. 1728– 1686 B.C.) with mighty weapons, and was his "gracious protecting genius." More than a thousand years later, in the days of Nabonidus (555–539 B.C.), she was still worshipped at Uruk in a gold-clad cella, driving a chariot to which were harnessed seven lions.[1]

The direct heir of Inanna in Mesopotamia was Ishtar, the great goddess of love and war in the Akkadian pantheon. The identity of the two is attested by the fact that in some Akkadian texts the two names are used interchangeably. In the Babylonian Ishtar, however, a certain shift occurred in the balance between the virginal and promiscuous poles of her character: her virginal aspect was underplayed, while her promiscuity was emphasized to the extent of making her a divine harlot. In many texts Ishtar is spoken of as the "Cow of the Moon-God Sin," and in this capacity she ruled over the plants, watered them and made them grow. An incantation for childbirth tells of this "Cow of Sin" that she was impregnated by a "restless young bull," and had great difficulty in bearing her young, until two genii of heaven helped her. In her human form, her love easily turned to hate: she first loved then destroyed, a long line of divine, human, and animal paramours, including a lion, a horse, a bird, a gardener, several shepherds, the hero Gilgamesh, Tammuz, etc. She also was the wife of human kings, such as Sargon of Agade. Her influence extended over all mankind and the entire animal kingdom: when she entered the Nether World, neither man nor beast copulated; when she emerged, all of them were again seized by sexual desire. But she was also the mother of the country, who said of herself, "It is I myself who gave birth to my people," and the mother of several gods among whom the Fire-god was the first born. One of her titles was "sweet-voiced mistress of the gods." Yet she was also "the most awesome of the goddesses," "Ishtar of the battlefield," clad in divine fire, carrying the melammu-headwear, who would rain fire on the enemies. It was she who gave victory to her lovers, the Babylonian kings, entrusting her mighty armed forces to them. Among all the arts of war she was specially interested in charioteering: in the early stages of her career she tried to win the love of Gilgamesh by promising him "a chariot of lapis and gold," and more than a millennium later, in the Ptolemaic period, she was still known as "mistress of horses, lady of the chariot." When not engaged in love or war she was sitting, awe-inspiringly, on her lion-throne.[2]

The Canaanite Anath, with whose exploits we have become acquainted above in Chapter II, is so close in character and attributes to Inanna and Ishtar that she must be considered as merely the western variant of the great Mesopotamian goddess.

The Persian counterpart of the great virginal-wanton-motherly-warrior goddess was Anahita. Although the phonemic resemblance between "Anath" and "Anahita" is purely coincidental, the worship of Anath may have spread as early as the 1st millennium B.C. from the Mediterranean shore as far east as the upper reaches of Euphrates, as indicated by the name of an Assyrian township, Anat (today Ana), a few miles lower down on the river from Dura Europos. The worship of Anahita, Herodotus informs us (in a passage in which he makes the curious mistake of writing "Mithra" instead of "Anahita"), was learned by the Persians from the Assyrians. Other Greek authors state that the cult of Anaitis (as they referred to Anahita) corresponded in every respect to the Babylonian cult of Ishtar, and that the representations of Anaitis were shaped after those of Ishtar.

In the Avesta, the sacred writings which ancient Iranian tradition attributes to Zoroaster (who probably lived in the 10th century B.C.) but which did not assume their extant form until the early Sassanian period (3rd–4th centuries A.D.), an entire chapter (Yasht v) is devoted to her. Her full name was Ardvi Sura Anahita, or "The High, Powerful, Immaculate," and she is described as "a beautiful maiden, powerful and tall, her girdle fastened high, wrapped in a gold-embroidered cloak, wearing earrings, a necklace and a crown of gold, and adorned with thirty otter skins." She is, thus, unmistakably a virgin goddess, like her Sumerian, Akkadian, and Canaanite counterparts. Yet her virginity, as theirs, did not prevent her from being also the goddess of fertility: she was the goddess of the fertilizing waters, of a supernatural spring, located in the region of the stars, from which flow all the rivers of the world. She was the one who multiplies the herds and wealth, gives fertility, easy childbirth, and ample milk to women, and purifies the seed of men. She was invoked by marriageable girls and by women at the time of childbirth. Nor was she lacking in the attributes of the harlot, and in her sanctuary at Erez in Akilisene, which contained her golden statue, the daughters of the noble families of Armenia used to prostitute themselves to strangers before their marriage. In Lydia, where she was identified with Cybele, the Great Mother, as well as in Armenia and Cappadocia, because the bull was sacred to her, she was confounded with Artemis Tauropolos. And finally, just as Inanna, Ishtar, and Anath, Anahita too was the goddess of war, who rode in a chariot drawn by four white horses. Wind, Rain, Clouds, and Hail, bestowed victory on the combatants and gave them sturdy teams and brave companions. Because of this warlike character of hers, she was identified by the Greeks also with Athene, while as the goddess of fertility she appeared to them as identical with Aphrodite. Most commonly, however, she was called in the Hellenistic world the "Persian Diana" or "Persian Artemis." In astrology, the Iranians themselves regarded her as the personification of the planet Venus. Her cult, according to Berossus, was introduced among the Persians by Artaxerxes II (404–362 B.C.), who built for her altars and set up her statues in Babylon, Susa, Ekbatana, Persepolis, Baktra, Damaskos(?), and Sardes. From these places, Persian influence carried her cult westward into the Greco-Roman world. At a later period, she was considered the daughter of Ormuzd, and the benefactor of all mankind, mother of all wisdom and queen.[3]

2. THE MATRONIT IN POPULAR-MYTHICAL VIEW

The same four traits of chastity and promiscuity, motherliness and bloodthirstiness, characterize the Matronit, the daughter-goddess of Kabbalistic literature.

According to Kabbalistic theory, the Matronit is but the lowest of the ten Sephirot, the mystical aspects or emanations of the Godhead which, to some extent, correspond to the Gnostic *aeons*. Yet whatever the primary meaning and origin of the Matronit as a theosophic concept, she has been built up in Kabbalistic literature, and especially in the late 13th century Zohar—the holiest book of Kabbalism—into a palpable individuum whose acts, words, and feelings only make sense if she is considered a true mythological deity. Whatever the intention of the authors of Kabbalistic treatises in creating or developing the female divine figure of the Matronit, one thing is certain: among the Kabbalists there could have been very few, who, while reading or hearing about her uninhibitedly described exploits, were nevertheless able to visualize that she was nothing but an aspect of the manifest nature of the one and only Deity. For the masses of Kabbalists—and Kabbalism was a religious *mass* movement among the Jews from the 15th to the 18th centuries—she undoubtedly assumed the character of a discrete divinity, in other words, she was taken as a goddess, separate and distinct from the male deity who, when contraposited to her, was referred to as her husband, the King. The *popular-mythical,* as against the *scholarly-mythical* view of the Matronit had a marked resemblance to the popular Mariolatry of the Latin countries, where the Virgin is not the Jewish woman whose womb God chose to reincarnate

Himself in human form—as the official Catholic doctrine has it—but the Mother of God, herself a goddess, who through the ages never ceased to perform miracles, and to whom, therefore, direct and personal adoration is due. This, precisely was the light in which the Matronit appeared to the uneducated or semieducated Kabbalistic Jews; in contrast to the divine King who, following the destruction of the Jerusalem Temple, withdrew into the remote heights of heaven and made himself inaccessible, the Matronit remained down here on earth, continued to be directly concerned with the welfare of her people, and could be approached directly, any time, any place. She thus supplied the psychologically so important female divine figure in Judaism, a religion in which this element had been submerged for many centuries prior to the emergence of Kabbalism.

The relatively late reappearance of the goddess—I say reappearance because, as we have seen in the first two chapters, in Biblical times goddesses did figure prominently in popular Hebrew religion—is in itself a remarkable feat of religious resurgence. Even more remarkable, however, is the reappearance in the figure of the Matronit of the four basic traits of chastity, promiscuity, motherliness, and bloodthirstiness, which place her right alongside the great ancient Near Eastern love-goddesses.

3. THE VIRGINAL MATRONIT

Little can be said about the first of these cardinal features in the portrait of the divine Matronit. Virginity, after all, is a state shared by all human and divine females in an early stage of their life history. It becomes remarkable only if, after reaching full nubility, a woman prefers to remain a virgin and actually preserves her virginal state in an environment, whether earthly or Olympian, where the general atmosphere is one of intensive sexual activity or even promiscuity. It becomes more than remarkable if the feminine figure in question herself engages in such promiscuous sexual activity and yet, at one and the same time, retains her virginity. Yet this is precisely the paradoxical chastity characterizing several ancient Near Eastern goddesses, and this is the trait shared with them by the Matronit.

The Virgin Mary, to whom reference has already been made earlier, also belongs to this category of female divinities, and her veneration can be adduced as an additional example which will further facilitate our understanding of the paradoxical virginity of the Matronit. Mary bore Jesus to God, and several other sons and daughters to her earthly husband Joseph, yet she nevertheless remained *"The* Virgin" and is adored as such to this day. Similarly with the Matronit, who paradoxically retained her virginity while being the lover of gods and men. Her virginity is spoken of in the Zohar in both figurative expressions and direct statements. The Biblical verse about the "red heifer, faultless, wherein is no blemish, and upon which never came yoke," [4] is applied to her and explained as meaning that the forces of Evil could never overpower the Matronit, "neither Satan, nor the Destroyer, nor the Angel of Death," all of whom represent the forces of Hell.[5] In contrast to the pagan goddesses who all are said to have succumbed to Satan, she, the Shekhina, is a cup full of blessing of which nobody has as yet tasted, unimpaired, that is, virginal. No stranger is permitted to draw near her, he who tries to approach her suffers the penalty of death.[7] In one aspect the Shekhina is identical with the Holy Land, and in this capacity she was never defiled or enjoyed by a stranger.[8]

4. THE LOVER OF MEN AND GODS

In sharp contrast and logical contradiction to this picture of the virgin Shekhina is the one which depicts her as being enjoyed, in addition to the divine King who was her lawfully wedded husband, also by

Satan, other gods, heroes of Biblical history, and
many other men. Yet, and this again is a feature she
has in common with ancient Near Eastern love-goddesses, no blame is attached to her because of any of
these sundry unions. A goddess behaves in accordance
with her divine nature, and the human laws of sexual
morality simply do not apply to her—this is the common attitude that finds expression in both the ancient
Near Eastern and the Kabbalistic myths. As the father-
god El says in an Ugaritic mythical poem ". . . there is
no restraint among goddesses." [9]

In the early mythical ages, we are informed in the
Zohar, Jacob became the first husband of the Matronit. However, while Jacob was alive, the union was
not consummated because, inveterate polygamist that he
was, he continued to have marital relations with his
two wives and two concubines even after the goddess
attached herself to him. Therefore, only after his
death, when his spirit entered the Beyond, did Jacob
couple with the Matronit.[10]

With her second husband, things were different.
This was none other than Moses, who, once she became his wife, separated himself from his earthly helpmate, Zipporah. Having done this, he was allowed
to achieve what Jacob never did: to copulate with the
Matronit while still in the flesh.[11]

We hear nothing of the Matronit from the death of
Moses—when she took him on her wings and carried
him from Mount Nebo to his unknown burial place
four miles away [12]— to the time when the Temple was
built in Jerusalem. As Solomon labored on the construction of the Sanctuary, the Matronit made her own
preparations for her union with her divine husband,
the King: she prepared a house for him in which he
could take up joint residence with her and which, in a
mystical way, was identical with the Jerusalem Temple
itself. When the great day arrived, her father and
mother adorned her so that her bridegroom should
become desirous of her.[13]

The King and the Matronit were not only brother
and sister, but twins; in fact, Siamese twins, who

emerged from the womb of the Supernal Mother in the androgynous shape of a male and a female body attached to each other back to back. Soon, however, the King removed his sister from his back, and she, after a futile attempt to reunite with him in the same position, resigned herself to the separation and to facing the King across a distance.[14]

By human standards a marriage between brother and sister would have been incestuous; not so in the heavenly realm: there, a Zoharic text informs us, no incest prohibitions exist, and thus it was completely proper and licit for the King and the Matronit to marry.[15]

The wedding, a veritable *hieros gamos,* was celebrated with due pomp and circumstance. The Matronit, surrounded by her maidens, repaired to her couch set up in the Temple, there to await the coming of the groom. The curtains round about were decorated with myriads of precious stones and pearls. At midnight, the tinkling of bells he wore around his ankles announced the coming of the King. As he approached, he was accompanied by a host of divine youths, and the maidens of the Matronit welcomed him and them by beating their wings with joy. After singing a song of praise to the King, the Matronit's maidens withdrew, and so did the youths who accompanied him. Alone, the King and the Matronit embraced and kissed, and then he led her to the couch. He placed his left arm under her head, his right arm embraced her, and he let her enjoy his strength. The pleasure of the King and the Matronit in each other was indescribable. They lay in tight embrace, she impressing her image into his body like a seal that leaves its imprint upon a page of writing, he playing betwixt her breasts and vowing in his great love that he would never forsake her.[16]

Some say, that as long as the Temple stood the King would come down from his heavenly abode every midnight, seek out his wife, the Matronit, and enjoy her in their Temple bedchamber. The Sacred Marriage thus became a daily, or rather midnightly, ritual, performed not by the human representatives of the god and the goddess who usually figured in the ancient Near Eastern New Year rituals, but by the two deities themselves. This divine union had unsurpassed cosmic significance: on it depended the well-being of the whole world.[17]

Others say that the King and the Matronit coupled only once a week, on the night between Friday and Saturday. In true mythical fashion, this weekly divine union served as the prototype, in other words, as the mythical validation, of the traditionally practiced weekly union between pious husbands and wives.[18] In the Kabbalistic view, when the learned men, familiar with the heavenly mysteries, couple with their wives on Friday nights, they do this in full cognizance of performing a most significant act in direct imitation of the union which takes place at that very time between the Supernal Couple. If the wife conceives at that hour, the earthly father and mother of the child can be sure that it will receive a soul from the Above, one of those pure souls which are procreated in the divine copulation of the King and the Matronit.[19]

But even more than that. When a pious earthly couple performs the act, by doing so they set in motion all the generative forces of the mythico-mystical universe. The human sexual act causes the King to emit his seminal fluid from his divine male genitals, and thus to fertilize the Matronit who thereupon gives birth to human souls and to angels.[20] The passage in the Zohar in which this particular thought (or mythologem) is expressed is so replete with symbolic expressions calculated to obscure its true meaning that one gains the impression of purposeful avoidance of clarity in order not to offend sensibilities. The King's seminal fluid is referred to as a "river"; the Shekhina or Matronit as "the Sea" or "Living Creature"; the King's male genital is called "the sign of the covenant," and so forth. Yet the meaning of the whole passage is nevertheless clear: it speaks of the sexual union between the King and the Matronit, and the resultant procreation by them of souls and angels.

Yet another version, still preoccupied with the times of divine copulation, speaks not of a weekly, but of an annual cycle. Every year, we are told, the people of Israel sin with tragic inevitability which enables Samael, the Satan (or Azazel), to bend the Matronit to his will. Samael, in the form of a serpent, or riding a serpent, lurks at all times near the privy parts of the Matronit, in the hope of being able to penetrate her. Whether or not he succeeds in thus gratifying his desire depends on the conduct of Israel. As long as Israel remains virtuous, Samael's lustful design is frustrated. But as soon as Israel sins, as they, alas, are bound to do year after year, their sins add to Samael's power, he glues himself to the Matronit's body "with the adhesive force of resin," and defiles her. [21]

Once this happens, the Matronit's husband, the King, departs from her and withdraws into the solitude of his heavenly abode. This unhappy state of affairs continues until, on the Day of Atonement, the scapegoat, which is destined to Azazel,[22] is hurled to its death down a cliff in the Judaean Desert. Samael, attracted by the animal offered to him, lets go of the Matronit, who thereupon can ascend to heaven and reunite with her husband, the King.[23]

The union between the Matronit and the King is described most graphically in a manuscript entitled *Sefer Tashaq,* written in the early 14th century by a Spanish Kabbalist known only as R. Joseph. The central portion of this book is a mystical interpretation of the meaning of the letters of the Hebrew alphabet, including the Tetragrammaton, and an abstruse description of the body of the Matronit. The following brief excerpts are taken from the discussion of the mystical meaning of the letters *zayin* (ז) and *het* (ח).

> After the completion of the holy body of the Holy One, blessed be He, which is the Covenant [23a] of the Holy One, blessed be He, He pours out the good oil [23b] to the Matronit. . . . The letter *het* is open to receive the male, that is, the letter *zayin,* which is called the Covenant. . . . The letter *het*

hints at the Matronit: as the woman is closed on three sides and is open on the fourth side to receive her husband, so the letter *het,* which is the Matronit, is open to receive the *vav,* the King, the Lord of Hosts. For the legs of the *het* are the legs of the Matronit, which are open, and the beam on top is the body of the Matronit. And the *zayin* is the Covenant in relation to the *het,* and it is complete, and the letter *het* is as in the human body with its two legs spread out, and the body on top is the beam and this is its image:

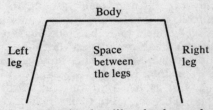

Moreover, woman is also like the letter *he* (ה), but in the letter *he* the son does not cleave to her,[23c] while in the *het* he does cleave and suck from her. Likewise when Metatron, the great and precious prince, does not suck from the Matronit, he is called *he*—there is a space between the legs, for he does not cleave to the Matronit. But when he sucks from the Matronit and cleaves to her in union, he is called *het* and is called Metatron.[23d] Thus far the mystery of *het.* And how many holy chariots has each letter, for each letter is in the image of the Holy One, blessed be He.[23e]

A new chapter in the life of the Matronit opened when her bedchamber, the Temple of Jerusalem, was destroyed. Since her husband, the King, was wont to copulate with her only in the Temple, its destruction meant the sudden disruption of the heretofore intensely pursued love-relationship between the two.[24] This event was a stark tragedy for the divine lovers. The Matronit was banished from her holy abode and

from the Land of Israel, the King intoned a bitter
lament over his great loss, and the Sun and Moon and
all that is above and below mourned and cried with
him.[25] The separation of the King and the Matronit
denuded them of each other and both remained in a
state of "shameful nakedness." [26] Moreover, since it
is a cardinal principle of the physical as well as the
metaphysical universe that "blessings are found only
where male and female are together," the King, when
he thus became deprived of his Matronit, lost stature
and power, was no longer King, nor great, nor potent.[27]

Soon, however, in true male fashion, the King was
no longer able to endure the misery of solitude, and
he let a slave-goddess take the place of his true queen,
one of the handmaidens of the Matronit who used to
"sit behind the hand-mill." This slave-concubine, who
was none other than Lilith, now assumed rule over the
Holy Land, just as the Matronit had ruled over it in
former times. This act, more than anything else, caused
the King to lose his honor.[28]

As to the Matronit, her misery consisted not only
in losing her husband and being banished from her
palace and land, but she had to resign herself to being
violated in her exile by other gods. And although these
unions were involuntary on her part, once the other
gods were able to take possession of her, she became
tied to them, and the children of those other gods, the
gentiles, were able to suckle from her just as the Children of Israel had done while the Temple still stood.[29]

Yet whether at home or in exile, the Matronit is
irresistibly attracted to the pious men of Israel, and
especially when they are engaged in either of the two
most meritorious pursuits: the study of the Law and
the performance of good deeds. Men of such caliber
make it a rule to sleep with their wives only on Friday
night: throughout the six days of the week they live
as if they had been castrated and devote themselves to
their holy works. But, in doing so, do they not run
the risk of unblessedness, since "blessings are found
only where male and female are together"? No, be-

cause whenever these men are away from their wives, the Shekhina couples with them. Likewise, when such sages keep away from their wives because of the latter's menstrual impurity, or when they are on a voyage, the Shekhina joins them; never are they deprived of the blessed state of male and female togetherness.[30]

Above (p. 143), we have seen that in the Kabbalistic view Rachel, the beloved wife of Jacob, was identified with the Shekhina. Since Rachel is the suffering mother of Israel, and the Shekhina (or Matronit) is the personification of the Community of Israel (see below, Section 5), the identification of the two had a deep emotional appeal. A special mystical *Kavvana,* a procedure of intense mental concentration, was recommended by Isaac Luria (1534–1572), the leading Kabbalistic master of 16th-century Safed, for the purpose of bringing about the reunification of the exiled Rachel-Matronit with her husband, God the King. This Lurianic *Kavvana* is described by Jacob ben Hayyim Tzemah (d. after 1665), a Kabbalist and physician, in his anthology of the customs of Luria:

> One must concentrate with a complete concentration on two things, as a result of which one will be beloved Above and well-liked Below, and a thread of charm will be drawn over him on that day, and he will be accepted into the sacred hall of the Matronit. At first he should concentrate on this: at the beginning of the night, when he goes to sleep, he should think and concentrate on raising up his soul into the mystery of the Matronit and into the mystery of the Female Waters, in order to make Lea copulate with Jacob. And when midnight arrives, he no longer has to cause the Female Waters to rise, and therefore at that time he should concentrate a second time, this time on participating in the anguish of Rachel, for at that time she descends down below, into the [world of physical] creation. Therefore he should at that time weep for half an hour or more about

the anguish of Rachel and her banishment and her exile, and about the destruction [of the Temple]. And it is especially proper to concentrate on this: Since we sinned, we cast the souls into the husks [i.e., into the unclean physical world] and forced Rachel, who is the Shekhina, to go down into exile among the husks to gather those souls. . . . Because of our many sins she was forced to descend into exile, and thus we caused her all this. And especially he who is from the root of Cain, in whom there is much of the filth of the serpent [see below, p. 209] into which the souls are sunk, does well to cry and wail much, for he has a greater share in that treacherous act [of causing the exile of the Matronit] than the other roots. . . . And thereafter, from midnight on, let him occupy himself with the Torah until the light of morning. And you should concentrate on bringing gratification and elevation to the Shekhina, to Rachel, who stands outside. And you should bring about her restoration through the Torah with which you occupy yourself at that time, so that she be restored by the time dawn breaks, [and be able and ready] to ascend together with the ascent of the morning prayer, to copulate with her husband [i.e., God] through the power which you added to her during the night. And then you will be called Groomsman of the Matronit, if you concentrate on this unfailingly to participate in her anguish and to restore her.[30a]

5. THE MOTHERLY MATRONIT

The third characteristic of the virginal and wanton love-goddesses of the Ancient Near Eastern religions, as we shall recall, is their motherliness. By an apparently paradoxical combination of traits, the same goddess who remains eternally virginal and who is insatiable in her sexual appetite, is also the mother image, the woman who bears, suckles, rears, and protects both gods and men.

In Kabbalistic mythology the trait of motherliness originally belonged to the second person in the tetrad, the Mother-goddess, the progenitress of both the Son-King and the Daughter-Shekhina,[31] but it was transferred to the Daughter, as a few references will show. The Shekhina-Matronit, we read in the Zohar, is the (spiritual) mother of Israel, and as such she is the embodiment of the "Community of Israel" (the Hebrew term for which, Knesseth Yisrael, has the feminine gender). She lovingly suckles all the Children of Israel, thereby providing them not only with nourishment but also with complete well-being. She is, in fact, called the "Lower Mother" in relation to her people, and in contradistinction from her own mother, who is the "Supernal" or "Higher" Mother. The motherly nature is so strong in the Matronit that she is unable to turn away even from the gentile children foisted upon her: after her exile from Jerusalem, when the "other Gods," that is, the deities of the pagans, had their will on her, she gave suck to the heathens just as she had wet-nursed Israel.[32]

6. THE WARLIKE MATRONIT

The fourth characteristic of the virginal-wanton-motherly ancient Near Eastern goddesses is their bloodthirstiness. In the old mythological texts the maiden goddess of sexual love is often described as possessed of the most appalling cruelty. The close to three millennia which had elapsed between those myths and the period in which the Matronit of the Kabbala flourished have, of course, left their mark. In the medieval sources, the warlike traits of the Matronit are drawn with greater restraint. Yet the archaic feature of bloodthirstiness is clearly recognizable in the Kabbalistic references to the Matronit as the chieftain of the divine armies, and the leader of the supernal forces against the opposing human and infernal powers of evil.

It would be futile at this stage to search for connecting links between the bloodthirsty goddesses of the 3rd and 2nd millennia B.C. and the warlike Matronit of the 13th century A.D. The idea of a warlike deity was, of course, nothing strange to Biblical Hebrew faith, but, in keeping with the officially embraced monotheism, all supernatural belligerence was attributed to Yahweh, who therefore is referred to as a "man of War," a slayer of dragons, and a victor over human enemies whose life-blood crimsons his garments.[33] In Talmudic times (1st–5th centuries A.D.), although the chastised and subjugated Judaism of the Roman and Byzantine eras had long ceased to think of god as a warrior, a late faint echo of the ancient pagan goddesses of destruction can perhaps be heard in one of the traits attributed to the Shekhina, the personified Presence of God, imagined as a female entity. She was said to take the souls of exceptionally meritorious individuals who were to be spared the bitterness of being mowed down by the the Angel of Death.[34] The remarkable thing in this idea is not the combination of compassion and the snuffing out of human life, but that this function or mercy killing was assigned to the female Shekhina. It was, however, only in the Kabbala that the Shekhina, now conceived as a truly mythical female deity, assumed a character reminiscent of the ancient Near Eastern bloodthirsty goddesses.

In the Zohar it is the Shekhina-Matronit to whom the King entrusts all his warlike activities: when he wishes to take revenge on the idolatrous nations, the Forces of Evil awaken, and the Shekhina becomes filled with blood and metes out bloody punishment to the sinners.[35] In her wars against the pagans the Matronit commands myriads of supernatural soldiers falling into many categories, such as "lords of supernal faces," "lords of eyes," "lords of weapons," "lords of lamentations," "lords of trembling," and other armed warriors with six faces and six wings, all of whom gird terrible swords, whose clothes are blazing fire, and whose flaming scimitars fly all over the world. This was the army which the Matronit led against the Egyptians in the days of the Exodus.[36]

In fact, the King completely renounced all direct control of his forces and placed them under the command of the Matronit. He entrusted to her all his weapons, spears, scimitars, bows, arrows, swords, catapults, as well as all his fortifications, wood, stones, and subordinated all his warlords to her, saying: "From now on, all my wars shall be entrusted to your hands." In keeping with this mandate, when the Great Overlord of the Egyptians, who was none other than Samael, leading his six hundred chariots manned by angry warriors (or "accusers," because this battle was, of course, a spiritual rather than a physical contest), charged the fleeing Israelites, it was the Matronit who led the defense and drove the attackers into the sea. Several generations later, when Sisera attacked the Children of Israel, it was again the Matronit into whose hands the enemy's chariots were delivered and who uprooted them from the world.[37]

In a Midrash which represents a later Hebrew version of the ancient apocryphal Book of Enoch (written probably in 150 B.C.), a passage deals with the theme of the warlike Matronit. The Hebrew book in question is called *Sefer Hekhalot* ("Book of the Heavenly Halls"), as well as *Sefer Hanokh* ("Book of Enoch"); it belongs to the rich *Hekhalot* literature which flourished beginning with Talmudic times, and was known to the author of the Zohar and other Kabbalists. Its frame is the visit that Rabbi Yishma'el paid to the heavenly halls, where he was met and guided by Metatron, the chief "angel of the Face," who is none other than Enoch after his translation. The passage referred to reads as follows:

R. Yishma'el said: Metatron, the angel, the prince of the Face, said to me: In the seven halls stand the four chariots of the Shekhina, and before each hall stand four camps of the Shekhina, and between each two camps flows a river of fire, and between each two rivers the camps are surrounded by mists of purity, and between each two of them stand pillars of brimstone, and between each two pillars are wheels of flame which surround them, and between each two wheels there are flaming torches. . . .[37a]

While the interest of the author, like that of the *Hekhalot* literature in general, is focussed on the description of the marvels seen in the heavenly halls, the idea that the Shekhina-Matronit is in charge of the heavenly chariots and armed camps is clearly attested here as being pre-Zoharic.

As in the glorious past, so in the mystical present of the long exile, the miserable Galuth, the Shekhina-Matronit is the warlike defender and deliverer of Israel. But her power to defeat Israel's enemies depends ultimately on Israel herself. The Shekhina-Matronit is always present in the midst of Israel ready to protect it from all sides and against all nations. But when Israel sins, it thereby weakens the hands of the Shekhina, her strength fails, and the great commanders of the other nations, that is, their heavenly guardians, gain the upper hand. But as soon as Israel repents the Shekhina becomes filled with strength; she shatters the power of all those great commanders, destroys the armies of Israel's enemies, and takes revenge on them.[38]

Closely related to the warlike aspect of the Zoharic Shekhina-Matronit is her appearance as an enormous and monstrous being described by the author of the Zohar in terms borrowed from the Midrashic picture of the Behemoth. This mythical cosmic animal is said in the Midrash to be eating every day the grass of the Thousand Mountains and devouring the many beasts that pasture on their slopes, to be drinking in one single gulp all the waters of the Jordan and quenching its thirst from the huge river Jubal, which issues from Paradise.[39] This mythologem is elaborated in two Zoharic passages which describe the Shekhina-Matronit as a cosmic woman monster for whom the Thousand

Mountains are but one single bite, who swallows in one gulp the waters of a thousand rivers, whose terrifying arms stretch out in 24,000 (or 25,000) directions, with her claws ready to tear or kill. In her hair are caught thousands of shields, while her hair itself streaks down and away from her, earning her the epithets "Moon with the hair" and "Comet with the tail." From this long, Lilith-like hair issue hosts of frightful and threatening warlords grouped under such peculiar names as "lords of weights," "lords of severity," "lords of insolence," and "lords of lords," all of whom are also called "lords of purple." No one can escape from the cruel punishment meted out by them, or by the Shekhina herself.

From between the legs of this terrifying woman monster emerges an equally terrifying son, the chief angel Metatron, who reaches from one end of the world to the other, and issue two daughters who are none other than the two infamous queens of the she-demons, Lilith and Naamah.

It is consonant with this terrible aspect of the Shekhina-Matronit that her old Talmudic role of death bringer is also remembered and revived in the Zohar, which repeatedly asserts that the words of the Book of Proverbs (5:5) "Her feet go down to death" refer to the Shekhina, symbolically represented by the forbidden tree which for Adam was a "tree of death." [40]

The warlike, monstrous, and bloodthirsty aspect of the Matronit leads us back, for a moment at least, to the question of connections between Kabbala and Hinduism (cf. above, p. 149). The probability of a connection between the two, and especially between the Kabbala and the Tantric and Shivaic teachings of India, has been further developed in my book *The Jewish Mind* (1977), in which, among numerous other topics, I discuss Kali, the beautiful, but at the same time monstrous, Hindu goddess who is one of the many manifestations of Shakti and who thus far has been mentioned only in passing here (p. 133). Just as Kali is conventionally depicted as black, to emphasize her frightening character, so the Shekhina also, says the

Zohar, "at times tastes the other, bitter side, and then her face is dark." [40a] Marvin H. Pope, in his monumental new commentary to the Song of Songs (in which, incidentally, he devotes 26 pages [pp. 153–79] to a summation of the argument presented in the first edition of the present book), goes even further in calling attention to the similarities between Tantric hymns to the black and beautiful goddess Kali and certain passages in the Song of Songs (especially 1:5). [40b] After an extensive and interesting discourse on "black and beautiful," Pope surveys the surprisingly numerous black goddesses and dwells on the "most notorious of all," Kali of India, who is "beautiful, ever young and virginal, and at the same time horrendous, violent, destructive and insatiable in her thirst for blood and flesh, wine and sexual intercourse." Unquestionably, the verse "I am black and beautiful, O daughters of Jerusalem" (Songs 1:5) is strongly reminiscent of certain Hindu hymns celebrating the swart beauty of Kali, and especially the lines "Dark art Thou like the blue-black cloud/Whose face is beauteous as that of Samkarshana [i.e., Shiva]." [40c] These comparisons add a new dimension, an unsuspected historical depth, to the relationship between Kabbalism and Hinduism.

Another aspect of this relationship is that, despite the geographic distance that separated the Spanish Jews from India, intrepid Jewish authors such as the Kabbalist traveled Abraham Abulafia (see p. 149), his contemporary the Kabbalist translator and author Isaac Albalag, and others did to some extent familiarize the Spanish Kabbalists with Hindu thought and doctrines. [40d]

7. MARY AND THE MATRONIT

An interesting parallel to the warlike aspect of the Matronit is represented by the development of the Virgin Mary not only into the supreme ruler of the world but into the patroness or goddess of Christian armed might. At the opening of the Council of Ephesus in 431 A.D., Cyril of Alexandria delivered a sermon in which he described Mary as the mother and virgin "through whom the Trinity is glorified and worshipped, the cross of the Savior exalted and honored, through whom heaven triumphs, the angels are made glad, devils driven forth, the tempter overcome, and the fallen creature raised up even to heaven." [41]

Lest one think that the triumph of heaven and the driving forth of devils attributed to Mary was regarded as taking place on a spiritual plane only, let us refer to Narses (c. 478–c. 573), the Byzantine general and officer of Emperor Justinian, who looked to Mary for direction on the field of battle, expecting her to reveal to him the time and hour of attack,[42] and the Emperor Heraclius (c. 575–641), who bore her image on his banner.[43] As early as 438, a portrait of the Virgin, attributed to St. Luke, was sent from Jerusalem to Pulcheria, and subsequently this portrait came to be regarded as a kind of palladium and accompanied the Byzantine emperors to the battlefield until the capture of Constantinople by the Turks in 1453.[44] In the West, the German Knights (*Deutscher Ritterorden*) chose the Virgin as their patroness.[45]

Pope, in his commentary to the Song of Songs, has pointed out that this role of the Virgin Mary as war-goddess and the use of her picture as a palladium and battle standard

> developed early from the identification with the goddess Athena-Victoria. The Emperor Constantine worshiped Athena and Apollo, who appeared to him at Autun before the Battle of Milvian Bridge. Constantine's *labarum*, under which sign Christianity became a religion of conquest, had as its base the saltire or cross chest bands of the soldier and the war-goddess, which continue to this day as the symbol of the Queen of Battles on flags and military uniforms.[45a]

Mary, like the Matronit, was considered as having taken over the royal, governing, and controlling functions of God to the extent that her sovereignty actually eclipsed that of God. She was regarded as the imperatrix of the universe, the ruler of the world, the mistress who commands, and the queen of heaven and earth.[46] John of Damascus (ca. 750) called her the sovereign lady to whom the whole creation had been made subject by her son, so that it be preserved through her.[47] St. Peter Damian (1007–72), the Italian cardinal and Doctor of the Church, calls her *deificata*, i.e., "the deified one," and two hundred years later, Mechthild of Magdeburg (c. 1210–c. 1285), the German mystic, goes so far as to call her "goddess." [48]

The parallel between Mary and the Matronit extends to other aspects as well. Like the Matronit, Mary was also considered the spouse of God; like her, she came to be regarded as the mother of men in a general, mystical sense; and like her, she assumed the position of the intermediary between God and men through whom led, if not the only, at any rate the best and easiest, way to God. The old pagan goddess to whom the Israelites sacrificed cakes [49] reawakened among the Christians to new life in the Mary whom the Kollyridians, a 5th-century sect of zealous women, worshiped by carrying cakes in a procession in her honor; [50] and among the Jews in the Matronit-Shekhina, whose identity with Asherah was recognized by Moses Cordovero in 16th-century Safed.[51]

8. THE MEANING OF THE MATRONIT

We discussed a few of the traits which make up the four aspects of the Matronit—her chastity, her promiscuity, her motherliness, and her warlikeness (or bloodthirstiness)—which are the most important components of her personality. The fact that precisely the same four aspects characterize also the ancient Near Eastern love-goddesses, and that their traces can be rediscovered in the Virgin Mary, makes us pause. Whence, we feel compelled to ask, this resemblance, this persistence of the paradoxical goddess-figure in ostensibly and avowedly monotheistic religions? In trying to answer, the alternative of diffusion *versus* independent invention immediately offers itself. The possibility of diffusion is, of course, present: the prototype was the Sumerian Inanna, whose features can be clearly recognized in the Babylonian Ishtar, the Canaanite Anath, and the Persian Anahita. Hebrew monotheism may have been unable to exorcise the tenacious goddess, and it is not at all impossible that, even if she slumbered for several centuries, she awoke and reclaimed some of her old dues in the figure of Mary in Christianity and in that of the Shekhina-Matronit in Talmudic and Kabbalistic Judaism. Yes, not at all impossible. But how can one prove it, short of the most elaborate research? And if a connection were proven, what would be gained thereby? There still would remain the question of why precisely *this* goddess achieved such a fabulous secondary career, among all the others just as readily available in the rich ancient Near Eastern pantheons? To answer this, we have to shift from comparative mythology to psychology, and once we do this, the question of diffusion *versus* independent invention becomes irrelevant. For whether or not the Matronit (and Mary) goes back ultimately to Inanna, her coming to life in new and very greatly changed religious environments shows that she answered a psychological need in medieval Ashkenazi or Sephardic Jewry as she had in Sumer of the 3rd millennium B.C. How can this psychological need be made tangible?

In trying to answer this question, we shall, of necessity, concentrate on the Matronit-Shekhina, the medieval Kabbalistic goddess-figure, with whom this chapter deals. If we want to consider what the Matronit-Shekhina meant psychologically, we must view her entire mythical character comprised of the four major traits discussed above. They present the Matronit-Shekhina as the mythologically objectified projection of the all-round woman, the woman who takes on all the shapes, aspects, and appearances of the human female needed by the male of the species not only for biological survival but equally for his psychological existence. The character of his need, which accompanies him from birth to death, from cradle to grave, changes as he lives out his allotted span. No soon is he born of her, than he wants to be clasped to her ample, motherly breast and given suck by her. As he grows, he needs her protection and direction. As soon as he becomes aware of woman as the opposite sex, he must have her shine on his emotional horizon in virginal purity. When he has to struggle with enemies or is beset by adversity, he relies, in fact or in fancy, on her to fight the forces of evil that oppose him. When he smarts under frustration or is discouraged by failure, he imagines her as the furious female who can do for him what he himself cannot do, fearlessly plunging into attack and fighting his battles. In the routine of regulated marital sexuality, she imparts metaphysical, even cosmic, significance to the act. When homelife becomes monotonous and stale, she is there with the thousand painted faces of her allure and the ever-present promise of her availability. And when the ultimate exhaustion overcomes him, it is the hope of her last kiss which makes him forget the bitterness of dying and instead think of death as the beginning of a new life in a happy Beyond.

The Matronit is thus the projection of everything a woman can be in order to sustain man. She symbolizes in her manifold aspects the great affirmation of life, the basic satisfactions one derives from existence, the comforts one finds in mother, nursemaid, lover, bride, wife, wanton seductress, warrior-protectress, and opener of the gates of the Beyond.

The fact that the image does not lack its contradictory features, betrays something of the male's ambivalence in his relationship to woman. The Matronit, in common with the great ancient love-goddesses, is both virgin and wanton. Virgin, because man must idealize woman: he wants *his* woman to be virginal, to have waited for him through countless aeons, and to remain virginal and chaste even while yielding to his embrace, and to his alone. Wanton, because at the same time, he imagines the woman whose body holds the promise of lust for him as the embodiment of desirability, loved by men and gods, as one who not merely yields to him but arouses him, makes him follow her into and through the labyrinthine mysteries of love. And, paradoxically, but with a deep inner inevitability, he imagines his virgin bride and wanton woman to be one and the same person and projects both self-contradictory characters into one and the same goddess. A third feature with which the same goddess is embellished is that of the mother. This expresses, if not necessarily Oedipal inclinations, at least the desire to recapture in the beloved's embrace something of the happy security of the infant cuddled in its mother's arms.

As if this were not enough, the conflated image of the virgin-wanton-mother, in turn, appears as merely one of the two overall aspects united in the goddess: the love aspect, as against which she has another aspect, a cruel and frightening one, that of the pitiless warrior-goddess who sheds blood, extinguishes life, and enjoys doing this as much as she does making love. And, what is equally paradoxical, man feels himself attracted by the wrathful countenance of this goddess of battle and blood as much as to the virgin-wanton who beckons to him with her chaste-experienced smile, or to the mother who offers him her ample, nourishing breasts.

The goddess thus speaks to man with four tongues: keep away from me because I am a Virgin; enjoy me because I am available to all; come shelter in my motherly bosom; and die in me because I thirst for your blood. Whichever of her aspects momentarily gain the upper hand, there is a deep chord in the male psyche which powerfully responds to it. Her voices enter man and stir him; they bend man to pay homage to her and they lure man to lose himself in her, whether in love or in death.

Chapter VII

LILITH

No she-demon has ever achieved as fantastic a career as Lilith, who started out from the lowliest of origins, was a failure as Adam's intended wife, became the paramour of lascivious spirits, rose to be the bride of Samael the Demon King, ruled as Queen of Zemargad and Sheba, and ended up as the consort of God himself. The main features of Lilith's mythical biography first appear in Sumerian culture about the middle of the 3rd millennium B.C. What she meant for the Biblical Hebrews can only be surmised, but by the Talmudic period (2nd–5th centuries A.D.) she was a fully developed evil she-demon, and during the Kabbalistic age she rose to the high position of queenly consort at God's side.

1. THE BACKGROUND

The earliest mention of a she-demon whose name is similar to that of Lilith is found in the Sumerian king list which dates from ca. 2400 B.C. It states that the father of the great hero Gilgamesh was a Lillu-demon. The Lillu was one of four demons belonging to a vampire or incubi-succubae class. The other three were Lilitu (Lilith), a she-demon; Ardat Lili (or Lilith's handmaid), who visited men by night and bore them ghostly children; and Irdu Lili, who must

have been her male counterpart and would visit women
and beget children by them.¹ Originally these were
storm-demons, but because of a mistaken etymology
they came to be regarded as night-demons.²

Lilith's epithet was "the beautiful maiden," but she
was believed to have been a harlot and a vampire
who, once she chose a lover, would never let him go,
but without ever giving him real satisfaction. She was
unable to bear children and had no milk in her
breasts.³ According to the Sumerian epic *Gilgamesh
and the Huluppu Tree* (dating from ca. 2000 B.C.),
Lilith (Lillake) built her house in the midst of the
Huluppu (willow) tree which had been planted on
the bank of the Euphrates in the days of Creation. A
dragon set up its nest at the base of the tree, and the
Zu-bird placed his young in its crown. Gilgamesh slays
the dragon with his huge bronze axe, whereupon the
Zu-bird flees with its young to the mountain, and
Lilith, terror-stricken, tears down her house and es-
capes to the desert.⁴

A Babylonian terra-cotta relief, roughly contemporary with the above poem, shows in what form
Lilith was believed to appear to human eyes. She is
slender, well-shaped, beautiful and nude, with wings
and owl-feet. She stands erect on two reclining lions
which are turned away from each other and are flanked
by owls. On her head she wears a cap embellished by
several pairs of horns. In her hands she holds a ring-
and-rod combination.⁵ Evidently, this is no longer a
lowly she-demon, but a goddess who tames wild beasts
and, as shown by the owls on the reliefs, rules by
night. (See Plate 31.)

In the ensuing centuries Lilith's shape changed
again. A 7th-century B.C. tablet found at Arslan Tash
in northern Syria shows her as a winged sphinx, across
whose body is written the following inscription in
Phoenician-Canaanite dialect:

> O, Flyer in a dark chamber,
> Go away at once, O Lili!

These lines are part of an incantation text used to help women in childbirth [6]—one of many extant from the period of the Assyrian Empire and the new Babylonian Kingdom—and they show that by that time the myth of Lilith had all the major features which were elaborated to their fill 2,000 years later by Kabbalistic Judaism.

2. ISAIAH 34:14

One brief reference to Lilith, and a doubtful one at that, is all that is found in the entire Bible. Isaiah, in describing Yahweh's day of vengeance, when the land will be turned into a desolate wilderness, says:

> The wild-cat shall meet with the jackals
> And the satyr shall cry to his fellow,
> Yea, Lilith shall repose there
> And find her a place of rest.[7]

The Mesopotamian and North Syrian material surveyed above supplies the background to this prophetic allusion. Evidently, Lilith was a well-known she-demon in Israel of the 8th century B.C., whose name had only to be mentioned to conjure up the beliefs current about her. That she is said to find a place of rest in the desert seems to tie in with the episode recorded in the Sumerian Gilgamesh fragment: after Lilith fled into the desert, she evidently found repose there.

3. THE TALMUDIC LILITH

The information about Lilith contained in the Talmud and the Midrashim of the Talmudic period is meager. One passage states that she had wings [8]; another, that she had long hair.[9] On this basis Rashi

(Shlomo Yitzhaqi), the medieval Talmud commentator
(1040–1105), concluded that the Lilin (masculine
plural of Lili, whose feminine singular is Lilith), have
human form, except that they have wings, in contrast
to the demons who have completely human form and
eat and drink like humans, and to the spirits who
have neither body nor form.[10] It thus appears that, as
far as her overall appearance was concerned, Lilith
looked very much like the Cherubim. This detail will
become significant in connection with the Zoharic
myth about the relationship of Lilith to the Cherubim.

Somewhat more is known about the life history of
Lilith and her nefarious activities, as they were
imagined in the Talmudic period. Lilith, we learn, was
Adam's first wife. However, Adam and Lilith could
find no happiness together, not even understanding.
When Adam wished to lie with her, Lilith demurred:
"Why should I lie beneath you," she asked, "when
I am your equal, since both of us were created from
dust?" When Lilith saw that Adam was determined to
overpower her, she uttered the magic name of God,
rose into the air, and flew away to the Red Sea, a
place of ill-repute, full of lascivious demons. There,
Lilith engaged in unbridled promiscuity and bore a
demonic brood of more than one hundred a day.
God, however, sent after her three angels, Senoy,
Sansenoy, and Semangelof by name,[11] who soon located
her in the same wild waters in which the Egyptians
were to drown in the days of the Exodus. The angels
gave her God's message, but she refused to return.
When they threatened drowning her in the sea, she
argued: "Let me be, for I was created in order to
weaken the babes: if it is a male, I have power over
him from the moment of his birth until the eighth
day of his life [when he is circumcised and thereby
protected], and if a girl, until the twentieth day." The
angels insisted however, and in order to make them
desist, she swore to them in the name of God: "Whenever I shall see you or your names or your images
on an amulet, I shall do no harm to the child." Moreover, she gave her consent to the death of one hundred

of her own children day after day—which is the reason why that many demons die every day. This agreement between the three angels and Lilith is the basis for writing the names Senoy, Sansenoy, and Semangelof on amulets hung around the necks of newborn babes: when Lilith sees the names, she remembers her oath and leaves the child alone.[12]

However, in spite of her determined refusal to return to Adam, Lilith soon became attracted to him again, and managed to sleep with him against his will. In the meantime Adam had received Eve as his wife, was persuaded by her to eat from the fruit of the Tree of Knowledge, and was expelled from the Garden of Eden with the curse of death hanging over his head. When Adam became aware that because of his sin God decreed mortality upon him and all his future descendants, he embarked upon a period of penitence which lasted for 130 years. He fasted, refrained from intercourse with Eve, and, in order to mortify his flesh, wore a belt of rough fig twigs around his naked body. He could not, however, control his involuntary nocturnal emissions, which were brought about by female spirits who came and coupled with him and bore him spirits, demons, and Lilin. At the same time, male spirits came and impregnated Eve, who thus became the mother of innumerable demon children. The spirits thus procreated are the plagues of mankind.[13]

It should be noted that the succubae and incubi who sought out Adam and Eve in the 130 years of their self-imposed separation remain anonymous in all the sources dating from the Talmudic period. Yet there is basis to assume that Lilith was regarded as one of Adam's succubae, because her seduction of Adam must have served as the mythical prototype and validation of the belief in her power over men who spent a night alone in a house. The danger to which such a man would expose himself was regarded as so acute that Rabbi Hanina, the 1st century A.D. teacher, warns: it is forbidden for a man to sleep alone in a house, lest Lilith get hold of him.[14]

4. LILITH OF THE BOWLS

The relatively scanty Talmudic material about Lilith is complemented by much richer data contained in Aramaic incantation texts found in Nippur in Babylonia, some 50 miles southeast of modern Hilla in Iraq. Excavations conducted by the University of Pennsylvania brought to light dozens of bowls inscribed with magical texts, several of which are directed against Lilith or Liliths. The bowls date from about 600 A.D.; in other words, they are about a hundred years younger than the text of the Babylonian Talmud (which was compiled ca. 500 A.D.). But there is every reason to assume that such incantations against Lilith were not the product of the 6th century but go back to earlier periods. In Nippur of the 6th century, there was an important Jewish colony (in addition to Mandaeans and other groups), and some of the most interesting bowls were, by their own incontrovertible evidence, inscribed and used by Jews. While the Talmud contains the views of the learned elite about Lilith, these bowls show what she meant for the simple people. It is surprising to see to what extent the sages and the quacks shared the fear of Lilith and the belief in her evil nature.

From a synopsis of the incantation texts it appears that Lilith was regarded as the ghostly paramour of men and constituted a special danger for women during many periods of their sexual life cycle: before defloration, during menstruation, etc. A mother in the hour of childbirth and her newborn babe were especially vulnerable, and therefore had to be protected from the Liliths. The home, arches, and thresholds were favorite haunts where the Liliths lurked ready to pounce on anybody foolish enough to go unprotected. A rough drawing sketched on a Jewish bowl shows Lilith naked, with long loose hair, pointed breasts, no wings, strongly marked genitals, and chained ankles. At night, the female Liliths join men, and the male

Lilin women, to generate demonic offspring. Once they succeed in attaching themselves to a human, they acquire rights of cohabitation, and therefore must be given a *get*, or letter of divorce, in order that they may be expelled. Jealous of the human mates of their bedfellows, they hate the children born of ordinary human wedlock, attack them, plague them, suck their blood, and strangle them. The Liliths also manage to prevent the birth of children by causing barrenness, miscarriages, or complications during childbirth. As Montgomery aptly put it over half a century ago, "the Liliths were the most developed products of the morbid imagination—of the barren or neurotic woman, the mother in the time of maternity, the sleepless child." [15]

Let us now turn to a few examples illustrating the manner in which these magic incantations are phrased. The first is the text of the bowl which carries the sketch of Lilith described above (see Plate 32). It reads as follows:

> In the name of the Lord of salvations. Designated is this bowl for the sealing of the house of this Geyonai bar Mamai, that there flee from him the evil Lilith, in the name of 'Yahweh El has scattered'; the Lilith, the male Lilin and the female Liliths, the Hag [ghost?] and the Snatcher, the three of you, the four of you, and the five of you. Naked are you sent forth, nor are you clad, with your hair dishevelled and let fly behind your backs. It is made known to you, whose father is named Palhas and whose mother Pelahdad: Hear and obey and come forth from the house and dwelling of this Geyonai bar Mamai and from Rashnoi his wife, the daughter of Marath.
>
> . . . Be informed herewith that Rabbi Joshua bar Perahia has sent the ban against you. . . . A divorce-writ [*gita*] has come down to us from heaven, and therein is found written your advisement and your intimidation, in the name of Palsa-Pelisa ["Divorcer-Divorced"], who renders to thee thy divorce and thy separation, your

divorces and your separations. Thou, Lilith, male
Lili and female Lilith, Hag and Snatcher, be under
the ban . . . of Joshua bar Perahia, who has thus
spoken: A divorce-writ has come for you from
across the sea. . . . Hear it and depart from the
house and dwelling of this Geyonai bar Mamai
and from Rashnoi his wife, the daughter of Marath.
You shall not again appear to them, either in a
dream by night or in slumber by day, because
you are sealed with the signet of El Shaddai, and
with the signet of the House of Joshua bar Perahia
and by the Seven who are before him. Thou
Lilith, male Lili and female Lilith, Hag and
Snatcher, I adjure you by the Strong One of
Abraham, by the Rock of Isaac, by the Shaddai
of Jacob, by Yah [is] his name . . . by Yah his
memorial . . . I adjure you to turn away from
this Rashnoi, the daughter of Marath, and from
Geyonai her husband, the son of Mamai. Your
divorce and writ and letter of separation . . . sent
through holy angels . . . the Hosts of fire in the
spheres, the Chariots of El Panim before him
standing, the Beasts worshipping in the fire of
his throne and in the water. . . . Amen, Amen,
Selah, Halleluyah! [16]

Only a few comments are needed for the complete
understanding of this text. Its intent is clear: Lilith
and her company are adjured to leave the house of
Geyonai and his wife Rashnoi, never again to return.
The Liliths are given a letter of divorce and sent
naked, just as Gomer was by her husband Hosea.[17]
In another bowl, both female and male demons are
given their *get* (letter of divorce) in order thus to rid
the house and its inhabitants of them:

This is the *get* for a demon and spirits and
Satan . . . and Lilith in order to banish them
from . . . the entire house. Yah . . . cut off the
king of the demons . . . the great ruler of the
Liliths. I adjure you . . . whether you are male

or female, I adjure you. . . . Just as the demons
write letters of divorce and give them to their
wives and do not again return to them, so take
your letter of divorce, accept your stipulated
share [*ketubba*], and go and leave and depart
from the house. . . . Amen, Amen, Amen,
Selah.[18]

A medieval story, preserved in Hebrew and Arabic
versions, tells of a youth, Dihon ben Shalmon, who
marries the daughter of Ashmodai, then gives her a
get (letter of divorce), whereupon she kills him with
a kiss.[19] Rabbi Joshua ben Perahia, whose name is
invoked several times in the Nippur bowl, was an
early-1st-century B.C. sage, who evidently was believed,
by the 6th century A.D., to have been a powerful
exorciser of demons. The divine names and epithets
are either traditional Jewish or very close to them.
The concluding lines show that certain elements of the
Merkabah ("Chariot") mysticism [20] were familiar
matters in 6th-century Nippur.

Another, considerably later text is a classic example of a magic ritual whose integral part is its own
validation by reference to a myth. It reads as follows:

Shadai

Senoy, Sansenoy, Semangelof, Adam, and the
Ancient Eve. Out Lilith.[21]

In the name of Y, the God of Israel, the
Cherubim-sitter, whose name lives and endures
forever. The prophet Elijah was walking on the
road and met the Evil Lilith and all her band.
He said to her: 'Where are you headed for, O
you Unclean One, and you Spirit of Defilement,
and all your band, where are they going?' And
she answered and said to him: 'My lord Elijah,
I am on my way to the house of a woman in
childbirth, Mercada . . . ,[22] daughter of Donna, to
give her the sleep of death and to take her child
which is being born to her, to suck its blood, and

to suck the marrow of its bones, and to seal its flesh.' And the prophet Elijah, blessed be his memory, said to her: 'With a ban from the Name (i.e., God), blessed be He, be you restrained and be you like unto a stone.' And she answered and said to him: 'For the sake of Yahweh, release me from the ban and I shall flee and swear to you in the name of Y, the God of Israel, that I shall desist from this woman in childbirth and her child which is being born to her, and shall surely not harm her. And every time that they mention my names, or I see my names written, I and my band shall have no power to do evil or to harm. And these are my names: Lilith, Abitar, Abiqar, Amorpho, Hakash, Odam, Kephido, Ailo, Matrota, Abnukta, Shatriha, Kali, Taltui, Kitsha.' And Elijah answered her: 'Behold, I adjure you and all your band in the name of Y, the God of Israel, [which name in its] numerical value [equals] 613 [or the number of the religious commandments], [the God of] Abraham, Isaac, and Jacob, and in the name of his Holy Shekhina, and in the name of the ten Seraphim, Ophanim, and Holy Beasts, and the ten books of the Law, and by the might of the God of the Hosts, blessed be He, that you and your band go not to injure this woman, or the child she is bearing, neither to drink its blood, nor to suck the marrow of its bones, nor to seal its flesh, nor to touch them, either their 256 limbs, nor their 365 ligaments and veins. Just as she cannot count the stars of heaven, and cannot dry up the waters of the sea. In the name of Him who rent Satan, Hasdiel, Shamriel.[23]

The efficacy of the ritual is ensured by reciting the first occurrence of a similar rite, performed by a mythical hero, in this case the prophet Elijah. The structure of the text is identical with the one which validates the efficacy of an amulet inscribed with the names of

Senoy, Sansenoy, and Semangelof by telling the story of how these three angels extorted a promise from Lilith to keep away from all places where their names are displayed. As we shall see later, the thirteen additional names of Lilith reappear in medieval Jewish magic.

On a third incantation bowl the name "Lilith Buznai" appears several times.[24] Some four centuries later this name, in the form "Pizna," reappears in the Midrash Abkir. The context of the bowl says: "Charmed art thou, Lilith Buznai and all the goddesses . . . and the 360 Tribes, by the word of the granddaughter of the angel Buznai." Evidently, Buznai was the individual name of a female numen, who is described interchangeably as a Lilith and an angel; she was regarded as a goddess and had a granddaughter who was antagonistic to her. A similar enmity, as we shall see later, existed between the Elder Lilith and the Younger Lilith, according to Kabbalistic mythology.

Lilith's fame and fear of her spread from Babylonia to the East, into Persia, where magic bowls were used against her by various strata of the population, much in the same fashion as in Babylonia. As in the case of the bowls discussed above, the Persian bowls also talk of Lilith in the singular, as well as of plural "Liliths," as a category of female, harmful, and dangerous demons, in conjunction with male "devils" and male "demons." The following bowl inscription is written in Aramaic, around a picture of Lilith, similar in execution to the one referred to earlier though differing in detail (Plate 33): [25]

You are bound and sealed, all you demons and devils and Liliths, by that hard and strong, mighty and powerful bond with which are tied Sison and Sisin. . . . The evil Lilith, who causes the hearts of men to go astray and appears in the dream of the night and in the vision of the day, who burns and casts down with nightmare, attacks and kills children, boys and girls—she is

conquered and sealed away from the house and
from the threshold of Bahram-Gushnasp son of
Ishtar-Nahid by the talisman of Metatron, the
great prince who is called the Great Healer of
Mercy . . . who vanquishes demons and devils,
black arts and mighty spells and keeps them away
from the house and threshold of Bahram-Gushnasp, the son of Ishtar-Nahid. Amen, Amen,
Selah. Vanquished are the black arts and mighty
spells, vanquished the bewitching women, they,
their witchery and their spells, their curses and
their invocations, and kept away from the four
walls of the house of Bahram-Gushnasp, the son
of Ishtar-Nahid. Vanquished and trampled down
are the bewitching women, vanquished on earth
and vanquished in heaven. Vanquished are their
constellations and stars. Bound are the works of
their hands. Amen, Amen, Selah.[26]

The evidence of the names of the man for whom
the bowl was inscribed and his mother seems to indicate that he was a follower of the Parsi religion. As
the text itself shows, Lilith was supposed to threaten
Bahram-Gushnasp as a result of a magic spell cast
on him and his house by witches who were Lilith's
devotees.

In the text of another bowl from Persia, this one
written in Mandaic (pagan Aramaic), Lilith is rendered
harmless by a still more powerful incantation. She is
adjured to cease haunting the house of a certain Zakoy
and is immobilized as follows:

Bound is the bewitching Lilith with a peg of iron
in her nose; bound is the bewitching Lilith with
pincers of iron in her mouth; bound is the bewitching Lilith, who haunts the house of Zakoy,
with a chain of iron on her neck; bound is the
bewitching Lilith with fetters of iron on her hands;
bound is the bewitching Lilith with stocks of stone
on her feet. . . .[27]

5. THE BIRTH OF LILITH

While the major characteristics of Lilith, as we have just seen, were well developed by the close of the Talmudic period, it remained for Kabbalistic mysticism to establish a relationship, and quite a close one at that, between her and the deity. In the six centuries that elapsed between the Babylonian Aramaic incantation texts and the early Spanish Kabbalistic writings, Lilith must have greatly extended her influence, for when she reappears in the 13th century she not only commands considerably greater attention but is surrounded by a larger retinue, and her life history is known in much greater mythological detail.

Her birth, to begin with, is described in a number of alternative versions. According to one, she was created before Adam—in fact, on the fifth day of Creation, because the "living creature" with whose swarms God filled the waters [28] was none other than Lilith.[29] Another version, which ties in directly with the earlier (Talmudic) Lilith image, recounts that she was created by God in the same manner in which, shortly before, he had fashioned Adam. That is to say, God again turned to the earth to obtain raw material, but this time, instead of using the clean earth which was the substance of Adam's body, He— for reasons unknown—took filth and impure sediments from the earth, and out of these He formed a female. As was to be expected, this creature turned out to be an evil spirit.[30]

According to a third version, God originally created Adam and Lilith together in such a manner that the female creature was contained in the male. Lilith's soul was originally lodged in the depths of the Great Abyss, whence she was called forth by God and joined to Adam. When Adam was created and his body completed, a thousand souls from the Left (i.e., Evil) Side tried to attach themselves to him. But God let out a shout and thus drove them off. All this while

Adam lay there, a body without a soul, greenish in color. Then a cloud descended, and God commanded the earth to produce a living soul. This God breathed into Adam, who now was able to stand up, and, behold, his female was attached to his side. But God sawed his creature into two, whereupon Lilith flew off to the Cities of the Sea, where she still lurks ready to harm mankind.[31]

Yet another version considers Lilith not as a being created by God, but as a divine entity which emerged spontaneously, either out of the Great Supernal Abyss, or out of the power-aspect of God (the *Gevurah* or *Din*), which manifests itself chiefly in the divine acts of stern judgment and punishment. This stern, punitive aspect of God, one of His ten mystical attributes (*Sephirot*), has at its lowest manifestation some affinity with the realm of evil referred to as "the dregs of the wine," and it is out of this that Lilith emerged together with Samael:

> A mystery of mysteries: Out of the power of the glow of Isaac's noon (i.e., the *Gevurah*), out of the dregs of the wine, there emerged an intertwined shoot which comprises both male and female. They are red like the rose, and they spread out into several sides and paths. The male is called Samael, and his female [Lilith] is always contained in him. Just as in the side of Holiness, so in the Other [Evil] Side as well, male and female are contained in one another. The female of Samael is called Serpent, Woman of Harlotry, End of All Flesh, End of Days.[32]

In the mystical writings of the two brothers Jacob and Isaac Hacohen of Segovia (Castile), which antedate the Zohar by a few decades, Lilith and Samael are said to have been born by an emanation from beneath the Throne of Glory, in the shape of an androgynous, double-faced being, corresponding in the spiritual realm to the birth of Adam and Eve, who also were born as a hermaphrodite. The two androgynous twin-couples not only resembled each other, but both "were like the image of what is Above": that is, reproduced in a visible form the image of the androgynous deity.[33]

Yet another version connects the birth of Lilith with the creation of the luminaries, carefully avoiding, however, any statement to the effect that God actually created her. The "first light," which was the light of Mercy (another of the ten Sephirot), appeared when, on the first day of Creation, God said "Let there be light." [34] When this light became hidden, Holiness became surrounded by a husk of Evil. This idea is expressed by the statement that "a husk [qelipah] was created around the brain," and this husk, in turn, spread and brought out another husk, and this was none other than Lilith.[35]

6. LILITH AND THE CHERUBIM

As soon as Lilith was born, or emerged in one of the mysterious ways described above, her longing for male companionship manifested itself. She began to fly about, soaring up into the heights of heaven and again swooping down, until she reached the Cherubim who surrounded God's throne and who, because their faces were like those of small boys,[36] are called in the Zohar "small faces." To them Lilith attached herself, impressing herself into their bodies, and once she succeeded in doing this, she refused to separate from them. But when God created man, which He did in order to bring this world to completion, He forcibly detached Lilith from the Cherubim and made her descend to earth. Lilith, thinking that she would become Adam's helpmate, approached him, but again she was frustrated. For, attached to Adam's side was Eve, whose beauty resembled the beauty of Above. When Lilith saw the complete image of Adam and Eve together, she understood that she had no chance, and fled back up to heaven to reattach herself to the

Cherubim. However, by this time the watchers of the
Gate of Above barred her way, and God, addressing
a stern rebuke to her, cast her into the depths of the
sea.[37]

7. LILITH AND ADAM

As noted above, the older sources do not state
clearly that it was Lilith herself who, after her Red
Sea sojourn, returned to Adam as his succuba. The
later sources, however, know it for a fact that this,
indeed, did happen. Adam, we read in the Zohar,
succeeded in impregnating Lilith during their early
short-lived connubium; then, not having been a suitable helpmeet for him, Lilith left him,[38] to return after
a while and force herself upon him. Before doing so,
however, she managed to attach herself to Cain and
to bear him numerous spirits and demons.[39]

The first medieval source to give the myth of Lilith
and Adam in full was the lost Midrash Abkir (ca.
10th century), which was followed by the Zohar and
later Kabbalistic writings. Adam, we learn, was a
perfect saint, and when he understood that because
of his sin—or, as a consequence of Cain's fratricide—
death came into the world, he separated from Eve,
slept alone, and fasted for 130 years. But Lilith, whose
name is Pizna [40]—or, according to the Zohar, two
female spirits, Lilith and Naamah—found him, desired
his beauty, which was like that of the sun disk, and
lay with him. The issue of these unions were demons
and spirits, called "the plagues of mankind," who lurk
underneath doorways or in wells and latrines, and
lead men astray.[41]

According to the mythical cosmology of the German-
born Palestinian Kabbalist Naphtali Herz ben Jacob
Elhanan (lived in the second half of the 16th century),
in the second of the seven earth-layers, counting from
the bottom, dwell

the giant human figures, tall of stature, who were born of Adam in the 130 years during which he begot demons, spirits, and Lilin. Lilith used to come to him against his will and conceive from Adam [and she bore these beings]. And they are always sad and full of sorrow and sighs, and there is no joy at all among them. And these hosts can multiply [and ascend] from that earth to this world upon which we stand, and [here] they become harmful spirits, and [then] they return there. . . .[42]

That Adam begot with Lilith spirits, demons, and Lilin became a commonplace in the mystical literature of the 14th to 17th centuries, often with the added explanation that it was Adam's own sin which made it possible for Lilith to overcome him against his will.[43]

8. LILITH THE SUCCUBA

The next period in Lilith's life was spent in two activities: seducing men and killing children. As to the first, a passage in the Zohar puts it as follows:

She [Lilith] roams at night, and goes all about the world and makes sport with men and causes them to emit seed. In every place where a man sleeps alone in a house, she visits him and grabs him and attaches herself to him and has her desire from him, and bears from him. And she also afflicts him with sickness, and he knows it not, and all this takes place when the moon is on the wane.[44]

Spontaneous nocturnal emission is the visible sign of Lilith having succeeded in arousing the desire of a man in his sleep and of having satisfied her own lust through him. In doing this, she assumes the shape of either a mature woman or a young virgin. The issue of such unions are evil spirits:

> She forsakes the husband of her youth [i.e., Samael] and descends to earth and fornicates with men who sleep here below, in the uncleanness of emission. And from them are born demons, spirits, and Lilin, and they are called 'the plagues of mankind.' [45]

However, Lilith is well capable of seducing men not only in their sleep but also while awake. Once she succeeds, she turns from a beautiful seductress into a cruel fury and kills her victim:

> She adorns herself with many ornaments like a despicable harlot, and takes up her position at the crossroads to seduce the sons of man. When a fool approaches her, she grabs him, kisses him, and pours him wine of dregs of viper's gall. As soon as he drinks it, he goes astray after her. When she sees that he has gone astray after her from the path of truth, she divests herself of all ornaments which she put on for that fool. Her ornaments for the seduction of the sons of man are: her hair is long and red like the rose, her cheeks are white and red, from her ears hang six ornaments, Egyptian cords and all the ornaments of the Land of the East hang from her nape. Her mouth is set like a narrow door, comely in its decor; her tongue is sharp like a sword, her words are smooth like oil, her lips red like a rose and sweetened by all the sweetness of the world. She is dressed in scarlet, and adorned with forty ornaments less one. Yon fool goes astray after her and drinks from the cup of wine and commits with her fornications and strays after her. What does she thereupon do? She leaves him asleep on the couch, flies up to heaven, denounces him, takes her leave, and descends. That fool awakens and deems he can make sport

with her as before, but she removes her ornaments and turns into a menacing figure. She stands before him clothed in garments of flaming fire, inspiring terror and making body and soul tremble, full of frightening eyes, in her hand a drawn sword dripping bitter drops. And she kills that fool and casts him into Gehenna.[46]

Lilith attempted to play this trick on Jacob, but she was no match for him: "Jacob went to her and came to her place . . . and saw all the ornaments of her house, but escaped from her, whereupon her male, Samael, attacked him and fought him but could not prevail upon him." [47]

Even when a man wishes to engage in lawful sexual intercourse with his wife, the menace of Lilith is present:

And behold, that hard shell [i.e., embodiment of evil], Lilith, is always present in the bed linen of man and wife when they copulate, in order to take hold of the sparks of the drops of semen which are lost—because it is impossible to perform the marital act without such a loss of sparks—and she creates out of them demons, spirits, and Lilin. . . . But there is an incantation for this, to chase Lilith away from the bed and to bring forth pure souls . . . in that moment, when a man copulates with his wife, let him direct his heart to the holiness of his Master, and say:

'In the name of God.
O you who are wrapped in velvet [i.e., Lilith],
You have appeared.
Release, release!
Neither come nor go!
The seed is not yours,
Nor in your inheritance.
Go back, go back!
The sea rages,

Its waves call you.
I hold on to the Holy One,
Wrap myself into the King's holiness.

Then let him cover his head and his wife for
one hour. . . .[48]

Some forms of unholiness in sexual intercourse are
described by R. Naphtali as follows:

Lilith, God preserve us, has dominion over
children who issue from him who couples with
his wife in candlelight, or with his wife naked,
or at a time when he is forbidden to have intercourse with her. All the children who issue from
such unions, Lilith can kill them anytime she
wishes, because they are delivered into her hands.
And this is the secret of the children's smiling
when they are small—because of Lilith who plays
with them.[49]

The counterpart of the magic efforts to protect
men from the nocturnal enticements of Lilith, the
succuba, is an incantation whose purpose is precisely
the opposite: to obtain a succuba for the night with
the help of that other demon-queen, Igrath bath
Mahalath. The formula is contained in a 15th-century
text which reads as follows:

'I adjure you, Ograth [i.e., Igrath] bath Mahalath, Queen of the Demons, with the great,
strong and terrible Name, with the name of his
holy angels, and with the name of Bilar the
heroic, King of the Demons, that you send to me
X, daughter of Y, the beautiful maiden from
among your maidens who follow you, whose
number is like the number of the days of the
year, and with the name of Metatron and Sandal-
phon, *AAA NNN SSS*.' And this must be done
either on the eve of Sunday or on the eve of
Wednesday. And one must have a separate room,

and a clean white bed and clothes, and the room
and the bed should be fumigated with aloe wood.
And the knowledgeable will understand.[50]

An incantation such as this must have been employed by Rabbi Joseph della Reina in making Lilith
herself his lover. This Rabbi Joseph seems to have
been a known Spanish Kabbalist who about 1470
attempted to bring about the redemption of Israel by
means of a great magico-mystical ritual. Having failed
in his noble but extremely dangerous attempt to slay
Satan, whose machinations prevented redemption, so
the story goes, Joseph despaired of the powers of
saintliness and turned to evil ways, bending the forces
of the Other Side to his will. The full, folklorically
embellished version of Joseph's story written by Solomon Navarro (b. 1606) contains an account of
Joseph's love affairs, first with Lilith and then with
the Queen of Greece (whence his surname, Della
Reina):

And after this, Rabbi Joseph reached the city
of Zidon and dwelt there. And he corrupted his
ways, after seeing that his plan [to bring the
Messiah] had failed. And especially after hearing
the terrible heavenly voice, he despaired of the
World to Come, made a covenant with the evil
Lilith, and delivered himself into her hands, and
she became his wife. And he made himself impure
with all impurities, to the extent of using for
evil the Holy Names and the other names and
incantations he knew. And he adjured spirits and
demons every night to bring him what he wanted.
And this is how he conducted himself many days,
until he became enamored of the wife of the
King of Greece more than of any other woman.
And he had her brought to him almost every
night, and in the morning he commanded [the
spirits] that they return her.
And it came to pass one day that the queen
told the king that 'Every night in my dream they

take me to a place and a man lies with me, and in the morning I find myself in my bed, and I am soiled with an effusion of semen, and I do not know whence this came to me.' The king understood the matter, sent for the magicians, and ordered them to watch in the house of the queen with other women, and said to them that they should be prepared and ready with incantations and names of impurity, so as to stop those who would come to take the queen. And they did so and sat watching.

And in that night the demons came as commanded by Rabbi Joseph, and the watchers instantly sensed it and performed acts and adjured them so that they should know what was the matter and what it was about. And the demons said: 'We are emissaries of Rabbi Joseph, who dwells in Zidon.' Instantly the king sent a commander of the army with letters and a present to the Prince of Zidon [asking him] that he should immediately send him Rabbi Joseph alive, [to enable the king] to take revenge on him by subjecting him to severe torture. And it came to pass that when Rabbi Joseph saw that the evil had overtaken him—and he knew it from the mouth of the demons he had sent even before the writing reached the prince of Zidon—he went and threw himself into the sea and died.[50a]

9. LILITH THE CHILD-KILLER

Following her rejection by the Cherubim, Lilith remained in the depths of the sea until Adam and Eve sinned,

when the Holy One, blessed be He, brought her up, and she obtained power over those children —the 'small faces' of mankind—who deserved to be punished because of the sins of their fathers.

She roams all over the world, then approaches the gates of the Garden of Eden and observes the Cherubim watching over the gates. She sits down there, next to the flame of the sword, since it was from that flame that she originated. When the flame turns around [indicating that the world has entered into a phase of punishment], she rushes off and again goes roaming all over the world to seek out the children who deserve to be punished. And she smiles at them and kills them. . . .[51]

After the completion of her raids on mankind, Lilith returns to the cities of the sea, her headquarters. Only when ultimately God will destroy the Evil Kingdom of Rome, will she move there to take up her abode in the eternal ruins.[52]

In the meantime, Lilith

goes out into the world and seeks out children, and she sees the children of mankind and attaches herself to them to kill them and to draw herself into their souls. And as she is about to go into such a soul, three holy spirits [i.e., the three angels Senoy, Sansenoy, and Semangelof] appear there, and they soar toward her and take that soul from her and place it in front of the Holy One, blessed be He, and there [the children] study in front of Him.[53]

Thus, even if the angels are unable to save the child's life, they at least save its soul. To make sure that one's child is in no way harmed by Lilith, one must perform the act of procreation itself in holiness:

If a man is in a state of holiness, he has no fear of her [Lilith], because the Holy One, blessed be He, sends those three holy angels whom we mentioned, and they watch over the child [which is being conceived] and she cannot harm him. . . .

But if a man is not in a state of holiness, and he draws out a soul from the side of uncleanness, then she comes and plays with that child, and if she kills it, she penetrates that soul and never leaves it.[54]

Although the above quotations were taken from the Zohar, the practice of protecting a mother and her newborn child from Lilith with the help of the three angels Senoy, Sansenoy, and Semangelof is considerably older not only in the East but also in the West. The famous mystical treatise *Sepher Raziel* (*Book of Raziel*), written or compiled in all probability, by Eleazar ben Judah ben Kalonymos of Worms (1176–1238), contains, e.g., several such incantations. On folio 43a of the 1701 Amsterdam edition, one finds the following instructions:

Tried and proven for protecting the mother and her child from sorcery and the Evil Eye, and so that in the hour of the birth no demon and evil plague should be able to overpower her and her child . . . the seventy names of angels are, as is well known, very efficacious for all kinds of protection. And also the following names and their drawings, as Adam saw them and drew them, are very good for the protection of the mother and child. (See Figure 1.)

On the very next page of the *Book of Raziel* are listed the names of the seventy angels, and under them is a sketch showing twice the three angels Senoy, Sansenoy, and Semangelof. It is difficult to make out what the three sketches on the right side represent, but on the left the intention seems to be to show them as bird-headed beings. Over the sketches of the angels the words "Adam and Eve, Out Lilith!" appear twice, and under the picture follows the incantation text, which reads as follows (my translation from the Hebrew):

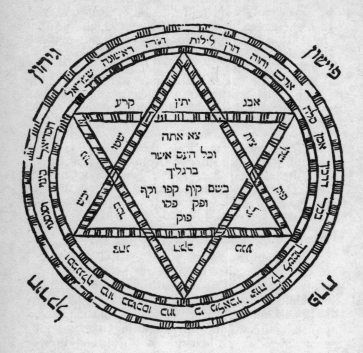

Figure 1. Amulet to protect woman in childbirth from Lilith. (From *The Book of Raziel*, folio 43a.)

In the name of *EHYE WHA AA BB AO MAK AAA*.

I adjure you First Eve [here an epithet of Lilith] in the name of Him Who is your Creator and in the name of the three angels whom your Creator sent after you and the angel in the isles of the sea, to whom you swore that wherever you will find their names you will cause no harm, neither you nor one of your cohorts and servants, and that [you will not damage] anybody who wears their names. Therefore, in their names

and seals set down here, I adjure you and your
cohorts and your servants that you cause no harm
to the woman in childbirth, N. daughter of N.,
nor to the child who was born to her; neither
during the day nor during the night, neither
through their food nor through their drink,
neither in their head nor in their heart, neither
in their 248 limbs, nor in their 365 sinews. By
strength of these names and figures, I adjure you
and your cohorts and your servants." (See Figure 2.)

Figure 2. Amulet to protect woman in childbirth
from Lilith. (From The Book of Raziel, folio 43b.)

As we see, the *Book of Raziel* follows the classical
pattern of incantation rituals which carry in themselves the guarantee of their effectiveness by re-
counting, or at least referring to, a validating myth.
Reference to the old myth about Lilith and the three
angels is all that is needed in order to endow the
apotropaic measure with unfailing potency.

The myth of Lilith the child-killer remained a potent

factor in the lives of the tradition-bound Jews down to the 19th century. To protect the newborn boy-child against Lilith, they would draw a circle with natron or charcoal on the wall of the birth room and write within it: "Adam and Eve. Out Lilith!" At the same time, they would write the names of the three angels Senoy, Sansenoy, and Semangelof on the door of the room: [55]

> If children laugh in their sleep, or if they laugh while they are awake but alone, this is a sign showing that Lilith is playing with them, and especially when this happens on the night of the new moon. Whoever notices that they laugh will do well to tap them on their nose with his finger and say: 'Go hence, Pelonith [i.e., Lilith], you have no portion or inheritance here, you have no satisfaction here!' Then let him recite the entire *'Wihi no'am'* prayer, and do thus three times. . . .[56]

Solomon's dominance over Lilith, which became an integral part of medieval Jewish and Muslim Arab demonology, retained an important role in Middle Eastern Jewish exorcisms as recently as the early 20th century. Raphael Ohana writes in his collection of magical remedies:

> In another manuscript book I found written the following: Protection from Lilith. Draw a Seal of King Solomon, peace be upon him, who adjured Lilith that when she would see his seal she and her cohorts would flee, and that she would have no permission to hurt him. And if it be placed on a house, she would not enter it, neither she nor any one of her band. If it be engraved upon pure silver, it is even better. And this is its shape: [57] (See Figure 3.)

> The same magic Seal of Solomon protects also the sick against Lilith, if it is ascertained that it is she who caused the ailment.[58]

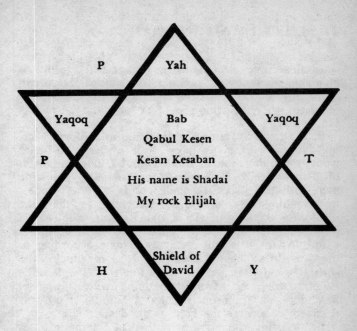

P Yah

Yaqoq   Bab   Yaqoq

                    Qabul Kesen

P   Kesan Kesaban   T

                    His name is Shadai

                    My rock Elijah

                    Shield of
H   David   Y

Figure 3. The magic Seal of Solomon. (From Raphael Ohana, *Mar'eh HaYeladim*, p. 94a.)

The same book contains two further suggestions as to methods one can employ in order to safeguard a woman from Lilith:

> If you place a needle close to the wick in the lamp which is in the house of the woman in childbed, she will be safe from the entry of Lilith. Also, if she take the measure which is used to measure the wheat, and place it close to the bed, and if Lilith is there, she will sit on that measure and will not move from her place until they remove that measure from there. (From a Babylonian manuscript book.) [59]

10. LILITH AND NAAMAH

Lilith's companion in many of her evil exploits is
Naamah, another high-ranking she-demon. Her origin
is obscure, but as her name Naamah ("the Charmer")
indicates, she is a demoness of extraordinary, irresistible beauty.

In the earlier, Talmudic-Midrashic mythology, Naamah is still taken to have been a flesh-and-blood
woman, the daughter of Lamech and Zillah, and sister
of Tubal-Cain,[60] who earned her name by enticing
men with the sweet, sensual sounds of her cymbals
to worship idols, although, according to the lone
dissenting opinion of Abba bar Kahana, she was a
pious and well-mannered woman who became Noah's
wife.[61] Naamah is still a human female according to
those myths which tell about her role in seducing the
sons of God. She was so beautiful that she led the
angels astray, and from her union with the angel
Shamdon, or Shomron, sprang Ashmodai, who was
destined to become the king of the devils.[62]

From being the human mother of Shamdon's demonic brood, Naamah was transformed by the Kabbala
into a semi-human, deathless being who, like Lilith,
fulfills the double task of seducing men and strangling
children in their sleep. She was so beautiful that

the sons of man, and even the spirits and demons,
went astray after her. R. Yitzhaq said: Those
sons of God, 'Aza and 'Aza'el, went astray after
her. R. Shimeon said: She was the mother of the
demons, for she came from the side of Cain, and
she, together with Lilith, was appointed over the
askara [strangulation] of children. R. Abba said
to him: Did you not say that she was appointed
to play with people? He answered: True; she
comes and plays with people, and at times she
bears them spirit-children, and to this day this is
her task. R. Abba said: [Since we know that the

demons] die like humans, how can she still be
alive? He answered: Right, but Lilith and Naamah, and Agrath, the daughter of Mahalath who
came from their side, all continue to live until
the Holy One, blessed be He, eradicates the
spirit of uncleanness from the world. . . .

Come and see: This Naamah was the mother
of demons, and from her side come all those
demons who lie with men and take the spirit
of desire from them, and she makes sport with
the men [in their sleep] and causes them to emit
seed.[63].

Naamah and her brother Tubal-Cain were descendants of Cain, and the latter was, of course, the son
of Satan by Eve:

In the hour when Adam with the supernal
image, with the holy image, descended, and those
of Above and Below saw him, they all approached
him and made him king over the world. After
the Serpent came upon Eve and injected his
impurity into her, she gave birth to Cain. From
there descended all the generations of the sinful
in the world, and also the demons and spirits
came from there. Therefore, all the spirits and
demons are half human, while their other half
comes from the supernal angels. Also, all the
other spirits which were born of Adam are, likewise, half from Below and half from Above.
After they were born of Adam, he begot on those
spirits daughters who resembled the beauty of
those Above and the beauty of those Below. . . .

And there was one male who came into the
world from the spirit of Cain's side and he was
called Tubal-Cain. And a female came with him
after whom the creatures went astray, and she
was called Naamah. From her came other spirits
and demons, who hang in the air and announce
things to those others who are found below. It
was this Tubal-Cain who brought murder weapons

into the world. And as to Naamah . . . she is
alive to this day, and her dwelling is among the
waves of the Great Sea.[64]

In a mythical image, reminiscent of Dante's In-
ferno, the Zohar describes Naamah's beauty, which is
irresistible even to the most horrid nocturnal monsters: In the darkness of the night, great monsters pursue Naamah: they are Afrira and Qastimon, the two
chieftains of the demonic world, who "swim about in
the Great Sea and, when night falls, fly away from
there and come to Naamah, the mother of the demons,
after whom the early divinities went astray. They try
to approach her, but she leaps away six thousand
parasangs, and takes on many forms in the eyes of
men, in order to seduce them." [65]
Once Naamah arrives in our own world,

she makes sport with the sons of man, and conceives from them through their dreams, from the
male desire, and she attaches herself to them. She
takes the desire, and nothing more, and from
that desire she conceives and brings forth all
kinds of demons into the world. And those sons
whom she bears from men visit the women of
humankind, who then conceive from them and
give birth to spirits. And all of them go to the
first Lilith and she brings them up. . . .
At times it happens that Naamah goes forth
in the world in order to have intercourse with the
sons of man, and a man is found in bounds of
desire with her and awakens from his sleep and
gets hold of his wife and lies with her, and his
urge stems from that desire which he had felt
in his dream. In such a case the child which is
procreated comes from the side of Naamah, because in her desire he was conceived. When Lilith
comes and sees this child, she knows what happened, and she attaches herself to him and rears
him like those other children of Naamah, and she

comes to him many times but does not kill him. . . .
For each time when the moon renews itself in
the world, Lilith comes and visits all those whom
she rears, and makes sport with them, and that
man suffers damage at that time.[66]

While Lilith and Naamah thus have become unmistakably evil spirits, at least once more in history
they assumed human form. This happened when, in
order to try Solomon's wisdom, they took the shape
of two prostitutes and went to Solomon asking for his
judgment in their quarrel over the surviving child.

Then came two harlots to King Solomon, and
they were Lilith and Igrath [according to other
sources: Lilith and Naamah]. Lilith, who strangles
the children because she cannot set up for herself, from one of them, a screen to be a hiding
place for her [?]. And the other is Igrath. . . .
One night David was asleep in the camp in the
desert, and in his dream Igrath coupled with
him and bore Adad [identical with Hadad the
Edomite]. And when they asked him, 'What is
your name?' he answered, 'My name is Ad, Ad
is my name' [*Ad sh'mi* in Hebrew], and they called
him Ashm'dai. He is Ashmodai, the King of the
demons who deprived Solomon of his kingdom. . . .[67]

King Solomon, it may be remarked here, "had
dominion over the demons, spirits, and Lilin, and knew
the language of each . . . and when his heart was
merry with wine, he would command the wild animals,
the fowl of heaven, and the creeping things of the
earth, as well as the demons, spirits, and Lilin, to
dance before him." [68]
It was due to Solomon's power over the demons
that he was able to resist the Queen of Sheba, who
was none other than Lilith.[69] Another country over
which Lilith reigned was Zemargad.[70]

11. LILITH AND SAMAEL

As we have seen, according to a Zoharic myth, Lilith and Samael emerged in an androgynous form out of the "dregs of wine" of the divine punitive power.[71] Another version which was also current in Kabbalistic circles in the Middle Ages is silent as to Lilith's provenance, but makes her Samael's wife, and the first among his four wives, to boot. Bahya ben Asher ibn Halawa, the early-14th-century Kabbalistic Bible commentator (died 1340), reports the myth as follows:

> Four women were the mothers of demons: Lilith, Naamah, Igrath, and Mahalath. Each one of them has her own hosts and classes of spirits of uncleanness, and they have no number. And it is said that each of them rules on one of the four *Tequfot* [i.e., the vernal equinox, the summer solstice, the autumnal equinox, and the winter solstice] of the years, when they gather on a lofty peak near the Mountains of Darkness. Each of them rules on her *Tequfa*, from the hour of sunset until midnight, they and all their hosts. But King Solomon ruled over all of them and called them [his] slaves and slave-women and used them according to his will. And these four women are the wives of Esau's heavenly patron [i.e., Samael], and following his example, Esau himself took four wives, as explained in the Pentateuch.[72]

Nathan Spira (died 1662) transmits an interesting variant of the same theme. The four women become the "rulers," in the sense of heavenly patrons, of four kingdoms:

> Know that there are seventy heavenly patrons, one appointed over each nation, and they all are under the rule of Samael and Rahab. Rahab was

given as his share all the borders of Egypt, which
measures 400 by 400 parasangs. Samael was
given four kingdoms, and in each of them he has
a concubine. The names of his concubines are:
Lilith, whom he took as his consort, and she is
the first one; the second is Naamah; the third,
Even Maskith; and the fourth, Igrath, the daughter of Mahalath. And the four kingdoms are:
first, the Kingdom of Damascus, in which is found
the House of Rimmon; second, the Kingdom of
Tyre, which is opposite the Land of Israel; third,
the Kingdom of Malta, which formerly was called
Rhodus; and fourth, the Kingdom called Granata,
and some say that it is the Kingdom of Ishmael.
And in each of these four kingdoms dwells one
of the four aforementioned concubines.[73]

Mixed Egyptian-Arab-demonic descent is attributed
to Igrath in a late version of the myth of the four
she-demons who rule over the *Tequfot* (i.e., the two
equinoxes and the two solstices). When Ishmael grew
up, his mother Hagar brought him an Egyptian wife,

the daughter of Kasdiel, the Egyptian sorcerer.
And when Ishmael divorced her, as commanded
by his father, she was pregnant and gave birth
to Mahalath. And the mother and the daughter
remained together in that desert, which was full
of sorcery, and a demon named Igrathiel ruled
over it. This demon was attracted to Mahalath,
who was very beautiful, and she conceived and
bore a daughter whom she called Igrath, after
that demon. Thereafter Mahalath left the desert
and became the wife of Esau. But her daughter
Igrath remained in the desert, and she, Naamah,
Pelonith [i.e., Lilith], and Nega' rule over the
four *Tequfot*. Pelonith fornicates with all men,
Naamah only with the gentiles, Nega' only with
Israel, and Igrath is sent out to do harm on the
nights preceding Wednesdays and Saturdays. But

of those who fear God it is said, 'And Nega'
will not approach your tents.' [74]

The marriage between Samael and Lilith was arranged by the "Blind Dragon," who in Kabbalistic
mythology is the counterpart on high of "the dragon
that is in the sea." [75] "There is a dragon of Above who
is the Blind Prince, and he functions as the intermediary between Samael and Lilith, and his name is *Tan-
iniver* [Blindragon]. . . . It is he who arranges the
match between Samael and Lilith. . . ." [76]

Blindragon's place in the mystical hierarchy of
demons is described as follows:

> Asimon [a demon] rides on Naamah, and Naa-
> mah rides on Igrath, the daughter of Mahalath,
> and this Igrath rides on several kinds of spirits
> and bands of mid-day demons; and from the left
> there is the shape of a serpent riding on a blind
> dragon, and this dragon rides on Lilith the wicked,
> may she be destroyed quickly in our days, amen.[77]

However, the marriage of Lilith with Samael, also
known as the "Angel Satan" or the "Other God," was
not allowed to prosper. God was apprehensive lest they
fill the world with their demonic brood, and to prevent
this, he castrated Samael. This mythologem, found
in several 17th-century Kabbalistic books,[78] is based
on the identification of "Leviathan the Slant Serpent
and Leviathan the Tortuous Serpent" [79] with Samael
and Lilith, respectively, and on the reinterpretation of
the old Talmudic myth according to which God castrated the male Leviathan and killed the female in
order to prevent them from coupling and thereby
destroying the earth. Leviathan the Tortuous, or
crooked, Serpent is, to the Kabbalists, Lilith, "who
seduces men to follow crooked paths." [80] Once Samael
was castrated, Lilith, since "she could no longer couple
with her husband," took to satisfying her desire by
fornicating with men who experience nocturnal emissions.

In another 15th- or 16th-century Kabbalistic text the Midrashic statement that God "cooled" the female Leviathan is reinterpreted to mean that God made Lilith barren, so that she cannot bear offspring "but is mere fornication." [81]

12. THE TWO LILITHS

The idea that there are many Liliths is, as we have seen, very old. In the Babylonian incantation texts there appear male Lilin, in addition to the female Liliths, who are the heirs to the 3rd millennium B.C. Sumerian male and female demons similarly named. It remained, however, for the 13th-century Kabbalists to split the person of Lilith herself in two and to distinguish between an Elder and a Younger Lilith.

In the writings of R. Isaac Hacohen, a Spanish Kabbalist who flourished about the middle of the 13th century, we read that the Lilith who was born androgynously with Samael and who became the wife of that "Great Prince and Great King of all the demons," is Lilith the Elder. In addition to Samael, other demons as well are the bedfellows of this Lilith the Elder, who—and this is most remarkable—"is a ladder on which one can ascend to the rungs of prophecy." This can mean only one thing: that Lilith can help those whom she favors—or who gain mastery over her—to rise towards, or actually attain, prophetic powers. Another numinous figure introduced into this mythology is Qaftzefoni, the Prince and King of Heaven, whose wife is Mehetabel, the daughter of Matred.[82] The daughter of this mysterious couple is Lilith the Younger. There seems, however, to be some confusion between Lilith the Younger and Lilith the Elder, because it is the latter who is called Tzefoni ("Northerner"), which would make her, and not Lilith the Younger, the daughter of Qaftzefoni:

Know that all the jealousy and altercation

between the Princes of Quarrel and the Princes of Peace . . . is on account of Samael and Lilith who is called Northerner (Tzefonit), as it is written 'Out of the North, the Evil One shall break forth.' [83] Both of them [Samael and Lilith] were born in a spiritual birth as androgynes, corresponding to Adam and Eve—below and above two twin figures. And Samael and Lilith the Elder, who is the same as Tzefonit, are referred to as the Tree of Knowledge of Good and Evil. . . .[84]

The same mid-13th century author, Isaac Hacohen, also asserts that "on rare occasions Qaftzefoni couples with, and adheres to, and loves a creature whose name is Lilidtha," who in a mysterious way resembles Hagar the Egyptian; but whether this Lilidtha is identical with Qaftzefoni's own daughter, Lilith the Younger, cannot be established.

Now, Lilith the Younger became the wife of Ashmodai, King of the demons, and out of this union sprang the great prince Harba diAshm'dai ("Ashmodai's Sword"), who rules over 80,000 demons of destruction and numerous other demon offspring. However, "Lilith the Younger, who has the form of a beautiful woman from head to navel, and from the navel downward is flaming fire—like mother, like daughter—" aroused the desire of Samael. This caused intense jealousy between Samael and Ashmodai, as well as constant fighting between Lilith the Younger and Samael's wife, Lilith the Elder.[85]

Some three centuries after Isaac Hacohen, Moses Cordovero (1522–1570), a leader of the Safed Kabbalists, retells the myth of the two Liliths with the addition of a few interesting details: Lilith the Elder, he says, has 480 bands of demons under her command, the number being derived from the numerical value of the letters L Y L Y T (30,10,30,10,400) making up the name Lilith. On the Day of Atonement, Lilith the Elder marches out into the desert and, being the demon of screeching—her name taken as if derived from the verb Y L L, "to scream"—

spends the day there screaming. Samael, however, also has a concubine named Mahalath, the daughter of Ishmael,[86] who has 478 bands of demons at her disposal—again the letters of her name give the clue to this number (M H L T = 40,8,30,400)—and "she goes and sings a song and a paean in the Holy Tongue. And when the two meet, they fight, on the Day of Atonement, there in the desert, and they taunt each other, until their voices rise to heaven, and the earth trembles under their screams. And all this is brought about by God so that they should not be able to make accusations against Israel [on the Day of Atonement]. . . ."

Lilith the Younger is helped in her fight against Lilith the Elder by her own mother Mehetabel.[87]

The mythological motif of enmity between Lilith and her fellow-demonesses, and the resulting advantage for Israel on the Day of Atonement, is treated by other 16th-century Kabbalists as well. Abraham Galante (died 1560 or 1588), an important Safed Kabbalist and contemporary of Moses Cordovero, recounts the entire story of the annual encounter in the desert between Lilith and Mahalath, but gives a somewhat different characterization to one of the two chief she-demons: Mahalath, according to him, is shown by her name to have been a compulsive dancer: as she marches into the desert at the head of her bands of destructive angels, "she goes and dances and gyrates in ring dances" until she and Lilith fall upon each other and engage in a fierce battle.[88]

Lilith's bands, and presumably Lilith herself as well, were imagined in this period as being covered with hair from head to foot, including their faces, but as having a bald pate. Their fourteen names, derived directly from the older incantation texts,[89] are: Lilin, Abito, Abizo, Amo(z)rpho, Haqash, Odam, (I)Kephido, Ailo, Tatrota, Abniqta, Shatrina, Kalubtza, Tiltoi, Pirtsha.[90]

But, to return to the two Liliths: this idea is put forward in a different form by Hayyim Vital (1543–1620), a Safed Kabbalist and chief disciple of Isaac

Luria. He explains that the original "Lilith the stiff-necked" was the "garb," that is, the shell, the outer and evil part, of Eve, the wife of Adam. But he goes on to say, "there is an even more external [i.e., more evil] Lilith, who is the wife of Samael." In the sequel it is not clear whether Vital speaks of the first or the second Lilith when he says that "there was an angel who was expelled from heaven and he was called 'the flame of the revolving sword,' [91] and at times he is an angel and at times a demon called Lilith. And since the female rules at night, and the demons rule at night, she is called Lilith" [i.e., Nocturnal].

The notion that Lilith rules at night goes back to the Zohar, where the Biblical expression "dread in the nights" (*pahad ba-leloth*) [93] is explained as "Samael and his female," i.e., Lilith.[94] What is more interesting in Vital's thinking is that he regarded Lilith and the angel as interchangeable, as appearing once in the shape of one and once as the other, made tangible by the flame of the revolving sword. We shall recall that in the 6th-century A.D. Nippur incantation texts the same numen is called once "Lilith Buznai" and once "angel Buznai," [95] which is yet another example of the great antiquity of some of the ideas put forward by the medieval Kabbalists. The same idea underlies a passage contained in the Zoharic literature itself which reads: "Come and see: The Shekhina is at times called the Mother, at times the Slave-Woman [i.e., Lilith], and at times the King's Daughter." [96]

In other words, circumstances determine whether one and the same feminine divine essence assumes the form of a good or an evil numen. And, since circumstances constantly change, the goddess appears once as good and once as evil. In a different formulation of the idea, Lilith appears as the "nakedness" of the Shekhina, that aspect of her which preponderates in the period of Israel's exile: "When Israel was exiled, the Shekhina too went into exile, and this is the nakedness of the Shekhina. And this nakedness is Lilith, the mother of a mixed multitude." [97]

13. LILITH'S TRIUMPH AND END

The hour of Lilith's greatest triumph and the high point in her career came with the destruction of the Jerusalem Temple. When that catastrophe took place,

> the King [i.e., God] sent away the Matronit and took the slave-woman [i.e., Lilith] in her place. . . . Who is this slave-woman? She is the Alien Crown whose first-born God slew in Egypt. . . . She used to sit behind the hand-mill, and now this handmaid is heir to her mistress.[98] Rabbi Shimeon cried and said: 'The King without the Matronit is not called King; the King who attached himself to the slave-woman, to the handmaid of the Matronit, where is his honor? . . . He lost the Matronit and attached himself to the Other Place, which is called slave-woman. . . . And this slave-woman was destined to rule over the Holy Land of Below, as the Matronit formerly ruled over it. . . .'[99]

The Zoharic idea that the most terrible outcome of the destruction of the Temple and the exile of Israel was that because of them God was forced to accept Lilith as his consort in place of the Matronit, was further elaborated by R. Shlomo Alqabetz (ca. 1505–1584), the Safed Kabbalist and famous author of the Sabbath-song *Lekha Dodi* ("Come, My Friend"). In his mystical philosophy, Alqabetz attributes it to the sins of Israel that the Shekhina, Israel's mother, had to leave her husband, God, who is Israel's father, and go into exile together with her children. As a result of this separation, God the father consorted with "the slave-woman" (i.e., Lilith), and she became the mistress of His house. The situation was similar to that of a man who had a good wife, the mother of his sons, and then, in his wrath, he turned away from her and went in to her handmaid, who conceived and bore him a son.

"And it is known that there is no glory for a man except with his wife who was destined for him, but not by adhering to handmaids . . . through which he himself is reduced to a lower rung." Likewise, after the Shekhina in exile

> descended to be with us . . . her rival [Lilith] angers her greatly, and she sobs and sighs because her husband [God] does not throw his light upon her. . . . Her joy has fled because she sees her rival in her house, deriding her, to the extent that the mistress became a handmaid, and the handmaid mistress. And when our Father sees our Mother lying in dust and suffering because of our sins, He too becomes embittered in his heart and He descends to save her and make the strangers cease violating her. And now, can there be anybody who sees these things without rending his heart to repent and thus to bring back our Mother to her place and to her palace? . . .[100]

While thus the Zohar and the later Kabbalists who were influenced by it attribute God's degradation through coupling with Lilith to the cosmic consequences of the destruction of the Temple, the preZoharic gnostic Kabbalists, such as Moses of Burgos, placed the same divine Fall in the very days of Creation. For, they maintained, just as on earth below Lilith and Samael procreated demons and spirits with Adam and Eve, so in the Upper Realm "a spirit of seduction issued forth from Lilith and seduced God the King, while Samael managed to have his will on the Shekhina." [101]

Whatever the beginnings of this connubium between God and Lilith, it is to continue until the coming of the Messiah will put an end to it.

A voice is appointed to announce to the Ma-

tronit and say 'Rejoice greatly, O daughter of
Zion, shout, O daughter of Jerusalem, behold,
thy King cometh unto thee, he is righteous and
victorious, lowly and riding upon an ass.'[102]
. . . For he would be riding, until that time, in a
place which is not his, in an alien place . . . and
would remain lowly . . . for until that time the
Righteous One would remain without righteousness. But at that time [he and the Matronit will
again] couple with each other, and he will become
'righteous and victorious' because he will no
longer dwell in the Other Side [i.e., will no longer
be tied to Lilith]. . . . And God will restore the
Matronit to her place as in the beginning. And
what will the rejoicing be? Say, the rejoicing of
the King and of the Matronit. The rejoicing of
the King over returning to her and separating
from the slave-woman, and the rejoicing of the
Matronit over coupling again with the King.[103]

Those Messianic days will mark not only the re-
union of God and the Matronit and the rejection of
Lilith, but also the end of Lilith's existence. For, although Lilith has existed ever since the sixth or even
the fifth day of Creation, she is not immortal. In the
Days to Come, when Israel will take revenge on Edom,
both she and the Blind Dragon, who arranged the
match between her and Samael, will be killed.[104]

14. CONCLUSION

It is rather difficult to evaluate the position of
Lilith in Jewish religion, and her significance for the
Jewish believer. The very fact that as late as the 18th,
or even the 19th, century the belief in her not only
survived but remained a potent factor in religious
consciousness and conduct is in itself surprising. That
these beliefs and, in all probability, the practices as
well retained essentially the same form in which they

first appeared 4,000 years previously in Sumer is remarkable. A citizen of Sumer ca. 2500 B.C. and an East European Hassidic Jew in 1800 A.D. had very little in common as far as the higher levels of religion were concerned. But they would have readily recognized each other's beliefs about the pernicious machinations of Lilith, and each other's apotropaic measures for driving her away or escaping her enticements.

It is interesting, moreover, to note that both in ancient Sumer and in Kabbalistic Judaism Lilith's career ran very similar courses. She started out in both faiths as a lowly she-demon, whose activities were confined to the nether realms of existence, who was associated with impure nocturnal animals, and who pulled man down to her own base level. Then, in both religions, she succeeded in working herself up, as it were, to higher rungs on the scale of numina, until she became an undoubted goddess in Sumer and the consort of God in Kabbalism. Yet with all these advances in her career, the basic qualities of her personality never changed: she remained the beautiful seductress who joined lonely men in their nocturnal unrest, enjoyed sex with them, and bore them demonic offspring, while she also found enough time to play her lethal games with children, causing them to laugh happily in their sleep and then strangling them mercilessly so as to get hold of, and array herself in, their innocent souls. There can be little doubt that a she-demon who accompanied mankind—or at least a part of mankind—from earliest antiquity to the threshold of the Age of Enlightenment must be a projection, or objectification, of human fears and desires which, in a deeper sense, are identical with those of oft-mentioned "plagues of mankind" said in Kabbalistic literature to be the offspring of Lilith, but recognized by us as her psychogenic progenitors.

The meaning of Lilith becomes more easily comprehensible if one considers the basic similarity between her and the Matronit, the goddess of the Kabbala, whose image was described and analyzed in the previous chapter. Lilith, of course, is the embodiment of everything that is evil and dangerous in the sexual realm, while the Matronit is her exact opposite: a good, even saintly figure. Yet, at the same time, Lilith is also irresistibly attractive, while the Matronit is sternly forbidding and even warlike. A closer look easily discerns the mask-nature of these contrasting characterizations: behind the evil mask of Lilith and the good one of the Matronit, the numen, embodying man's fears and desires, is disconcertingly, yet reassuringly, the same. Her mythical biography, whether it treats her as Lilith or as the Matronit, remains fundamentally unchanged:

Both the Matronit (who is identical with the Shekhina) and Lilith originated, according to the Kabbalistic doctrine, from an emanation of the deity. We also recall the virginity of the Matronit. Lilith, too, is a virgin, or at least assumes at will the bodily form of a virgin when she joins the couch of a sleeping man who embraces her in his unconscious desire. Both the Matronit and Lilith are, on the other hand, promiscuous: no sooner is a man separated, even temporarily, from his wife than the Matronit joins him, couples with him, and thus restores him to that state of completeness which is the privilege and high blessing of the male and female together. Lilith does the same, with the difference, of course, that in contrast to the holy union of man and the Matronit, the union which Lilith enters into with man is an unholy defilement.

Both the Matronit and Lilith are queens: the Matronit, the heavenly queen of Israel; Lilith, the queen of Sheba and Zemargad.

The motherly aspect of both the Matronit and Lilith is expressed in their giving birth all the time to innumerable souls: although again, the souls brought forth by the Matronit are pure and enter the bodies of children conceived by husbands and wives in purity, while those issuing from Lilith are impure and become demons, "the plagues of mankind."

The Matronit, as we have seen, is a goddess of war also; she kills not only the enemies of God and Israel, but also takes the souls of pious men, substituting in

their extreme hour for the Angel of Death. Lilith, likewise, is a killer of men and of children, and the pleasurable laughter of her victims makes us more than
suspect that they enjoy death at her hands as much as
they would expiring through a kiss of the Matronit.

The Matronit was the wife of Jacob and Moses;
Lilith was the wife of Adam and Cain. The Matronit
was also the wife of God—her wedding with him having been signified by the dedication of the Temple of
Jerusalem. Lilith, too, became the wife of God, at the
hour that same Temple was destroyed. Both of them
were also enjoyed carnally by Samael the Satan—
the Matronit each time Israel sinned, and Lilith when
the Blind Dragon arranged a union between them.

Finally, the images of both the Matronit and Lilith
were split in two: a distinction was made between the
Upper Matronit and the Lower Matronit, and likewise
between the Elder Lilith and the Younger Lilith.

We thus recognize the identity of opposites in Lilith
and the Matronit or, as one may better put it, the
ambivalence of religio-sexual experience. The same
impulse or experience can, in the case of one man, be
good, and in the case of the other, evil. In the case of
one, an act can promote the blessed union between
God and his Matronit; in the case of the other, the
same act, or what seemingly is the same act, can result
in a strengthening of the powers of evil, of the Other
Side. Thus it is not only God's will that is inscrutable;
man's feet lead him also along unpredictable paths,
and he rarely if ever knows whether a step he takes
leads him toward God or away from Him.

The interplay between man and the two bafflingly
similar antithetical goddesses is indicative of the great
unity that exists between the realms of the divine and
the human in the mystical Jewish world-view. The All is
viewed as an inverted triangle poised precariously on
its apex, man. Over him, at the two corners of the
triangle's base, hover—at a distance that defies the eye,
yet so near as to almost merge with him—God and
the Goddess. God is one, but the Goddess, who is part
of him, is two: the Matronit and Lilith. She appears

like the revolving flame of the Cherubim's sword in the ancient myth: once she shows her Matronit face, once her Lilith visage. The flame revolves so fast that it is impossible to hold in one's eye a separate picture of either. Although God and the Goddess are one, innumerable strands of attraction and repulsion run back and forth between them, and likewise between man and the deity. Far from "keeping his silence and sustaining the world," this deity is moved by man as much as he moves man, he rejoices with man and suffers with man, and the two aspects of his female component constantly struggle for man and within man.

Chapter VIII

THE SABBATH—VIRGIN, BRIDE, QUEEN, AND GODDESS

The Sabbath, to which we now turn our attention, is an exceptional figure among the female divinities of Judaism. All the numinous images discussed so far were originally either foreign goddesses and demons (Asherah, Astarte, Anath, Lilith, Naamah) or had their beginnings in Jewish divine attributes which were conceptualized and personified (Shekhina, Matronit). As against them, the Sabbath is a unique example of a day of the week—or more precisely, the name and idea of such a day—having been developed into a female numen and endowed with the character of virgin, bride, queen, and goddess.

1. SABBATH AND SEX

The Biblical name Sabbath *(Shabbat),* designating the seventh day of the week, seems to have had some connection with the Akkadian *shabattu* or *shapattu,* the name for the feast of the full moon. Yet neither in Akkadian nor in any other ancient Near Eastern religion was there a weekly feast and day of rest in any manner comparable to the Sabbath.

From a passage in Deutero-Isaiah we learn in what way one was supposed to observe the Sabbath in the early post-exilic period:

If, because of the Sabbath, you turn away your foot
From pursuing business on My holy day,
If you call the Sabbath a delight
And God's holy and honored day,
If you honor it by not following your way
And by not seeking your business
Nor speaking thereof—
Then you will find delight in Yahweh,
And I shall make you ride high
Upon the hills of the earth
And I shall feed you with the heritage
Of your father Jacob—
For the mouth of Yahweh has spoken.[1]

The character and laws of the Biblical Sabbath are
validated by the myth of Creation: God created the
world in six days, and on the seventh, the Sabbath,
He rested; He blessed and sanctified it, and consequently it is the duty of every Israelite to do likewise
and to refrain from all work on that holy day.[2] With
the passage of time, the restrictive Sabbath laws became more and more stringent. By the 1st century
A.D., in some Jewish communities sexual intercourse
was included among the acts prohibited on the Sabbath, under the penalty of death.[3] While this prohibition was unable to take root in Judaism (in which, on
the contrary, the idea was soon to develop that intercourse with one's wife on Friday night was a sacred
duty), it became an important law in several marginal
Jewish sects such as the Samaritans, the Karaites, and
the Falashas.[4]

In Talmudic Judaism the performance of the marital
act on Friday night was considered a very old religious
law. According to a Talmudic tradition, one of the ten
ordinances introduced by Ezra was that one should eat
garlic on the eve of the Sabbath, because garlic makes
one happy, multiplies the semen, arouses love, and
kills jealousy.[5] Some sages attributed such importance
to the performance of the act on Friday night that
nothing was supposed to keep them from it. A legendary reflection of this is found in a Talmudic story

which tells of Yehuda ben Hiyya that he used to spend all his time in the house of study and return home only on the eve of the Sabbath. Whenever he thus went home, a pillar of fire could be seen preceding him. One Friday, however, he became so engrossed in his studies that he forgot about the time and remained poring over his books. When his father-in-law, Rabbi Yannai, waited in vain for the appearance of the pillar of fire, he said: "Turn over his bed, for Yehuda must be dead. Would he be alive, he would never have neglected his marital duty." These words had the effect of a command issuing by mistake from the mouth of a ruler, which is carried out before he can rescind it, and at that instant Yehuda died.[6]

Thus, as far as sexual intercourse on the Sabbath is concerned, the view that developed in the mainstream of traditional Judaism was diametrically opposed to that held, or to be held later, in several semi-Jewish sects. As we shall see in the course of this chapter, Kabbalism, building on the traditional Jewish view, developed its own approach, which endowed the performance of marital intercourse on the Sabbath with a special cosmic significance and turned the Sabbath itself into a veritable divine queen, the bride of God Himself.

2. THE SABBATH OF PHILO

Philo's comments on the Sabbath begin with a discussion of the significance of the number seven. He refers to the old Pythagorean comparison of the numbers with gods and, in particular, to the likening of seven to the virgin goddess Athena,[7] and utilizes it in his allegorical explanation of the sacredness of the Sabbath, the seventh day. The number seven, Philo points out, is the only one in the "decade" (i.e., the first ten digits) which is neither produced by multiplication with any other number nor produces one within the decade if multiplied by another. And, he goes on to say, "by reason of this, the Pythagoreans, indulging in myth, liken seven to the motherless and ever-virgin Maiden [i.e., Athena], because neither was she born of the womb nor shall she ever bear." [8]

Elsewhere Philo says that since

it is the nature of seven alone . . . neither to beget nor to be begotten . . . other philosophers liken this number to the motherless virgin Nike, who is said to have appeared out of the head of Zeus, while the Pythagoreans liken it to the Sovereign of the Universe: for that which neither begets nor is begotten remains motionless . . . [and] there is only one thing that neither causes motion nor experiences it, the original Ruler and Sovereign. Of Him, seven may be fitly said to be a symbol. . . . [9]

This rich symbolism of the number seven is transferred by Philo in its entirety to the seventh day of the week, the Sabbath. We are left in doubt as to whether this application was the idea of Philo himself or whether it originated with others. One of the two passages in which Philo discusses the symbolism of the Sabbath is explicitly stated to be a mere recording of what others have invented; the other is phrased so as to indicate that it contains original thoughts of his own on the subject. In the first he says:

Some have given to it [the seventh day, the Sabbath] the name of the virgin, having before their eyes its surpassing chastity. They also call her the motherless, begotten by the father of the universe alone [who is] the ideal form of the male sex with nothing of the female. It [seven] is the manliest and doughtiest of numbers, well gifted by nature for sovereignty and leadership. Some give it the name of 'season' (or: 'decisive time'), judging its conceptual nature from its manifestation in the realm of sense. . . . For seven reveals as completed what six has produced, and there-

fore it may be quite rightly entitled the birthday
of the world. . . .[10]

Sabbath as the motherless, chaste virgin does not,
of course, jibe well with the excellences of the day
marked by seven, "the manliest and doughtiest of
numbers"; but as to the sovereignty and leadership
which Philo also attributes to the Sabbath, these—as
we know from his speculations about the two Cherubim—he regarded as traits of the *female* component
of the deity. In the passage in which Philo presents
these ideas as his own, he indulges in an even less restrained sexual symbolism:

> The prophet [Moses] magnified the holy seventh
> day, seeing with his keener vision its marvelous
> beauty stamped upon heaven and the whole world,
> and enshrined in nature itself. For he found that
> she [the Sabbath] was in the first place mother-
> less, exempt from female parentage, begotten by
> the Father [God] alone, without begetting, brought
> to the birth, yet not carried in the womb. Sec-
> ondly, he [Moses] saw not only these, that she
> was all lovely and motherless, but that she was
> also ever virgin, neither born of a mother nor a
> mother herself, neither bred from corruption nor
> doomed to suffer corruption. Thirdly, as he
> scanned her, he recognized in her the birthday
> of the world, a feast celebrated by heaven, cele-
> brated by earth and things on earth as they re-
> joice and exult in the full harmony of the sacred
> number.[11]

Here we have a fully developed mythological picture of the Sabbath, whether arrived at by Philo himself or built upon traditions known to him from other
sources. The Sabbath is described as a daughter of
God, begotten by her Father alone without the participation of any female, and therefore motherless. She is
marvelous in her beauty, ever virginal, incorruptible,
but, at one and the same time, endowed with sover-

eignty and leadership. In these features, we shall recognize without difficulty some of the traits which also characterized other female numina of the Talmudic and Kabbalistic periods.

3. THE TALMUDIC ANTECEDENTS

In the Bible, the prohibition of working on the Sabbath is stated in general terms only. In the Mishna and the Talmud, all the activities which count as work, and therefore are prohibited on the Sabbath, are enumerated and discussed in considerable detail.[12] There can thus be no doubt that in the Talmudic period the Sabbath was of primary importance as the weekly day of rest, hallowed by God and observed by men with meticulous scrupulousness, as one of the pivotal religious duties of Judaism.

Yet, in addition to all the legalistic detail, there is one single passage in Talmudic literature which indicates that the personification of the Sabbath as a bride and a queen dates back to Talmudic times (the two sages mentioned in the passage in question lived in the 2nd and 3rd centuries A.D.):

> Rabbi Hanina used to wrap himself [in festive clothes] towards evening on Friday and say: 'Come, let us go to receive Sabbath the Queen.' Rabbi Yannai used to put on [festive] clothes on the eve of the Sabbath and say: 'Come, O bride, come, O bride!'[13]

Other Talmudic passages, while not addressing the Sabbath as a bride or a queen, clearly show that the sages of the Talmudic period related with extraordinary love and affection to the Sabbath day. Sayings such as "He who takes three meals on the Sabbath will be saved from three evils: the pangs of the Messiah, the judgment of Gehenna, and the war of Gog and Magog," or "He who celebrates the Sabbath with enjoyments will be given an inheritance without bounds" [14] express the spirit in which the Sabbath was regarded. Anecdotes about a pious man called "Joseph the Sabbath-lover" are adduced to illustrate the rewards one can expect to reap if one loves and honors the Sabbath.[15] The Sabbath is like the spice which endows the Sabbath meals with a delicious scent.[16] The importance of honoring the Sabbath with a festive table is repeatedly emphasized, and one sage, Rabbi Yose ben Yehuda, a Palestinian teacher of the 2nd century A.D., had this to say about it:

> Two ministering angels accompany a man on Sabbath eve from the synagogue to his house. One is a good angel, the other an evil one. As the man arrives in his house, if he finds the candle burning, the table set, and his bed made, the good angel says: 'Be it the will [of God] that it be like this on the next Sabbath!' And the evil angel answers 'Amen' against his will. If not, the evil angel says: 'Be it the will that it be like this on the next Sabbath!' and the good angel answers 'Amen' against his will.[17]

In a midrashic passage the Sabbath not only is personified but is contraposited to God:

> Rabbi Shimeon ben Yohai said: The Sabbath said before God: 'Master of the Worlds! Each day has its mate, but I have none! Why?' The Holy One, blessed be He, answered her: 'The Community of Israel is your mate.' And when Israel stood before Mount Sinai, the Holy One, blessed be He, said to them: 'Remember what I told the Sabbath: "The Community of Israel is your mate." Therefore, remember the Sabbath day to keep it holy.' [18]

The six weekdays, this Midrash in effect says, constitute three pairs, and the odd Sabbath day received

Israel as her mate. Israel was thus promised to the Sabbath in the days of Creation.

The common feature between the Talmud's and Philo's view of the Sabbath is that both personify her as a woman: Philo makes her the virgin daughter of God, who is also the sovereign and ruler of the world; the Talmud presents her as the bride of Israel and a queen.[19]

4. THE FALASHA SABBATH

The Falashas, the black Jews of Ethiopia, who preserved several sacred books in the Geez language from a period as early as the 4th century A.D., went one important step further than the Talmud in their view of the Sabbath: they not only personified, but they deified her. This development, as has been pointed out, "is analogous to what Hellenistic Jewish and subsequent Gnostic speculation has done with such a concept as wisdom." [20] However, the Falasha deification of the Sabbath has been carried to an extreme never duplicated in either Hellenistic Jewish or Gnostic portrayals of the figure of Hokhma-Sophia. The only true analogy to it can be found in the Kabbalistic Matronit and Sabbath figures of the 13th and 16th centuries, respectively.

The Falashas, whose presence in Ethiopia is first attested historically in the 12th century A.D., preserved a primitive Judaism which relies entirely on the Old Testament and the apocryphal Book of Jubilees, includes the practice of animal sacrifices, and knows nothing of the Mishna and the Talmud.[21] One must therefore assume that they were cut off from contact with the Palestinian-Babylonian-Egyptian mainstream of Jewish life prior to the destruction of the Second Temple in 70 A.D.

The Falasha book *Teezaza Sanbat,* or "Commandments of the Sabbath," is definitely a Jewish book written in Geez, the classical Ethiopian language, and dating in its present form from the 14th century, although it contains material which may go back to the 5th–7th centuries.[22] The framework of the book is the story of Creation, but its bulk deals with the greatness and the glory of the Sabbath of Israel, her adventures, acts, punitive expeditions, and intercessions with God. She is described as the daughter of God, a divine princess, to whom all the angels pay homage and who is exceedingly loved by God Himself. God, we read, "sanctified the Sabbath, glorified her, and blessed her through the Holy Spirit. . . . The Sabbath will rise from her seat on Friday at dawn. . . . the archangels will crown the Sabbath of God, and the priests of Heaven will leap for joy. . . ." Ninety thousand angels will crown the Sabbath of God and bring her down from on high. Because of her, all will rejoice like calves, and all the angels of Heaven will be glad because of the greatness, the splendor, and the glory of the Sabbath of God. The Sabbath will look upon the souls of the just in the garden, and they will rejoice on Friday.

> The souls of the sinners will love her [the Sabbath] in order that she may bring them out of Sheol [hell]. . . .
>
> God said to the archangel Michael: 'Go down to Sheol for the sake of the Sabbath rest.' When the Sabbath rises from the right hand of God, Friday at dawn, the angels rise immediately with the Sabbath and crown her. While they praise, glorify, and honor her, they fear and tremble greatly. . . .
>
> The Sabbath of Israel said to God, the Lord of Heaven and Earth: 'I brought Thee those who believe in me and Thee, show mercy to them for my sake.' God answered the Sabbath: 'I pity them for thy sake,' and He sent them away without shame or humiliation. . . .
>
> Sabbath means: I am God. 'It is not the day but I [who says it],' says God. . . .
>
> Sabbath said to God: 'Hearken to me, O Lord,

[and let me say] but one word. I was with Thee when Thou didst create the Heaven and didst establish the earth upon the rocks with Thy wisdom. . . . O Lord, give me Thy consent and send me not to the unjust, the slanderers, the quarrelsome, and the treacherous. Drive me not away towards those who strike me with their spittle, who sit in the sun, who wash not with water, who cover not their . . . who throw away their spittle, quench not their fire, and accept not my commandments. As to their women, they knead their dough, they cook, draw water, crush in the mortar, shout, neglect my commandments, and rebuke their neighbors. . . .'

On the day when God reprimands the children of Adam, the Sabbath will stand at the entrance of Hell in the valley of fire and will say: 'By God! May the just be not separated from the sinners before I separate them for my sake. I shall inform Thee of those who rest not and observe not my laws.' God said to her: 'Numerous are those who committed sins before me.' The Sabbath said to God: 'Remember not the sins of Thy servants after they observed Thy Sabbath. Thou hast given me for a witness to the people, and Thou hast said through the mouth of Thy servant Moses: "My Sabbath you shall keep, for it is a sign between you and me throughout your generations." [23] And Thou hast said: "You shall keep my Sabbath for it is holy and a rest unto you, and later it will be a witness. Their other faults will not be reprimanded. Verily, I shall forget their sins because of thee, my witness." Thou shalt not count them among the infidels because of their faults, and Thou shalt not couple them with the unjust. I conjure Thee by Thy glory. Thou hast granted it to me, and Thou wilt not deny it because of Thy justice. I, Thy Sabbath, rose on that day to deliver my menservants and maidservants from among the oppressors and the wicked, for I am merciful. How can he be clean that is born of woman? Not even the sun and the moon are clean before Thee.[24] O Lord, permit me to deliver my servants forever, without limit. Amen.'

God said to the Sabbath: 'I shall not confound thee and shall not refuse what thou hast asked of me. I grant thee everything that is thine. I say it truly in the name of my justice and of my Sabbath. And now, may they have respite from Hell on that day, since the Sabbath is the witness for those who observe it.' Sabbath said to God: 'Grant it to me.' [25]

After brief references to the glory of God, the creation of Adam, the Fall, and the covenant of Noah, the narrative dwells at some length upon the well-known myth of Abraham and Nimrod,[26] then returns to the sin of Adam, recounts the story of the Golden Calf, and finally takes up again the story of the Sabbath:

When the Sabbath rose from her seat on Friday morning, 640,000 angels followed her, and she worshiped the Creator. About 4,300 angels praised the Sabbath; 680,000 were to her right, 880,000 to her left. God conversed with the Sabbath. He gave the Sabbath [to Israel] to eat the fruits of the earth,[27] to drink, to rest, to worship, to pray, and to show mercy. God said: 'They to whom I gave thee shall descend with thee. They who praise not, are not submissive, invoke not God on my Sabbath, and transgress my laws and commandments shall be coupled with the wicked.'

And God said: 'They who honor thee are as if they honored me, who dismiss thee are as if they dismissed me, who serve thee are as if they served me, who receive thee as if they received me, who make of the Sabbath a day of delight are considered as if they had made a loan to me. . . .'

The Sabbath said to God: 'From Thee come the commandments and the law. . . .' God said: 'May [the angels] descend with thee.' The Sabbath said to God: 'Hearken to me, only one word.' God said to his Sabbath: 'Yes, I listen to thee. He who celebrates thee and honors thee more than the other days will not have his sins remembered.[28] He who gives alms on the Sabbath, who receives thee after being washed in water, I permit thee to take him from me. To him who gives alms on the Sabbath of God, I shall give the forty-nine gifts I gave to thee.'

The Sabbath left the camp of God. God said to the angels, his servants: 'Go, descend with her.' He sent them, and the angels followed, numbering 240,000. They brought her to earth. They reported the deeds of men to God. . . .

God saw [all this] and said: 'The [Sabbath] shall never be worn out, the fruit of the Sabbath shall not perish. Praise me all people.'. . .

The Sabbath descended from Heaven to the earth on Friday at the ninth hour [and remained] until Sunday at the rising of the sun so that the earth might see the deeds of the Sabbath. . . .

The Sabbath said to Michael, Gabriel, Ruma'el, and Uriel: 'Bring to me all those who are mine, who believe in me, who neglect me not, who observe me and accept me.' Michael ran with his hosts, descended and seized all those who belonged to the Sabbath, as the Sabbath had told him. The hosts of Michael fought with the hosts of Berna'el, and with their nails they took these hypocrites, the host of Hell, by the throat. They drove them to the bottom of Sheol and slapped them on the cheeks. They overpowered the hosts of Berna'el and subjugated them according to their deeds. Michael then ascended to the Sabbath and said to her: 'The riders of Hell assailed me and took me by force.'

Thereupon the Sabbath said to God: 'O Lord, my Creator, give me power over those who love me, and over those who are mine, and withhold not my servants from me!' God said to the Sabbath: 'I shall give thee all those who are mine,

as thou has asked me . . . for those who fear God,
the Sabbath will stand before Him [and defend]
the children of Adam on the last day. And she
will say to God: 'On that day I shall be witness
for those who fear me and know me. And as for
those who disregard me and know not God, the
hosts of Berna'el will seize them and will throw
the sinners into Hell.'

The story now returns to the days of creation which
came to a conclusion with the Sabbath, and the choice
of Israel, whose special task was to keep the Sabbath.

God said to his Sabbath: 'Go, descend to the
earth.' And the Sabbath descended from the highest heaven to the earth in the midst of Jerusalem.
Abel, Enoch, and Melchizedek, the great priest,
received her. And all the angels of God crowned
her, and then they dispersed in the midst of
heaven after having departed from her throne. . . .
When God questions the inhabitants of the
earth upon the day of His arrival [the day of the
Last Judgment], the Sabbath will stand before
Him on behalf of those who fear Him. . . .
Sabbath said to God: 'Thy name is great forever. Thy name is gracious.' God said to the Sabbath: 'I am gracious for those who belong to thee.'
The Sabbath will rise on the day on which God
questions those who fear Him and those who fear
Him not. Then the Sabbath will intercede for
those who belong to her and will say to her Creator: 'These are my people; these are my inheritance; these are they who walk in my path, who
love me, who believe in me, who neglect Thee
not, who find delight in Thee. Now they will enjoy eternal rest. Amen. . . .' [29]

The personification of the Sabbath is a strong element also in another Falasha writing, the so-called
Abba Elijah. In it we read that God gave the Sabbath
the following names: Luminous, Glorified, Honored,

Beautiful, Resuscitating, Rejoicing, Beloved, and
Guardian; and that the name Sabbath itself means "I
am God alone." [30]

So far the old Falasha myth of the Sabbath.

In Ethiopian Jewish and Christian folk belief there
is a certain parallelism between Mary and the Sabbath.
In an Ethiopian folksong the Sabbath and Mary are
considered mothers of a certain hero, while Michael
and Gabriel are his fathers.[31] And a Falasha made the
following statement: "The mediatrix of the Christians
is Mary; ours is the Sabbath." [32]

To recapitulate the main features of the Falasha
Sabbath: she is one of the earliest creations of God but,
in a mystical sense, is also identical with God, which
does not, however, prevent her from engaging in dis-
cussions with God. She is also a queen, crowned by
the angels and seated on her throne. Those who observe the Sabbath rest and love her are her people,
whom she claims from God and whom she rescues
from the Last Judgment even if they sinned. To love
and honor the Sabbath is the same as loving and
honoring God. She orders the archangels to engage in
a battle with the hosts of Satan ("Berna'el") in order
to save the pious from his clutches. She is so terrifying
in her glory that even the angels tremble when they
look at her. In brief, she is a veritable goddess.

5. THE KABBALISTIC SABBATH

As might be expected, the laconic Talmudic allusions to the Sabbath as bride and queen were seized
upon by the Kabbalists and developed into a Sabbath mythologem, upon which then was built one of
their most important mystical rituals. Although the
peak of Sabbath adoration was reached only in the
16th century in the Safed center of the Palestinian
Kabbalists, the trend towards it was heralded as early
as the 12th century in both poetic and doctrinal exposition.

Abraham ibn Ezra (1092–1167), the famous Hebrew scholar and poet who lived in Spain, Italy, and France, describes in a treatise entitled "Epistle of the Sabbath" that on the night of the 14th of Tebeth, 4919 (December 7, 1158), while sojourning in England, he had a dream in which a man handed him a myrrh-scented letter, saying, "Take this letter which the Sabbath sent you." The poet opens the letter and finds in it a poem in which the Sabbath describes herself as "the crown of the religion of the precious ones" and goes on to enumerate her excellences, such as:

> I am the delight of males and females,
> In me rejoice the old and the young.[33]

A century later, a certain Menahem ben Jacob composed a poem in which he addressed the Sabbath as queen and bride. This poem was still reprinted in 19th-century editions of the complete prayer book.[34] The lines

> How sweet is your rest, O you Queen Sabbath,
> Let us hasten toward you, come, O anointed bride,

are closely reminiscent of the famous 16th-century Sabbath song *Lekha Dodi,* which was to supplant all the earlier poetic praises of the Sabbath and of which more will be said below.

Also in the 13th century, some Jewish mystics introduced a heterosexual notion into the Sabbath concept, justified by the two verbs which open the Fourth Commandment in the parallel versions of Exodus and Deuteronomy, respectively: "Remember the Sabbath day to keep it holy"; [35] and "Observe the Sabbath day to keep it holy." [36] The Book of Bahir, the mystical Bible commentator Nahmanides (Moses ben Nahman, 1194–1270), and the Zohar all reiterate the idea that the words "Remember" and "Observe" refer to two Supernal Sabbaths, one masculine, the other feminine. As the Zohar puts it: " 'The children of Israel shall keep the Sabbath' [37]—this refers to the night, the mystery of the female; and 'Remember the Sabbath day' [38] refers to the day, the mystery of the male." [39]

The feminine Sabbath is, moreover, mystically identified with the Shekhina, or the Sephira of Kingship, while the male Sabbath is the *Yesod* ("Foundation") or *Tif'eret* ("Beauty"), i.e., the male aspect of the deity. Since the Shekhina is also identified with the Community of Israel, in this manner the Shekhina becomes the bride, or mate, of the Sabbath *Yesod*. [40]

If we recall that Philo already had discerned a "manly and doughty" aspect in the Sabbath, in addition to her feminine aspects of virginity, beauty, and sovereignty, we find that the Kabbalistic distinction between a male and a female Sabbath is, again, an idea which has its roots in antiquity.

Elsewhere the Zohar describes the preparations one is supposed to make for reception of the Sabbath, the queen and bride, in proper fashion, in order thereby to induce her to come and, at the same time, banish her dark rival Lilith:

One must prepare a comfortable seat with several cushions and embroidered covers, from all that is found in the house, like one who prepares a *huppa* [canopy] for a bride. For the Sabbath is a queen and a bride. This is why the masters of the Mishna used to go out on the eve of Sabbath to receive her on the road, and used to say: 'Come, O bride, come, O bride!' And one must sing and rejoice at the table in her honor. And more than this: there is yet another mystery. One must receive the Lady [i.e., the Sabbath] with many lighted candles, many enjoyments, beautiful clothes, and a house embellished with many fine appointments, for through this rejoicing and these arrangements one causes the Evil Handmaid [i.e., Lilith] to remain in the dark, hungry, crying and wailing, wrapped in mourning clothes like a widow. For when the one is fulfilled, the other is destroyed. The Good Inclination is the

Holy Matronit, the Holy Kingdom which descends on the Sabbath . . . and the King proceeds to receive her with many hosts. And the Evil Inclination, the Evil Handmaid, remains in the darkness like a widow without her husband, without a chariot. Those about whom it is said that they offered sacrifices and burnt incense to the Queen of Heaven and the stars, which I [God] have not commanded them to do, they worship the Evil Maid who rules on the eve of Sabbaths and Wednesdays. What did they do? They took dark clothes, and darkened the lights and made a mourning on the Sabbath eves. . . .[41]

It is a peculiar, yet again almost inevitable, coincidence that the same night on which the pious prepare to receive Queen Sabbath, and on which God Himself proceeds to unite with her, should also be the time when Lilith roams and seduces men. It is up to man, the passage quoted above seems to say, to make his choice between the holy bride, the Sabbath, and the unholy one, Lilith.

Pope, after quoting the foregoing two paragraphs in his commentary to the Song of Songs, adds:

The passage, however, by implication, says even more than this. Patai, in his chapter on Lilith makes it clear that she is none other than the evil aspect of the same Goddess whose good side is the Matronit. The mention of the worship of the Queen of Heaven, with allusion to Jer. 7:18, 44:17–19, makes it clear that the reference is to the persistence of the old-time religion, the cult of the Great Goddess, older by millennia than the revelation of the name of the God of Israel. The issue here is whether one performed similar rites in the name of the Queen of Heaven, Inanna-Ishtar, Anat, Atargatis, Venus, or in the name of Yahweh and his Sabbath Bride.[41a]

Less than a hundred years after the Zohar, the

idea of the Sabbath as God's bride and of God as the Sabbath's bridegroom, was elaborated and made explicit by David ben Joseph Abudarham, a commentator of the prayers and the benedictions, who lived in Seville about the middle of the 14th century. In his exposition of this thought, Abudarham adduces evidence from the special Sabbath prayers, which he reads as alluding to the betrothal of the divine couple. "The Sabbath," he says, "is called bride, and God is called bridegroom." This can be concluded from the fact that the words "You [God] sanctified the seventh day to your name," included in the Friday evening prayer, actually mean "You betrothed the Sabbath day to Yourself." [42] Similarly, the prayer beginning with the words "Moses rejoiced" was included in the Sabbath liturgy because it refers to the rejoicing of the bridegroom, God, over the bride, the Sabbath; and the prayer "You are one" was included because it refers to the union of bride and groom.[43]

The Zoharic image of God the King proceeding with his innumerable hosts to receive his bride the Sabbath, the Holy Matronit, was subsequently translated into a central weekly ritual among the Safed Kabbalists of the 16th century. They developed the custom of leaving the town on Friday toward dusk and proceeding to the adjacent hills and fields in order to receive the Sabbath in the open. While approaching the queen and bride, the spirits of the marching group would rise to a near-euphoria, and they would begin to intone the *Lekha Dodi*, the Sabbath song which was universally accepted later and is sung to this day in every synagogue on Friday evening. The poem was written, with liberal borrowings from earlier versions, by Shlomo ben Moshe Halevi Alqabetz (ca. 1505–1584), a member of the Safed group of Kabbalists. Like all poems of this sort, the *Lekha Dodi* too is replete with Biblical phrases and allusions to religious ideas, with which one must be thoroughly familiar in order to get its full meaning. The literal prose translation which follows is offered with this author's apologies, in full

awareness of his inability to do justice to the poetic
and emotional qualities of the Hebrew original.

> Come, my friend, to meet the Bride,
> Let us receive the face of Sabbath.

'Observe' and 'Remember' in one utterance,
The Only God let us hear.
God is one and His name is one,
For renown, glory, and praise.

> Come . . .

Come, let us go to meet Sabbath,
For she is the source of blessing,
Pouring forth from ancient days.
The act was the end, in thought the beginning.[44]

> Come . . .

King's temple, royal city,
Arise, leave the destruction behind,
Long have you sat in the vale of tears,
Now He will show mercy unto you.

> Come . . .

Shake off the dust, arise, put on
The garments of your glory, O my people!
Through the Son of Yishai the Bethlehemite,[45]
Draw nigh to my soul and redeem it!

> Come . . .

Awake, awake, for your light has come!
Arise and shine!
Wake up, wake up, sing a song!
God's glory was revealed to you.

> Come . . .

Be not ashamed, be not confounded.
Why are you humble, why do you sigh?
The poor of my people will find refuge in you,
And the City will be rebuilt on her mound.

> Come . . .

Your spoilers will be despoiled,
All your destroyers will be removed,
Your God will rejoice over you
As the bridegroom rejoices over the bride.

      Come . . .

You will spread out to the right and left
And the Lord you will adore.
Through the Man, the Son of Perez,[46]
We all shall be happy and rejoice.

      Come . . .

Come in peace, O crown of her husband,
In joy and in jubilation,
Amid the faithful of the chosen people,
Come, O Bride, come, O Bride!

      Come, my friend, to meet the Bride,
      Let us receive the face of Sabbath.

In addition to this paean, in which the Sabbath is described as God's bride and God as the Sabbath's husband, Psalms 29 or 95–99 were also recited, and sometimes even musical instruments were played. The fields in which all this took place were, through the arrival of the Sabbath-Shekhina, turned into the "sacred apple orchard," which in itself is a mystical manifestation or aspect of the Shekhina,[47] a sacred grove sanctified by the union of God with His bride and producing the souls of the just. The festive procession going to receive the Sabbath outside the town resembled in both form and spirit the processional fetching of the bride in traditional Middle Eastern Jewish weddings by the entourage dispatched by the bridegroom's family to escort her to the wedding canopy.

Pope, in his commentary to the Song of Songs, surmises that this Kabbalistic custom of receiving the Sabbath in the open followed

an ancient custom of devoting the evening of Friday (Frī[g]day, Frīg being the old Teutonic love-goddess corresponding to Venus) to venereal activity. . . . The emphasis on the open country and the fields outside the town suggests alfresco amour under the benign glow of the Venus star (which helps one to understand the French expression for 'out-of-doors,' *à la belle étoile*, the beautiful star being Venus). The Bride and Queen greeted at dusk in the open country around Safed, we may plausibly surmise, was the epiphany of the Evening Star, Ishtar-Venus, Queen of Heaven. The question of the Canticle (8:5a): 'Who is this ascending from the steppe?' is thus answered. The vesper sortie into the field recalls the invitation of the Canticle (7:12–13): 'Come, my love, let us hie to the field . . . there will I give you my love.'

So far so good. But in the subsequent two sentences Dr. Pope makes a surmise which forces us to part company with him:

The euphoria of the procession as they marched to the field singing the hymn composed by Solomon Alqabetz, 'Come my love to meet the Bride/ The presence [face] of Sabbath let us receive,' could lead to 'lightheaded' activities if both sexes were present.

Just what was done by the devout mystics after they got to the field is not entirely clear, but one may imagine that in the popular observances there were those who tarried to indulge in the kind of celebration congenial to the Love Queen.[47a]

As far as one can conclude on the basis of what we know of the life of the Safed Kabbalists—and whether learned or not, all the Jews of Safed were Kabbalists in the 16th century—these Friday evening excursions to the fields must have been purely a masculine affair. Thus the open countryside, which mystically assumed the character of the "sacred apple orchard," could have been the scene of nothing more than a highly emotional, but at the same time purely mystical-imaginary union between the male participants in the procession, as representatives of the Community of Israel, and the Holy One, blessed be He, the Divine Bridegroom of that community and of the Sabbath. The passage from the Song of Songs (8:5) quoted in this context by Pope, "Under the apple tree I aroused you, there your mother conceived you," certainly contributed its share to the development of the concept of the "sacred apple orchard," and, as Pope pointd out (p. 193), may in turn have had something to do with the old pagan worship in sacred groves. But in the course of the more than two millennia that had passed since that Biblical scene, Jewish sensibilities had become highly refined, so that any kind of group "celebration congenial to the Love Queen" would have been totally abhorrent to the 16th-century Kabbalists.

By that time, and especially in a Muslim environment such as represented by the town of Safed, the strict separation of the sexes had long been an entrenched and inviolate rule among the Jews. Public intermingling of men and women, whether in the synagogue, in the fields, or elsewhere, was entirely out of the question. This communal emphasis on segregation of the sexes meant that unmarried young men had to, and did, find outlets in clandestine relationships or encounters with women. If and when such affairs became public knowledge, their least consequence was utter disgrace. While no accounts of the sexual behavior of the Safed Jews are extant, there are contemporary documents which allow us to conclude that clandestine illicit sex was the most frequent among the transgressions for which a sinner was believed to incur the punishment of *gilgul*, or transmigration of his soul into the body of an animal or another human.[47b]

However, clandestine offenses against an oppressively severe sexual code are one thing, and public sexual celebrations are quite another. While we can thus be practically certain that such group happenings could not, and did not, take place, we have every reason to assume that in those Friday evening excursions to the "sacred apple orchard" there was a strong admixture of erotic elements and libidinous arousal, which did not lead to any sexual activity until later that night, however. Since one of the focal endeavors in the religious life of the Kabbalists was to sanctify, by mystical interpretation, the legitimate sexual relations between husband and wife, whatever libido may have been aroused by the Friday evening group celebrations in the open fields around Safed was channeled into the licit and recommended satisfaction of marital sex after midnight.

Following the end of the evening prayers, the men would return home to be received by their wives—the wife in this instance became for the husband the earthly representative of the Shekhina, with whom he was about to perform that night the sacred act of cohabitation in imitation of, and in mystical sympathy with, the supernal union between God the King and His wife, the Matronit-Shekhina-Sabbath. The return from the synagogue to the home on Sabbath eve was also the occasion on which it was proper to show due reverence to the mother; of Isaac Luria, the great leader and master of the Safed Kabbalists, it is reported that upon entering his home he used to kiss reverently the hands of his mother.

Now the husband would approach the table and pick up two bunches of myrtle, each consisting of three twigs, prepared for the bride and the groom, and then circle the table—all rites imitative and symbolic of observances performed at actual weddings—and sing welcoming songs to the two angels of peace who were believed to accompany him home from the synagogue. The chanting of Chapter 31 (Verses 10–31) of the Book of Proverbs, which followed, had a double significance. Ostensibly, it was meant as a paean to the "woman of valor," the good wife and mother whose very presence in the house, quite apart from all the care she lavished on her family, made it possible for the husband to live a complete Jewish life, in accordance with the oft-reiterated teachings of the Kabbala about the blessed state of male-female togetherness. Beyond that, however, there was a deeper meaning: the "woman of valor" whose excellence is described in the twenty-two alphabetically arranged verses was interpreted as being none other than the Shekhina herself, the divine Matronit, whose image thus was mystically merged with that of the man's own wife.

Next came the recitation of an Aramaic poem containing an invitation addressed to God the King to take part in the festive Sabbath meal. At some time during that meal or following it, the husband chanted another mystical Aramaic poem written by Isaac Luria and describing the union of God the King and his bride, the Sabbath-Shekhina.[48] The first six stanzas read as follows: [49]

Let me sing the praises of Him who enters the gates
Of the orchard of apple trees, holy are they.

Let us invite her [50] now, with a freshly set table,
With a goodly lamp which sheds light on the heads.

Right and left, and the bride in between
Comes forth in her jewels and sumptuous raiments.

Her husband embraces her, and with her *Yesod*,[51]
Which gives her pleasure, he presses her mightily.[52]

Cries and sighs have stopped and ceased,
New faces come, spirits and souls.

He brings her great joy, in a double measure,
Light pours upon her, and blessings on end.

Upon the completion of this song it is customary to this day among the Hassidic Jews who follow the ritual established by "the Holy Lion" (i.e., Isaac Luria) to say this Aramaic prayer:

Be it the will before the Ancient One, the Most Holy One, and the Most Secret One, and

the Most Hidden of All, that the Supernal Dew
be drawn from Him to fill the head of the Small
Face and to fall upon the Orchard of Holy
Apples, in radiance of face, in pleasure and in
joy for all.[53]

The several courses of the meal, the drinking of
wine, the numerous songs, the "words of Torah," and
the after-meal grace took so long that, by the time
the family rose from the table, it would be near
midnight. And this was as it should be, because it
had to be midnight when husband and wife retired
to bed in order not to violate the stringent Kabbalistic
rule prohibiting cohabitation prior to midnight of the
Sabbath. The background of this rule requires some
explanation.

6. THE MYSTICAL UNION

As we have seen in the first section of this chapter,
Friday night was considered in the Talmudic period
the proper time for scholars to fulfill the religious
commandment of marital intercourse with their wives.
This must have been an established custom, just as
was the daily performance of the marital act by men
of leisure, twice weekly by laborers, once a week by
donkey drivers, once in thirty days by camel drivers
(whose caravans returned home only once in thirty
days), and once every six months by sailors (whose
extended sea voyages enabled them to return home
only at such long intervals). The passage in the Mishna
which contains this information [54] is couched in the
form of a legal decision as to the frequency of marital
intercourse required of people from various occupa-
tions in fulfillment of the Biblical law which enjoins
a man not to diminish "the food, the raiment, and
the conjugal rights" of his wife.[55] The subsequent Talmudic specification to the effect that scholars must
have marital intercourse with their wives on Friday

nights underwent further refinements as to the precise
time most suited for performance of the act by scholars, and received its final codification as a religious
law by Joseph Caro (1488–1575), in his *Shulhan
'Arukh*, the last great and comprehensive Jewish code,
first printed in Venice in 1564–1565. Caro, who was
also an outstanding mystic and leader of the Safed
circle of Kabbalists, advises that the act should be
performed "neither in the beginning of the night nor
towards its end, lest the husband hear the voices of
people and be brought to thinking of another woman,
but in the middle of the night." [56] Although this explanation of the rule to perform the act in the middle
of the night is plausible enough, since thinking of
another woman while coupling with one's own wife
was considered a grave sin, there is much more to it
than Caro allows to meet the eye. As his Polish commentator, Abraham Abele Halevi Gombiner (1635–
1682), remarked about a hundred years later, "The
Kabbalists wrote awesome mysteries [about inter-
course] precisely after midnight. . . ." [57]

What these "awesome mysteries" were can be summarized from the basic writings of the Kabbala. They
consist of two parts: an earlier one, explaining the
mystical meaning of marital intercourse on Friday
night; and a later one, specifying the mystical significance of restricting marital intercourse to Friday
night after midnight.

The first is found in the Zohar, which casts its
teaching on the subject into the form of a reinterpretation of a passage in Isaiah: "Thus saith the Lord
concerning the eunuchs who keep My Sabbaths, and
choose the things that please Me, and hold fast to My
covenant: Even unto them will I give in My house
and within My walls a monument and a memorial
better than sons and daughters. . . ." [58] The "eunuchs,"
says the Zohar, are the scholars who study the Law
all week long and "castrate themselves for the duration
of the six days of the week, tiring themselves out with
the study of the Law, and on Friday night they spur
themselves to copulation because they know the su-

pernal mystery of the hour in which the Matronit couples with the King." The words "who keep My Sabbaths" mean that those scholars keep themselves waiting for the Sabbath. "Choose the things that please Me" refers to the time of the coupling of the Matronit. "Hold fast to My Covenant" means that they hold onto that part of the godhead which carries the sign of the Abrahamic covenant, the Sephira of the *Yesod*, which stands for the masculine member, and through which the King unites with the Matronit. The Zohar concludes the passage with the words, "Happy is the lot of him who sanctifies himself in this holiness and knows this mystery"—that is to say, happy is he who, knowing this mystery, sanctifies himself by coupling with his wife on Friday night at the time when the King couples with His Matronit and, by so doing, both imitates the divine act and brings it about, helping the godhead to achieve its mystical unity.[59]

The second part of the mystery, that which pertains to the precise time of copulation, is contained in the 16th-century elaboration of the Kabbalistic doctrine. Isaac Luria, in his discussion of the relationship between the King and the Matronit, whom he calls the Small Face and his Female, respectively, distinguishes two facets or persons in the latter: one, referred to by the name Leah, representing the lower aspect of the Shekhina-Matronit and reaching only as high as the chest of the Small Face; and the other, Rachel, the Shekhina's higher aspect, occupying a face-to-face position with the male deity from his chest upward. The Small Face, incidentally, is also called Jacob or Israel when in juxtaposition to Leah and Rachel.

The Small Face is engaged during the day, and during the night up to midnight, in copulation with Leah which is, mystically, of a low degree. From midnight on, on weekdays, and up to midnight on Fridays, a higher type of copulation takes place between the Small Face and Leah. After midnight on Friday, the Small Face and Rachel copulate, which is the highest kind of union of the male and the female in the godhead. This, therefore, is the time of grace in which a scholar should unite with his wife, making sure that he does so only after having pronounced the words: "I fulfill the commandment of copulation for the unification of the Holy One, blessed be He, and the Shekhina." [60]

Thus, for the Jew reared in the great mystical tradition of his faith, the Sabbath was a day whose pleasures, both physical and spiritual, amply compensated him for the drabness, narrowness, and frequent sorrowfulness of the weekdays. With the Sabbath, a queenly visitor entered even the humblest abode, which, due to her presence, was transformed into a royal palace, with the table set, the candles burning, and the wine waiting. The mistress of the house became mysteriously identified with the Queen Sabbath, who was also identical with the Shekhina, the divine Matronit, God's own consort. As for the master of the house, he felt his chest swell and his consciousness expand due to the "additional soul" which came down from on high to inhabit his body for the duration of the Sabbath. All these supernal presences made man and wife feel part of the great spiritual world order in which every act and word was fraught with cosmic significance, and in which the supreme command of the day was "Rejoice!" When midnight came, and the fulfillment of the commandment to rejoice on the Sabbath found its most intense expression in the consummation of the marital act, this was done with the full awareness not only of obeying a divine injunction, but also of aiding thereby the divinity himself in achieving a state of male-female togetherness which God is just as much in need of as man.

It is certainly a very far cry from the ancient Canaanite mass orgiastic festivals performed in honor of Astarte, the goddess of sexual love and fertility, to the mystically oriented and privately observed celebration of marital sex in honor of the Sabbath, the divine queen and consort of God. Yet, quite apart from the historic development which led from the first to the second in the course of nearly three millennia, one can discover in both at least one common feature which indicates their generic relatedness. Both observances are culturally conditioned and traditionally formulated responses to the basic human psychological need to elevate and sanctify the sexual impulse by attributing to the sex act a higher, a religious, a divine significance. In both, the act becomes more than the end-in-itself that in physiological reality it actually is; it becomes a sacrosanct observance directed at a loftier and greater aim: the exertion of beneficial influence upon the great ultimate realities of the metaphysical world. And in both it is a female deity whose invisible yet omnipresent countenance is supposed to light up into a benign and pleasurable smile when she observes the fervid performance of her favorite rite.

CONCLUSION

The foregoing eight chapters have not discussed all
the feminine numina who, in one period or another,
played a role in the history of Hebrew and Jewish religion. There were, in addition to those treated, such
concepts as the "Holy Spirit," closely akin to, yet
distinct from, the Shekhina; the "Community of Israel," a personified guardian spirit of the totality of
the Jewish people; and "Wisdom," God's earliest creation and playmate, who had her counterpart in the
Greek Sophia; none of these received more than
fleeting mention above in various contexts. Several
others were not even touched upon, such as the
"Word," who also had a Greek counterpart in Logos;
the "Daughter Voice" (Bath Qol), through whom
God's will was made audible on earth; the Law
(Torah), God's beloved whom He made the bride of
Moses; the Earth (Adamah), considered in a literal
sense the mother of all living; the Mother City, and
especially Zion, regarded as the mother of the people;
and her counterpart, the Daughter of Zion, who represented the Mother's children, the people of Israel.[1]
All of these were personified, all were female, and all
partook, to a greater or lesser extent, of a numinous
character. If they were omitted from the present
volume, it was because they did not share, or shared

255

only to a minor degree, those traits which transform a numinous entity into a goddess, that is, into a truly divine being believed to possess a will of her own and to be capable of acting independently of any other divine power.

Such independent volition and capability of action was attributed to all the goddesses discussed. In reference to the early ones, those who established themselves in the Biblical Hebrew religious consciousness, the question of their dependence on or independence of Yahweh never had to be faced up to squarely. Asherah, Astarte, and Anath, on the one hand, and Yahweh (or Yahweh Elohim), on the other, inhabited two separate realms. Those who believed in the goddesses saw no incompatibility between the sway they held over certain areas of human life and certain departments of nature and the rule Yahweh exercised over others: in the polytheistic view of the divine, gods may compete with, and occasionally conspire against, one another, but they never cast a doubt on one another's existence. And as to those who believed in Yahweh only, for them the gods and goddesses worshiped by others were merely idols, devoid of any significance whatsoever, except the one baleful ability to lead men astray from the path of righteousness.

In the later period, the female divinities occupied a position in relation to God which was similar in one respect to that of Satan: they were capable of independent thought and action—surpassing by far the autonomy of angels, who were believed to be basically no more than the instruments of God's will. Yet there was, of course, the fundamental antithesis between good and evil which separated the Cherubim and the Shekhina from Satan and his cohorts. The independence of Satan's will from that of God was the result of his rebellion against his Master, and his opposition to God was always that of evil to goodness. Not so the female divinites, whose every independent act, even if it brought them into conflict with God, stemmed from their own, different, but equally valid, will to good.

The one exception to this rule is Lilith, the female embodiment of evil, Satan's companion, more deadly than any male devil could ever be. Her realm, dark and sinister, yet full of dangerous allure, stands beyond the control of God. The most powerful archangels, unable to subdue her, could only strike a bargain with her which left her ample room to pursue her nefarious activities.

The world peopled by these goddesses is calculated not only to repel the orthodox believer in the one and only God, but also to frustrate the logical mind. It is not unlike that old orchard of mysteries which the Talmud warns against exploring in the form of the story about the four sages who "entered the Pardes," three of whom came to a bad end. If one is armed only with the sword of logic, one runs the grave risk of being caught on the horns of not one but several dilemmas: not only that of reconciling the existence of the omnipotent, one and only God with the existence of other equally, or almost equally, potent divinities, and female ones to boot; but also that of rendering two opposing wills-to-good accordant with each other; and that of distinguishing between the good and evil goddess, who is perhaps, after all, but one wearing two different masks.

It is, however, in the nature of religious truth that it transcends logical verities. Faith, luckily for man, can grasp truth intuitively and on a deeper (or, if you wish, higher) level, a level far beyond the reach of the laborious, step-by-step advance of logical thinking. The religious truth of the existence of a once-harmonizing, once-discordant goddess side by side with a one-and-only and omnipotent God was triumphantly manifested in what can be called the Kabbalistic breakthrough. The mystical God-concept of the Kabbala, with its one and yet multiple deity, and its goddess image, the Matronit, whose wifehood to both God and man brought man nearer to God than he could ever get to a lone, patriarchal, male godhead, humanized God and, simultaneously, divinized man.

What ultimately emerges from this conspectus is

that, contrary to the generally held view, the religion of the Hebrews and the Jews was never without at least a hint of the feminine in its God-concept. At times, as in the Talmudic and even more so in the post-Talmudic periods, the female element in the deity was effectively pushed into the background. At others, as in the Biblical and again in the Kabbalistic eras, it occupied an important place in popular theology, occasionally even to the extent of overshadowing the male deity or the male component of the godhead. Only in the most recent times, after the Kabbalistic upsurge had subsided, and its last reverberations in Hassidism receded, did the female element disappear from the Jewish God-concept to leave it centered upon a strictly monotheistic, spiritual, and non-corporeal, but nevertheless masculine, godhead.

In conclusion, it may be appropriate to append here a comment for the purpose of putting the persistent sexual imagery of the Kabbala in its proper perspective. In the Middle Ages—and from the viewpoint of outlook, mentality, and imagery, the 16th-century Kabbalists were as medieval as the 13th-century originators of the Kabbala—there was nothing unusual about resorting to the symbolism of coitus in speaking of certain cosmic and divine events. Thus, for instance, in the cosmic realm, the conjunction of the sun and the moon—that is, the appearance of these two luminaries close to each other in the sky—was described verbally and visually as a man and a woman in sexual embrace, with an explicitness which today would be considered pornographic, but which in those days was taken for what it was intended: symbolic representations of an otherwise hard-to-imagine event.[2] Or, in the realm of the divine, let us recall the views of St. Peter Damian, the 11th-century cardinal and doctor of the Roman Catholic Church, who maintained that when the Virgin Mary matured, she possessed such charm and beauty that God, filled with passion for her, sang the *Canticles* in her praise, and that subsequently she was the golden couch upon which God, tired out by doings of men and angels, lay down to rest.[3] Two hundred years later, another Italian cardinal, the philosopher and ascetic St. Bonaventure, did not hesitate to call Mary "the Spouse of the Eternal Father." [4]

When viewed against this background, the sexual imagery of the union between God and the Sabbath, or between God the King and his consort, the Shekhina-Matronit—or, for that matter, between the Matronit and man—will appear neither offensive nor fantastic. The two-thousand-year-old Jewish tradition of viewing the relationship between God and man as one between husband and wife was, in the course of time, repeatedly transmuted, transformed, expanded, reapplied, and refined. What remained unchanged was the basic approach underlying it all: the overriding, irresistible tendency to view both the physical cosmos and the metaphysical world of the divine in human terms, which inevitably centered on the sexual reference, and thereby to reduce the great awesome mysteries, ever threatening to crush puny man, to a scale and form which he could grasp or with which, at least, he could grapple, thus gaining the self-assurance he needed to survive.

In strictly human terms, then, all the changing forms of the deity, the attribution to him of sexual qualities and functions, the early veneration of goddesses, their transformation into female divine attributes or manifestations, and their resuscitation at a time when they seemed dead and buried for over a millennium—all this served the one primal and permanent purpose, succinctly expressed first in the Bible and then repeated in numerous elaborations down to the present day: to safeguard human survival through any and every religious law, concept, idea, and endeavor. Let man, this view maintains, keep the statutes and ordinances, even those which bid him look up to a Brazen Serpent, in order that he may live by them.[5] It is under this imperative of life that the historical role of the Hebrew Goddess must be viewed and assessed.

Appendix

THE GODDESS IN
THE DURA SYNAGOGUE?

1. THE SYNAGOGUE AND ITS MURALS

Excavations conducted on a *tell*, close to the eastern frontier of northern Syria, on the right bank of the Euphrates some 40 miles to the south of its confluence with the Khabur, unearthed the remains of the town of Dura Europos. This was a Roman frontier post for about a century, and in 256 A.D. it fell to the advancing Persians. In order to buttress the city wall against the Persian onslaught, the Romans partly demolished the synagogue that had been built against the wall, and partly filled it with sand, mud, and rubble. It was due to this latter measure that the murals covering the inside walls of the synagogue remained undamaged through almost seventeen centuries, although as soon as excavation exposed them to the elements they began to deteriorate rapidly.[1]

An inscription found in the synagogue itself gives the date of its construction: it was built in 245 A.D., replacing an older and smaller synagogue that had occupied the site for a few decades. Sometime during the eleven years of its existence, all the interior walls of the synagogue were covered with the murals, whose discovery created quite a stir among historians of religion. That the Second Commandment was not interpreted by early Judaism as an absolute prohibition of all pictorial representation of humans and animals was known before the Dura Europos discoveries. But here was, for the first time, irrefutable historical evidence of the completely unrestrained use of polychrome painted murals showing scenes in which men and women appeared and interacted. Here were pictures illustrating Biblical stories, executed according to a master plan that utilized all the vertical wall surfaces of the synagogue, including its western walls, in whose center was a scallop-capped niche that originally must have contained the Ark. And, what is more, one of the largest and most elaborate murals flanking the Ark on the left and having the rescue of the infant Moses from the Nile as its subject is centered upon the naked figure of a woman! The Dura discoveries thus occasioned not only a correction in the traditional view of the Jewish historical attitude on representational art, but also a revision of the equally traditional ideas concerning Jewish modesty and bashfulness. It had to be conceded, at least, that Jewish communities existed that had assimilated and incorporated into their traditionally Jewish institutions the Hellenistic attitude to the naked human body and its pictorial representation in the service of religion. (See Plate 34.)

2. GOODENOUGH'S INTERPRETATION: ANAHITA

The three volumes of Goodenough's magnum opus, devoted to the interpretation of the symbolism of the Dura Europos synagogue,[2] contain the most exhaustive and penetrating analysis of the murals. Drawing on his unparalleled familiarity with the art of the Greco-Roman world in general, Goodenough has established beyond doubt that the naked woman, shown standing up to her thighs in the water of the Nile and holding the infant Moses in her arms, "startlingly resembles" the usual representations of the goddess Anahita, the most popular deity of Iran in the Sassanian period.[3] This observation, in itself, does not come as too great a surprise, because Dura Europos was a predominantly pagan city in which the Jews constituted but a small minority, and it was to be expected that their pictorial art should be subject to surrounding influences. As Goodenough points out, they spoke Greek, and their art had an undoubtedly Hellenistic base. Only two doors away from the synagogue, a wall painting found in a house shows Aphrodite (with whom Anahita was identified) with Eros beside her, and these two figures "startlingly resemble" the representation of the woman and the infant Moses.[4] Goodenough concludes that

> to paint the Moses scene the artist drew upon some painting of Aphrodite, who in Dura was probably often called Anahita, with the baby and with female attendants in their peculiar dress. So startling an invasion into the Moses story, for representation in a synagogue, would hardly have occurred as the mere borrowing of a form. The infant is indeed Moses coming out from the ark in the Nile, but he comes out to divine company in the arms of the goddess, herself quite as recognizable as though flagged with a written label.[5]

As to the three women standing above "Anahita," Goodenough says,

> I see no reason to doubt that following a Jewish tradition, or originally with himself, the master designer at Dura introduced the Nymphs deliberately and skillfully into the scene of the infant Moses, and did so in order to intensify the notion that Anahita-Aphrodite was drawing from the water a Wunderkind with royal nature at least 'hedged' with divinity.[6]

Goodenough thus argues that the synagogue muralist not merely borrowed the form in which Anahita was usually represented in the pagan paintings, but consciously took the figure of Anahita and introduced it into his painting as if saying: Look, Moses was a "divine child," as clearly proven by the fact that he was fetched out of the Nile by the goddess Anahita, who evidently would perform such a service to none other but a "divine child." The artist's purpose in doing so, Goodenough explicitly states, was to show that Moses was a "Wunderkind," a Miraculous Child, rivaling in his nature the pagan gods whom the Greeks and Romans liked to depict as "Wunderkinder." [7]

3. CRITICISM OF GOODENOUGH'S INTERPRETATION

Anahita, as we have seen above, was not merely the Persian counterpart of Aphrodite and of Artemis, but belonged to that ancient Near Eastern type of great goddesses who were virgins and wantons, loving mothers and cruel death dealers.[8] Could it be this goddess whom the Dura Europos muralist represented as holding the infant Moses in her arms? Is such an interpretation, as given by Goodenough, possible in the light of what we know about the Jewish attitude to pagan gods and goddesses?

We know that, following their penetration of Canaan, the Hebrew tribes adopted several local gods, or deities who held sway in neighboring countries, among them the goddesses Asherah, Astarte, and Anath (called the Queen of Heaven).[9] This was bitterly denounced by the Biblical authors and labeled as "awhoring after foreign gods." What, in fact, took place in the early Israelite period was an incorporation of Canaanite gods and goddesses into the popular (as well as court) religion of the Hebrews. However, this phase of their religious history came to an end in the 10th, or at the latest the 9th, century B.C., after which time no *new* foreign deity was able to gain a foothold among the Hebrews. They continued, to be sure, for several more centuries to serve the old gods who had won them over in the earlier, more malleable age, but no new adoption of foreign deities into popular Hebrew religion occurred.

After the Babylonian exile (586 B.C.), the "foreign" gods underwent a rapid decline among the Jews, although some of the old deities managed to live on, side by side with Yahweh, for another one or two centuries, especially in such relatively isolated places as the military outpost on the Upper Egyptian island of Elephantine. By the time the Hellenistic age arrived, in spite of all the attraction Hellenism held for the Jewish upper classes, it would have been completely out of line with this Jewish religious development, which by then was six or seven centuries old, to incorporate the worship of a new god into the Jewish religious structure. Individual Jews, of course, in every age, became temporarily or permanently attracted to the practices and doctrines of other religions. Apostasy and conversion to other faiths have dotted Jewish history for well over two thousand years. But never since the early Israelite period has Judaism admitted a new god.

These considerations alone contain a refutation of the interpretation of the naked female in the Moses panel of the Dura Europos synagogue as the representation of the goddess Anahita. Even if the 3rd-century Jewish community of Dura lay outside the mainstream of Jewish religious development,[10] the admittance of a pagan goddess in the form of her painted image on a synagogue wall would be totally impossible. As to the centers of Jewish religious development in Palestine and Babylonia, the fear of idolatrous contamination was so strong there that strenuous attempts were made to preclude any contact with idols. An illustration of this attitude can be found in the discussion that began when the Patriarch Gamaliel II (flourished about 100 A.D.), on the occasion of his visit to the Hellenistic city of Acre (north of Haifa), made use of a public bath which was decorated with a statue of Aphrodite. The question whether this was permissible still occupied the rabbis after several generations.[11] A Jewish community, such as that of Dura Europos, even if it was only remotely connected with the great Jewish religious centers of Palestine and Babylonia dominated by such a mentality, certainly could not tolerate the representation of a pagan goddess in its synagogue.

What the attitude of the Dura Jews themselves was toward the pagan gods worshiped by the gentiles of their town is clearly demonstrated by another mural in the synagogue. This shows the destructive effect the Ark of the Covenant had on the god Dagon of the Philistine city Ashdod (cf. Samuel 5:4). However, instead of showing the broken pieces of the statue of Dagon, the artist painted the broken images of the principal Palmyrene gods, which were worshiped at Dura. The meaning of this painting was correctly recognized by Goodenough when he remarked that the artist "succeeded very well in using the incident from [Book] I Samuel to show the collapse of paganism before the reality of Judaism, the collapse of paganism presumably as he knew it directly in Dura itself." [12] Elsewhere Goodenough repeats the same interpretation: "The gods of local paganism collapse before the Ark of the Covenant, the symbol of metaphysical reality in Judaism." [13] It is remarkable, indeed, that he remained unaware of the crass logical contradiction between this statement and the one that precedes it by only three lines, in which he says: "Moses is the divine baby here, with the three nymphs and Anahita-Aphrodite." How, one must ask, did Anahita-Aphrodite escape the fate of the other "gods of local paganism"? How could she be shown standing in triumphant nakedness over the ark (of Moses), when all her divine colleagues lie shattered under the Ark (of the Covenant)? One has only to pose this question in order to recognize that the woman holding the infant Moses in her arms cannot be the *representation* of Anahita-Aphrodite.

A comparison of the "Anahita-Aphrodite" picture with the Dura Europos synagogue murals in which the artist used Hellenistic elements, ideas, or motifs also vitiates Goodenough's interpretation. Neusner, following Goodenough, cites three examples of this artistic procedure.[14] One is the figure of David playing his lyre and surrounded by animals, in which the intrusion of the pagan Orpheus idea is unmistakable. The other is the figure of Moses shown leading the Children of Israel out of Egypt and carrying a staff, which, however, is portrayed as a club. Since the only two Greek heroes ever to carry a club are Theseus and Heracles, Goodenough argues that the Dura muralist "could have put it into Moses' hands only because of its immediate symbolic reference to their [i.e., Theseus' and Heracles'] special characters and to his [i.e., Moses']." [15] The third example cited by Neusner is that of Anahita-Aphrodite holding the infant Moses. However, there is a basic difference between Goodenough's interpretation of David-Orpheus and Moses-Heracles, on the one hand, and of the Anahita-Aphrodite figure, on the other. In the first two, we are shown pagan appurtenances with which the artist endowed the Biblical heroes whose pictures he painted. It was David whom he painted, although the manner in which he executed his painting made David's figure reminiscent of Orpheus. Similarly, in painting Moses, he made use of a feature associated with Heracles and Theseus. That the juxtaposition of the Greek and Hebrew heroes, implied by the borrowing of traits or paraphernalia from the former and attributing them to the latter, must have been based upon a current Jewish view influenced by Hellenism, cannot be doubted. In both cases, however, the Hellenistic features were absorbed and assimilated into the traditional Jewish concepts, which became enriched by them. What the artist says by means of the Hellenistic references is: Our David was a greater musician than Orpheus, our Moses a greater hero than Heracles.

If Goodenough were correct in his interpretation of the female figure holding the infant Moses, we would have to assume that the artist, in this single case, completely reversed the procedure he followed in the other pictures. For what Goodenough says is that this picture shows Moses being rescued by the pagan goddess Anahita-Aphrodite, that is to say, that the muralist in this case allowed a Biblical story to be assimilated into Greek or Hellenistic or Persian— but in any case, pagan—religious tradition and that he set down the result in his mural, quite uninhibitedly and for everybody to see. Had the artist actually had in mind what Goodenough ascribes to him, he would have been guilty of gross idolatry, and also the congregation that tolerated his mural in the synagogue would have been guilty of the same sin.

4. MOSES IN THE ARMS OF THE SHEKHINA

If the female figure holding the infant Moses in her arms is not Anahita, who then is she? Before seeking the answer to this question, let us again state clearly that part of Goodenough's interpretation which we accept. There can be no doubt that the muralist did engage in what Goodenough calls a "borrowing of form." In other words, he painted a female figure whose attributes and posture he borrowed from the current representations of Anahita-Aphrodite, and he did this in order to paint an image that could readily be recognized as a *divine* female. Once we accept that this was the artist's intention, we can easily understand why he "borrowed the form" of Anahita-Aphrodite: simply because there was no other form available to him in which to express the idea that a feminine deity cradled Moses in her arms. In Jewish artistic tradition there was certainly no prototype for the pictorial representation of a divine female; in the gentile environment of Dura, it was almost exclusively the Anahita-Aphrodite image that intruded upon the artist's consciousness.

Who then was this goddess-like figure into whose arms the muralist placed the infant Moses? Our answer is that she was the Shekhina.

This conclusion, startling though it may seem initially, can be supported by a number of considerations. The first of these is that the Midrash establishes a very close connection between Moses and the Shekhina, God's feminine aspect, which (or better, who) in the course of the Talmudic period achieved an increasing independence, and in the post-Talmudic period developed into a discrete feminine divinity.[16] In fact, no other human was represented as having had as intimate a relationship with the Shekhina as Moses. In the Kabbala, this relationship was to culminate in the statement that Moses, and he alone of all men, not only became the husband of the Matronit (=Shekhina), but copulated with her while still in the flesh.[17] In the earlier, Talmudic and Midrashic sources, this idea is adumbrated in the assertion that, of all men, Moses was the only one to whom the Shekhina spoke "every hour without setting a time in advance," and that therefore, in order to be always in a state of ritual purity and readiness to receive a communication from the Shekhina, Moses separated himself completely from his wife.[18]

When Moses died, the Shekhina, we are told, took him on her wings and carried him from Mount Nebo to his unknown burial place four miles away.[19] The Shekhina's function at the death of Moses is paralleled by her ministration to him at his birth. When the daughter of Pharaoh, we read in the Babylonian Talmud, found the ark of bulrushes in which his mother had placed Moses, and opened it, "she saw the Shekhina with him." [20] This tradition is quoted in the name of Rabbi Yose, son of Rabbi Hanina, a Palestinian teacher (Amora) of the second half of the 3rd century A.D., whose sayings are contained in both the Palestinian and the Babylonian Talmuds.

The second consideration is that the Midrash lifts the entire scene on the banks of the Nile out of the realm of the anecdotal, which characterizes it in the

Biblical narrative, into the realm of the miraculous and mythical. When the mother of Moses placed him in the ark, we read in the Midrash, she put a canopy over him, to take the place of his wedding canopy, because she feared that she would not be granted the sight of his *huppa*. When the handmaidens of Pharaoh's daughter tried to dissuade her from rescuing the child, the Angel Gabriel came and struck them to the ground. The ministering angels in heaven, with all kinds of arguments, reminded God that Moses must be saved. Gabriel gave Moses a blow, so as to make him cry and thereby awaken compassion in the heart of Pharaoh's daughter. Moses himself, although only three months old, had the voice of a youth, and he refused to take suck at the breasts of any Egyptian woman, saying(!): "The mouth which will speak with the Shekhina should suck an unclean thing!?" [21]

As for the daughter of Pharaoh, she did not just happen to go down to the river, but was compelled to do so by one of several divine acts. Some say that God sent a severe heat wave over Egypt, and all the Egyptians went down to the Nile to seek relief, among them Batya, the daughter of Pharaoh, with her maidens.[22] Others say that the daughter of Pharaoh suffered from leprosy, or from painful boils, so that she was unable to bear warm water. She therefore went down to the Nile to wash in its cool waves, noticed the ark, and the moment she touched it or the infant Moses, she was cured.[23] Still others say that she went down to the Nile in order to purify herself from the uncleanness of her father's idol worship and that, unbeknownst to her, she uttered words of prophecy on the banks of the river.[24]

When Batya saw that the touch of Moses cured her of her disease, she said, "This boy is a saint," and decided he must stay alive. Since he who keeps alive a single soul in Israel is considered by God as if he had sustained an entire world, the daughter of Pharaoh was taken under the wings of the Shekhina and was called the Daughter of God, Bat-Ya.[25]

Thirdly, it should be pointed out that the Midrash

literature abounds in passages clearly indicating that Moses was considered a "divine child." Miriam, the older sister of Moses, was possessed by the spirit of prophecy and foretold that her parents would give birth to a child who would become the savior of Israel. Thereupon Amram, who for three years had separated from his wife, approached her, and she conceived and bore Moses. When the child was born, the whole house became filled with great light, like the light of the sun and the moon. His parents saw that his appearance was like that of an angel of God. They circumcised him, called him Yequtiel (i.e., "My Hope Is God"), and hid him for three months. When they were no longer able to hide him in their home, his mother made him a little ark, which she placed, with Moses in it, among the reeds on the bank of the Nile.[26]

After taking him with her into the palace, Batya constantly kissed and hugged him, and she loved him exceedingly, for he was very beautiful. All the people at court desired to see him, and once they glimpsed him, they could not take their eyes off him.[27] Prenatal (or even preconceptional) annunciation, angelic countenance, light flooding the house, the healing touch, the ability to speak at the age of three months, irresistible charm and beauty—all these are features that unmistakably place the infant Moses in the "divine child" category.

The fourth consideration is the close association in the Midrash of the Shekhina with a sacred casket or ark. After accompanying Moses in the ark of bulrushes, the Shekhina dwelt in the Ark in which the Children of Israel carried the two Tablets of the Law in the desert. When the tribes rested, the Shekhina had her abode in the Tent of Meeting, the desert Tabernacle, or hovered over it. During these periods, and subsequently in the Land of Canaan, the Shekhina was most closely associated with the Ark of the Covenant. After Solomon completed the Temple in Jerusalem, the Shekhina hovered, or dwelt, over the Ark cover, between the two Cherubim. Some sages held that she was present in the Second Temple as well.[28] The Torah shrines in synagogues were the substitutes for the Ark of the Covenant, and after the destruction of the Second Temple (70 A.D.) the Shekhina, now in exile herself, sought out these synagogues to serve as her resting places. The significance of this association, Shekhina–Ark–Torah shrine, will become evident when we come to discuss the shape of the ark of bulrushes in the Dura synagogue mural.

Fifth and last, the Shekhina was closely associated with certain Babylonian synagogues. According to Abbaye (a Babylonian teacher who died in 339 A.D.), the Shekhina dwelt alternately in the Shaf Weyatibh synagogue of Nehardea and the synagogue of Huzal. Nehardea was one of the earliest centers of Babylonian Jewry, situated at or near the junction of the Euphrates and Nahr Malka rivers, some 200 miles southeast of Dura Europos; Huzal was located nearby. In these synagogues, the Shekhina was both audible and visible.[29]

Talmudic accounts thus place the Shekhina, in a visible and audible form, in synagogues only 200 miles distant from Dura Europos, and in the same period in which the Dura paintings were executed. As to the Midrashim summarized above under points one through four, although most sources in which they are found are centuries younger than the Dura murals, the oral tradition upon which they are based can easily go back into the 3rd century A.D., or even further. In these Midrashim, Moses is represented as a "Wunderkind"; and the Shekhina is closely associated with Moses, in that she is said to have been with him in the ark of bulrushes; to have spoken to him frequently, possibly daily, during the wandering of the Children of Israel in the desert; to have gone with him physically, dwelling in the casket or Ark containing the Tablets of the Law; to have been his bride; and to have carried him to his burial on her wings.

We have, of course, no way of knowing how much of these Midrashim was known to the Jews of Dura in general, and to their synagogue muralist in particular. There is, however, evidence to prove beyond doubt that some Midrashic embellishments of Biblical stories were known to the muralist, because he included them in his paintings. One case in point is his picturing one of Job's friends in kingly splendor, which conforms not to the Biblical text (in which Job's friends are not further identified), but to the Midrash which states explicitly that Job's friends were kings.[30]

A second example is found in the Moses panel itself, where the two midwives standing before Pharaoh at the right side of the picture are shown wearing the same dresses as worn by the mother and sister of Moses, appearing to the left. Identically clad figures denote the same person in the pictorial idiom of the Dura muralist (e.g., in the Exodus panel he shows Moses three times in identical garb, and in the Ezekiel panel he shows Ezekiel twice in identical garb); but the identifying of Shifra and Pua (the two midwives) with Jochebed and Miriam (Moses' mother and sister) is not Biblical, but Midrashic.[31] Here again the artist displays his familiarity with the Midrash, and these two instances make it probable or, at the very least, possible that in the scene showing the rescue of the infant Moses from the Nile he also illustrated a Midrash or, rather, the cycle of Midrashim that associates Moses with the Shekhina.

It seems to me that the cumulative force of the evidence adduced above indicates quite clearly that the intention of the artist was to stress the greatness, or even divinity, of Moses by showing him held safely over the water not by a foreign goddess, but by the divine female of Jewish tradition, the constant companion of Moses from cradle to grave, the Shekhina.

The Nile scene gave the artist the finest opportunity to show the infant Moses in the arms of the Shekhina. This was a scene in which, according to the Midrash, the Shekhina was present. However, the muralist could not show the Shekhina with Moses *inside* the ark; that would have been too difficult technically, if not impossible. He therefore proceeded to show the boy carried by the Shekhina, just as she carried him to his burial, a hundred and twenty years later when he died, substituting the figure of the divine female for the unnamed slave-girl whom, according to the Biblical account (Exodus 2:5), Pharaoh's daughter dispatched to fetch the child out of the Nile.

It remains to touch upon, albeit briefly, the nudity of the woman holding the infant Moses in her arms. This is undoubtedly the strangest, in the sense of least Jewish, feature in the entire pictorial cycle of the Dura synagogue. The very fact that the picture of a nude female was admitted into the synagogue shows to what extent the Jews of Dura were Hellenized, accustomed to the nude representation of the deities of their gentile neighbors, in temples as well as private homes. This circumstance made it *possible* for the artist to introduce the nude figure of a woman into the synagogue. What made it *necessary*, once he conceived the idea of showing the Shekhina with Moses, was that he had no Jewish, more modest example to follow in depicting the Shekhina, and that in borrowing the form of a gentile goddess he found only nude figures to copy. Thus the only way he could express that this woman, in contrast to the others appearing on the panel, was a divinity was to show her in the nude, while all the others were represented fully clothed.

5. THE ARK OF BULRUSHES, THE ARK OF THE COVENANT, AND THE TEMPLE

We have left to the last the question of the peculiar form the muralist gave to the ark of bulrushes in the Moses panel. The vessel is clearly not the little ark woven of bulrushes that Jochebed prepared for Moses (Exodus 2:3), which undoubtedly had a rounded, basketlike shape. What we see instead is a rectangular box, with a triangular gabled roof over its right end. The peculiar shape of the ark of bulrushes has caught the attention of Goodenough, who commented that the ark is sketched in a manner closely resembling the shape of the sarcophaguses found, e.g., at Beth Shearim, Israel. His explanation is that the artist intended to indicate that Moses, the Redeemer, had died and was reborn to new life.[32]

This explanation seems farfetched to me, because we have no evidence to show that the Dura muralist was familiar with the gabled sarcophaguses or that the idea of the infantile death and rebirth of Moses (a non-Jewish mythologem) was known to him. A much closer comparison would be between the shape of the ark of bulrushes and that of the Temple shown twice on the same wall. In fact, the ark of bulrushes is painted unmistakably in the shape of a miniature Temple.

The same shape was given to the Torah shrine or Ark in most Jewish representations from the 1st to at least the 10th centuries A.D. The oldest, found in the Jewish catacombs of Rome and dating from the 1st to 4th centuries A.D., show the Torah shrine as precisely such a miniature Temple with a gabled roof. In the Beth Alpha synagogue, a mosaic dating from the early 6th century A.D. shows the Torah shrine in the same form, as does a picture in a 10th-century Pentateuch manuscript from Egypt.[33] These examples, which could easily be multiplied, indicate that there was a firm tradition in Jewish art to represent the Torah shrine as a miniature Temple with a gabled roof. The Torah shrine, whose presence in any room turned it into a synagogue, actually symbolized, represented, and substituted for the Temple of Jerusalem, which was destroyed by the Romans in 70 A.D. In the Dura synagogue, the Torah shrine, or at least the niche in which it stood, did not have such a triangular gabled top but was capped by a rounded shell-like semidome. Corresponding to it, the Ark of the Covenant is also shown with such a shell-shaped rounded top. Yet this detail cannot alter the fact that the ark of bulrushes is shown in the shape of a miniature Temple, and it most probably is symbolic of the Temple or its predecessor, the desert Tabernacle.

We now recognize that just as the woman holding Moses in her arms represents the lifelong association of Moses with the Shekhina, so the ark of bulrushes in the shape of a miniature Temple or Tabernacle hints at the greatest religious feat performed by Moses: the building of the Tabernacle, the Sanctuary that served as the prototype for all subsequent Jewish Temples in Jerusalem. The desert Sanctuary was called *mishkan* ("dwelling") because Yahweh was believed to have "dwelt" (*shakhan*) in it or over it in a cloud.[34] It is this idea of the "dwelling" (*Shekhina*) of Yahweh that in time developed into the concept of the Shekhina, the "dwelling" or "presence" of God, as a separate, feminine divine entity. The nude woman in the Moses mural is shown raising her right arm over the Ark—this is how, with ingenious simplicity, the artist illustrates the mystical concept of the Shekhina hovering over the Tabernacle.

In recognizing that this is indeed what the Dura muralist had in mind in painting the nude woman holding the infant Moses in her arms, we find that in this picture he proceeded exactly as he did in the David-Orpheus and Moses-Heracles murals. As in those two, here also he enriched a Jewish character with features taken from the Hellenistic pictorial imagery of his environment. Far from allowing a pagan goddess to intrude into a Biblical scene, he assimilated, in this picture as well, certain Hellenistic features to embellish the Divine Female, the Shekhina.

6. CONCLUSION

The above considerations lead up to certain general conclusions with regard to the relationship of the Dura Europos Jews to Hellenism. These conclusions can be subsumed under two categories: first, the extent to which the Jews of Dura accepted Hellenistic cultural features; and second, the traits they rejected as incompatible with their own Jewish religious traditions.

The area from which the Jews of Dura were willing to accept cultural influences is presented in the synagogue murals as that of the pictorial representation of divine, or quasi-divine, heroes in the Hellenistic style. This is considerably more than a mere "borrowing of *form*," because it implies the assertion that the Biblical heroes and other Jewish figures depicted in a form borrowed from Hellenistic representational art were, in fact, as close to being divine as were the Greek heroes or deities whose attributes were borrowed for giving visual expression to the divine quality of the Jewish heroes and other figures.

The belief that some Biblical and post-Biblical heroes were superhuman and quasi-divine was an old Jewish tradition that went back to Biblical times and developed more fully in the post-Biblical period. It was certainly an old, established feature of Jewish religion by the time the Dura murals were painted.

We saw, above, some of the Midrashic traditions that surrounded the birth and infancy of Moses and that leave no doubt as to his quasi-divine character in Tannaitic and Amoraic belief. To them we may add the following generalizations: the typical hero, whether he lived in Biblical or post-Biblical times, was considered in the Talmudic (i.e., Tannaitic and Amoraic) tradition as being gigantic in bodily size, wielding superhuman strength, enjoying a much longer life-span than ordinary mortals, possessing extraordinary wisdom and beauty, having had (and prevailed in) encounters with angels and demons, and having the power to make even God Himself obey him.[35] People who had this mental image of their own "god-men," when they learned about Greek gods and heroes, felt no qualms over borrowing the latters' traits and attributes when it came to expressing in visual form the divine qualities of a Moses or a David, or depicting the divine female (or: the female in the divinity), the Shekhina.

As against this, the Jews of Dura were rooted firmly

enough in their Jewish traditions not to allow the pictorial representation of any pagan deity *as such* to intrude into their place of worship. In all the panels of the Dura synagogue there is not a single example of the representation of a pagan god as such. What are represented clearly and with unmistakable intent are the local idols (i.e., statues of the pagan gods), broken into pieces and lying scattered on the ground before the holy Ark of the Covenant of the God of David. To interpret the woman holding the child as Anahita holding Moses is therefore absurd. For the Dura Jews, Anahita was but another of those idols shown shattered in another panel. To represent her as a living deity and, to boot, as rescuing the infant Moses from the Nile would have been inconceivable.

We thus recognize, in the mirror of the synagogue murals, a community that was Jewish in its religious traditions and observances, whose Jewishness was sufficiently vital and self-assured to allow the assimilation of Hellenistic pictorial art as well as of features attributed by Greek religion to its gods, but that was, at the same time, tradition-bound enough in the manner of Talmudic Judaism to reject the very idea that the Greek gods could be anything more than lifeless images fashioned by human hands.

NOTES

Introduction

1. Cf. William F. Albright, *From the Stone Age to Christianity*, Baltimore: Johns Hopkins Press, 1940, pp. 92, 98, and 318–19, note 5.

2. Wilhelm Schmidt, *Origin and Growth of Religion*, London: Methuen, 1931, p. 287.

3. The following paragraph is based on a summary of the psychoanalytical interpretation of the goddess, very kindly communicated to me by Dr. Dorothy Zeligs of New York.

4. Erich Neumann, *The Great Mother*, New York: Pantheon Books, Bollingen Series XLVII, 1955, p. 12; cf. also pp. 3, 11.

5. *Cant. Rab.* to 7:8.

6. *Nehemia* 9:4.

7. *Zechariah* 5:8.

8. B. Yoma 69b; B. Sanhedrin 64a.

9. Cf. Moses Cordovero (1522–1570), *Pardes Rimmonim*, Sha'ar 'Erkhe haKinuyim, ed. Koretz, 1780, ch. 3, p. 120c: "Kingdom [i.e., the Shekhina] is called Asherah. . . ."

Chapter I. THE GODDESS ASHERAH

1. James B. Pritchard, *Ancient Near Eastern Texts* (hereafter: ANET) Princeton, 1955, pp. 131–34,138,140, 145,146,490.

2. William F. Albright, *Archaeology and the Religion of Israel*, Baltimore, 1942, p. 78.

3. *Enciqlopedia Miqra'it* (Jerusalem). s.v. Asherah; J. Halévy, *Revue des Etudes Juives* 12:112f.

4. Albright, *op. cit.* p. 78.

5. *Enc. Miqra'it*, s.v. Asherah; ANET, 483–84.

6. *Enc. Miqra'it*, s.v. Asherah.

7. See all the material ably presented by William L. Reed in his *The Asherah in the Old Testament*, Texas Christian University Press, Fort Worth, Texas, 1949, pp. 69–86.

8. *Judges* 3: 5–7.

9. The textual evidence as to the nature of "the Asherahs" is equivocal. The Asherahs are said to have been "made" (1 *Kings* 16:33; 2 *Kings* 17:26; 21:3; 2 *Chronicles* 33:3) which indicates that they were artifacts, made by human hands, and not merely natural trees as some scholars believe. The expressions to "set up" (*Isaiah* 27:9; 2 *Kings* 17:10; 2 *Chronicles* 33:19) or even "build" (1 *Kings* 14:23) an Asherah point to the same conclusion. Only once is an Asherah said to be "planted" (*Deuteronomy* 16:21) and the verb there probably means "implanted," that is, set into the ground as one would a pillar. On the other hand, the removal of Asherahs is called "cutting them down" (*Judges* 6:25,26,28,30; 2 *Kings* 18:4; 23:14; *Exodus* 34:13), "hewing them down" (2 *Chronicles* 14:2; 31:1; *Deuteronomy* 7:5), "breaking them into pieces" (2 *Chronicles* 34:4,7), "burning" (2 *Kings* 23:15; *Deuteronomy* 12:3), "exterminating" (2 *Chronicles* 19:3), "removing" (2 *Chronicles* 17:6), and "uprooting" (*Micah* 5:13) them.

10. *Judges* 6:25,28.

11. 2 *Kings* 21:3.

12. This is also the conclusion of Reed, *op. cit.*

13. *Judges* 6:25–32. The entire story of Gideon is most instructive in that it illustrates the irruption of Yahwist ideas into the midst of the pre-existing Baal and Asherah worship. The fact that Gideon needed the help of ten men (v. 27) in order to destroy the altar of Baal, cut down the Asherah and build an altar for Yahweh, indicates that the paraphernalia of the Baal and Asherah worship were quite sizable.

It might be pointed out here that there was a significant

difference between the image and the altar. The altar was "the altar *of* the Baal," it did not represent the god, but was merely dedicated to him. As against this, the wooden image *was* Asherah, it represented her in the manner in which a statue of an Egyptian or a Greek goddess represented that deity. It is therefore more than probable that the wooden image called "the Asherah" was carved or in some other way so fashioned as to indicate clearly that it stood for the goddess.

14. See sources in Reed, *op. cit.*, pp. 80–81, 87.

15. *Genesis* 30:10–13. Since Zilpah was Leah's handmaiden, it was Leah's right to name her children, just as it was Leah's right to introduce Zilpah into Jacob's bed. The text in *Genesis* is extremely laconic, and the exclamations made by Leah and adduced as explanations of the names given to the sons at their birth are purposely kept unclear. Nevertheless, the impression is gained that the names of Zilpah's two sons were originally felt to have had some connection with Canaanite deities. When the first son of Zilpah was born, Leah exclaimed: "By Gad (*baGad*)," and called his name Gad. When, shortly thereafter, Zilpah gave birth to a second son, Leah exclaimed: "By Oshri! (usually translated as "By my happiness!") For women will call me happy." And thus she named him Asher (*Genesis* 30:10–13). The prefix *b-*, used in both cases (*baGad* and *b'oshri*) is the one used when swearing by a god (cf., e.g., "By Yahweh," *Joshua* 2:12; *Judges* 21:7; 1 *Samuel* 24:22; 28:10; 2 *Samuel* 19:8; 1 *Kings* 2:8,23,42; "by Elohim," *Genesis* 21:23; 1 *Samuel* 30;15; *Nehemiah* 13:24; 2 *Chronicles* 36:13; *Isaiah* 65:16).

A deity by the name Gad was worshiped in Canaan, Palmyra, Phoenicia and Arabia as the god of good luck (cf. Robert Graves and Raphael Patai, *Hebrew Myths: The Book of Genesis*, New York, 1964, 45.2). No god by the name Oshri is known. Some scholars, therefore, assume that the text has been editorially emended so that the name of the deity invoked by Leah should conform more closely to the name Asher which it was supposed to explain, and that the original tradition had Leah exclaim: *basherah*—"By Asherah!" (Cf. Reed, *op. cit.*, pp. 80–81,87). The masculine name Asher may have been derived from Asherah, just as the masculine Astar was from Astarte in Canaanite mythology (cf. ANET, pp. 129,140; cf. also the Egyptian form Astar for Astarte, ANET, p. 250).

16. 1 *Kings* 3:2-3.

17. Cf. *Views of the Biblical World*, Jerusalem, 1960, vol. 2, p. 213; cf. 1 *Kings* 6:2-10, 15-38.

18. 1 *Kings* 7:13-50.

19. 1 *Kings* 11:4,6.

20. 1 *Kings* 11:2-4.

21. 1 *Kings* 2:46; 3:1.

22. 1 *Kings* 11:1,5.

23. Another consideration which speaks against the attribution of idolatry to Solomon's old-age weakness or folly is the accusation of idolatry leveled by the prophet Ahijah the Shilonite—an uncompromising Yahwist— against all Israel: "They have forsaken me," Ahijah says in the name of Yahweh, "and have worshiped Asthoreth the goddess of the Sidonians, Chemosh the god of Moab, and Milcom the god of the children of Ammon. . ." (1 *Kings* 11:33). We note that Ahijah accuses the Israelites of serving the same three foreign gods whose worship, according to the earlier passage, was introduced by Solomon in his old age. But while Solomon was said merely not to have gone "fully" after Yahweh, the people as a whole are charged by Ahijah with having "foresaken" Yahweh. It would, therefore, seem that while the royal court worshiped both Yahweh and other gods, the people did not worship Yahweh at all, but served only those other gods. It is hard to imagine that this should have come about as a result of the people imitating the court: popular religion in the Middle East was (and still is) notable for its slowness in accepting changes. It is far more likely that the popular idolatry of Solomon's day was by that time an old tradition which had spread among the Hebrews as a result of their prolonged contact with the nations of Canaan.

24. 1 *Kings* 11:5.

25. 1 *Kings* 11:33; 14:15.

26. 1 *Kings* 11:29-39.

27. 1 *Kings* 12:25-33.

28. I *Kings* 14:9, 15.

29. 1 *Kings* 16:32–33. In connection with Jezebel's father Ethbaal we again encounter the by now familiar confusion of Asherah and Astarte. From the account in the *Book of Kings* it is evident that Ethbaal and his family must have been the devotees of Asherah, for only this explains the introduction into Samaria of Asherah worship by Ahab in honor of his wife Jezebel, Ethbaal's daughter. Yet according to Menander, as quoted by Josephus Flavius (*Contra Apionem* 1.18), Ethbaal was the King of Tyre (and not of Sidon), and he was a priest of Astarte.

30. I *Kings* 18:19.

30a. Cf. R. Patai, "The Control of Rain in Ancient Palestine," *Hebrew Union College Annual*, vol. 14, 1939, pp. 251–86.

31. Verse 21.

32. 1 *Kings* 18.

33. 2 *Kings* 13:6.

34. 2 *Kings* 3:2.

35. 1 *Kings* 16:32.

36. 1 *Kings* 16:33.

37. 2 *Kings* 10:18–27.

38. 2 *Kings* 10:28–29.

39. 2 *Kings* 13:6.

40. 2 *Kings* 17:10–12,16–17.

40a. 2 *Kings* 23:15.

40b. *Hosea* 8:5–6.

41. 2 *Chronicles* 11:20,21,22; cf. 1 *Kings* 15:2, where Maacah's father is called Abishalom.

42. 1 *Kings* 14:31–15:2; 15:13; 2 *Chronicles* 11:20, 22.

43. 1 *Kings* 15:13; 2 *Chronicles* 15:16.

44. According to one set of sources, Asa was Abijam's brother (1 *Kings* 15:10; 2 *Chronicles* 15:16); according to another, he was his predecessor's son (1 *Kings* 15:8; 2 *Chronicles* 13:23).

45. 2 *Chronicles* 15:10.

46. 1 *Kings* 15:12,13; 2 *Chronicles* 14:2,4; 15:8,16.

47. 2 *Chronicles* 17:6.

48. 2 *Chronicles* 19:3.

49. 2 *Kings* 18:4; 2 *Chronicles* 24:2,17–18; 31:1.

50. *Isaiah* 17:8; 27:9.

51. *Micah* 5:11–13.

52. 2 *Kings* 21:3–7; cf. 2 *Chronicles* 33:3–7,15, 19.
53. Cf. above, p. 15.
54. *Deuteronomy* 7:5; 12:3; cf. *Exodus* 34:13.
55. *Deuteronomy* 16:21–22.
56. 2 *Kings* 23:4,6,7,13,14; cf. 2 *Chronicles* 34:3,4,7.
In 2 *Kings* 23:7 the masoretic text has "he demolished the houses of the *qedeshim* that were in the house of Yahweh, where the women wove houses (*batim*) for the Asherah." Apart from the question of how can houses be woven, stylistically it is well-nigh impossible that the word "house" should appear three times in one and the same sentence. The Septuagint has *"stolas,"* i.e. garments, for *batim*, which may be based on an original *badim*, i.e. "linens." The expression "(a person) clothed in linens" (*badim*) appears as a standing epithet for a mystical figure in *Ezekiel* (9:2,3,11, etc.) and *Daniel* (12:6,7). Thus it may well be that, from time to time, the Asherah statue was dressed in new linens, and that women considered it a pious act to busy themselves with weaving the material for these garments, on looms set up for this purpose in certain chambers in the Temple compound. The weaving of ritual vestments was a woman's task in Babylonian temples (cf. Woolley, *Antiquaries' Journal* 5:393), at Hierapolis in Syria (Lucian, *De Dea Syria* 42), and in Greece (Gressmann, *Zeitschrift für die alttest. Wissenschaft*, 1924, pp. 325 ff.). It seems that also in Ugarit the makers of sacred vestments had a role in the temple ritual (cf. John Gray, *The Legacy of Canaan*, p. 156, and *I and II Kings*, Philadelphia, Westminster Press, 1963, p. 507).

As to the *qedeshim*, most Biblical scholars consider the term to refer to sacred prostitutes of both sexes, and not merely males. I am inclined to read it as "male sacred prostitutes," for had the Biblical author wished to refer to both male and female functionaries he would, in all probability, have said *"qedeshim uqedeshot"* using both the masculine and the feminine plural forms of the noun *qadesh*. The function of the *qedeshim* had something to do with the fertility cult centering in the figure of the mother-goddess Asherah. Possibly, their services were made use of by childless women who visited the sanctuary in order to become pregnant. Such pilgrimages to holy places for the purpose of removing the curse of barrenness have remained an important feature of popular religion down to the present day among Moslems, Jews and Christians alike in all parts of the Middle East. The *qedeshim* may have also functioned in rites of imitative magic in the fertility cult, whose purpose was to ensure fruitfulness in nature, the coming of the autumn rains, the growth of the crops, the multiplication of domestic animals, etc.

Fertility goddesses had male attendants or priests in ancient Near Eastern religions, and, in the case of the *qedeshim* in the Jerusalem Temple, one of their tasks seems to have been to supervise the work of the women weaving linens for Asherah, which, therefore, was done in the chambers of the *qedeshim*.

57. *Jeremiah* 2:8,23; 7:9; 9:13; 11:13,17; 12:16; 19:5; 23:13,27; 32:29,35.

58. 2 *Kings* 23:13.

59. *Jeremiah* 17:2.

60. *Ezekiel* 8:1.

61. *Ezekiel* 8:1–18.

62. Cf. vv. 6,13,15.

63. The word "jealousy" undoubtedly refers to Yahweh: it is His jealousy that the image arouses. The word "image" (*semel* in Hebrew) first occurs in a Deuteronomic injunction prohibiting the making of "a statue (*pesel*), the form (*t'munah*) of any image (*semel*), the likeness (*tabnith*) of male or female; the likeness of any beast which is on the earth, the likeness of any winged fowl which flies in the heavens; the likeness of any fish which is in the water under the earth" (*Deuteronomy* 4:16–18). *Semel* therefore means here an image which represents a member of one of the four major realms of the animal kingdom, and which is made for idolatrous purposes.

In the *Book of Chronicles*, probably under the influence of Ezekiel's use of the term *semel*, the Asherah image set up by Manasseh is called, not merely "Asherah" as in the original account (2 *Kings* 21:3), but "the statue (*pesel*) of the image (*semel*)," and, the second time briefly "the image (*ha-semel*; 2 *Chronicles* 33:7,15). The identification of Ezekiel's "image of jealousy" with Manasseh's "image of Asherah" is implicit in the terminology of *Chronicles*.

Chapter II. ASTARTE-ANATH

1. ANET, 130.
2. ANET, 133.
3. ANET, 135.
4. ANET, 131.
5. ANET, 144.
6. ANET, 130, where, in view of the above-mentioned prosodic rule, the missing part of the name should be restored as "(Ana)th," rather than "('Ashtore)th" which is the first choice of H. L. Ginsberg.
7. ANET, 15.
8. ANET, 249–50.
9. ANET, 250.
10. W. F. Albright, *Amer. Journal of Semitic Languages and Literatures*, Jan. 1925, p. 82.
11. ANET, 249–50.
12. ANET, 250.
13. ANET, 320. Chemosh was regarded as the local Moabite manifestation of the deity known in many lands as Baal ("Lord") or Molech ("King"), as evidenced by the name Mesha king of Moab gave to one of the cities he built: he called it Beth-Baal-Meon, i.e. House of the Baal of Meon. It is not likely that a zealous devotee of Chemosh like Mesha would have named a city he built after another god. Cf. *Enc. Miqra'it*, s.v. Molech; ANET, 321.
14. ANET, 242, 328, 486 n.
15. ANET, 505.
16. ANET, 149; cf. p. 130.
17. Cf. the material assembled by H. Ranke in *Studies Presented to F. L. Griffith*, London, 1932, pp. 412–18; W. F. Albright, *Archaeology and the Religion of Israel*, Baltimore, 1942, index, s.v. Astarte.
18. Cf. above, p. 30.
19. I. e. Beth 'Ashtarah, *Joshua* 21:27.
20. 1 *Chronicles* 11:44.
21. E.g., 'Anathoth; see below, p. 38.
22. *Joshua* 9:10: 12:4; 13:12, 31; *Deuteronomy* 1:4; 1 *Chronicles* 6:56.
23. *Genesis* 14:5.

24. E.g., the 17th-century B.C. figurine from Nahariah, see Plate 9.

25. The original meaning of the word *'ashtaroth* can be established with the help of four passages in *Deuteronomy* (7:13; 28:4, 18, 51) in which it occurs in a poetic context. In each of the four passages the phrase "the *'ashtaroth* of your flock" is paralleled by "the increase of your kine." According to the rules of Hebrew prosody, the word "increase" (*sheger*) must have roughly the same meaning as *'ashtaroth*. On the other hand, *sheger* (which has its cognate verb-root in Aramaic meaning "to send forth") is a synonym of *rehem*, the well-known Biblical word for "womb" (*Exodus* 13:12). Thus both *sheger* and *'asharoth* can mean only "womb," or by transference "that which issues from the womb." Cf. U. Cassuto, *The Book of Exodus* (in Hebrew), Jerusalem, 1959, p. 105. From *"rehem"* is derived the Biblical Hebrew noun *"raham,"* meaning "she of the womb," or "girl" (*Judges* 5:30), and a similar Ugaritic noun meaning the same (Kramer, *Mythologies*, 187). Similarly, from *'ashtaroth* is derived the Canaanite name of the Goddess 'Ashtoreth, meaning "She of the womb," a most appropriate name for a goddess of fertility.

26. The name Baal is derived from a Semitic verb which originally meant "to take possession sexually."

27. When the goddess is styled "the maiden," this epithet is usually followed by her proper name Anath: "the maiden Anath." It seems that a knowledge of the original meaning of the name Astarte, namely "girl," lingered, and that it was therefore found clumsy to refer to the goddess as "the maiden Astarte" which would have meant "the maiden girl."

28. *Judges* 2:13.

29. *Judges* 10:6.

30. *1 Samuel* 7:3–4, 10–13; 13:10.

31. 1 *Samuel* 31:10.

32. *'Ashtoreth elohe Tzidonim, 1 Kings* 11:5, 33.

33. 2 *Kings* 23:13: *Shiqqutz.*

34. Cf. James B. Pritchard, *Palestinian Figurines in Relation to Certain Goddesses Known through Literature,* New Haven, 1943, pp. 1, 87.

35. *Joshua* 15:15; *Judges* 1:11; cf. *Joshua* 10:38–39; 12:13; 15:49; 21:15; 1 *Chronicles* 6:43.

36. W. F. Albright, *The Archaeology of Palestine*, Pelican Books, 1949, pp. 18, 43.

37. *Joshua* 15:15; *1 Kings* 8:6 etc.

38. *Joshua* 21:14; *1 Chronicles* 6:43.

39. Albright, *op. cit.*, pp. 105–06. The word "Asherah" on p. 106, line 1, should be emended to read "Astarte." Such a confusion between Astarte and Asherah occurs as early as *Judges* 2:13 and 3:7.

40. Cf. sketches of 15 such figurines in Albright, *op. cit.*, p. 133.

41. Albright, *The Excavations of Tell Beit Mirsim* vol. iii. (Annual of the American Schools of Oriental Research, New Haven, 1943, vol. xxi-xxii), p. 139; cf. pp. 138–41.

42. Albright, *The Archaeology of Palestine and the Bible*. New York, 1932, p. 110; *id., Journal of the Palestine Oriental Society*, 1931, pp. 123–24.

43. Cf. below, Chapter V.

44. Langdon, *Semitic,* p. 30; ANET 15,136,137,139, 140,142,146,151–53,249,250,254; Gordon, in Kramer (ed.), *Mythologies of the Ancient World*, 1961, pp. 187, 197–99; Albright, *Archaeology and the Religion of Israel*, pp. 75, 85, 197.

45. *Judges* 1:33; cf. *Joshua* 19:38.

46. *Joshua* 21:18; *2 Samuel* 23:27: *1 Kings* 2:26; *Jeremiah* 1:1, etc.

47. *1 Chronicles* 7:8; *Nehemia* 10:20.

48. *Judges* 3:31; cf. 5:6.

49. ANET, 130–31. For another explanation of the name Shamgar ben Anath, see Eva Danelius, "Shamgar ben Anath," *Journal of Near Eastern Studies*, July 1963, vol. 22, pp. 191–93.

50. Cf. above, p. 30.

51. *Jeremiah* 44:15.

52. *Jeremiah* 44:15–19.

53. *Jeremiah* 7:17–18.

54. Zimmern, *Keilinschriften und das Alte Testament*, 3rd ed., pp. 441 f., 425; ZATW 6, 301–08.

55. The mould and a modern cast made of it are pictured in *Views of the Biblical World*, vol. 1, Chicago-New York, 1959, p. 290.

56. A certain reinforcement for the above conjecture can be found in Rabbinic tradition according to which

the show-bread (*Lehem panim*) which was offered up daily in the Temple (*Exodus* 25:30) was baked in a mould, cf. Mishna Menahot 11:1; B. Menahot 94a, 97a; cf. Mishna Demai 5:45; Num. Rab. 4:14. The precise translation of the name of this bread-offering is "bread of the Face" (i.e., of God). This is how, e.g., Father de Vaux explains the meaning of the term in his *Ancient Israel*, New York-Toronto-London, 1961, p. 442. The mould in which the bread was baked must have given it a shape which had some relation to its name. If so, it becomes quite likely that the cakes for Astarte were prepared in a similar manner.

57. 2 *Kings* 23:13; cf. above, p. 32.

58. 2 *Kings* 22:3. According to the less plausible version of 2 *Chronicles* 34:3: in the eighth year of his reign.

59. *Jeremiah* 1:2.

60. Cf. *Enc. Miqra'it*, s.v. M'lekhet Hashamayim.

61. ANET, 491.

62. ANET, 491, n. 9.

63. For instance, when Arsames, the satrap of Egypt, left in 410 B.C. on a visit to Darius, the priests of the Elephantinian male god Khnub instigated the destruction of the temple of Yaho in Elephantine, cf. ANET, 492.

64. ANET, 491.

Chapter III. THE CHERUBIM

1. *1 Kings* 22:39.

2. See Lucas N. Grollenberg, *Atlas of the Bible*, London, 1957, figure 214; and E. Auerbach, *Wüste und gelobtes Land*, Berlin, 1936, II. pl. V.

3. Cf. Hugo Gressmann, *Altorientalische Bilder zum Alten Testament*, 2nd ed., Berlin-Leipzig, 1927, plate 497.

4. Cf. e.g. Hugo Gressmann, *Die Lade Jahves*, Berlin-Stuttgart-Leipzig, 1920, pp. 64–65; and *Enc. Miqra'it*, s.v. K'rubh.

5. Cf. *Enc. Miq.*, s.v. K'rubh.

6. *1 Samuel* 1:24.

7. *Exodus* 25:17–22; 37: 6–9; *Numbers* 7:89. The

size of the Cherubim is not stated, but one can reach an estimate on the following basis: The height of the Ark was 1½ cubits (2¼ feet), and, we are told in *Exodus* 25:10,20, that the wings of the Cherubim covered the Ark from above. If we assume that the Cherubim knelt on both sides of the Ark in a position resembling that of the genii of the Samarian ivory plaque, their height in this position must have been about 5 feet, so as to allow their wings to meet over the Ark. This would give us also a wing-length of about 5 feet (from the shoulder of the Cherub to the tip of the wing), in which case the wing would extend horizontally beyond the knee about 2 feet, and the 3¾ feet (or 2½ cubits) length of the Ark would have precisely enough room in the space between the knees and under the wings of the Cherubim.

8. *Exodus* 26:1, 36:8. Each of these curtains measured 28 cubits (42 feet) from top to bottom and 4 cubits (6 feet) in breadth (*Exodus* 26:2; 36:9). If, as seems probable, each curtain was decorated with one pair of Cherubim, the latter must either have been pressed closer together than the Cherubim over the Ark, or were smaller in size. The curtains were many-colored: fine twined linen, blue, purple and scarlet, "the work of the skilful workman" (*Exodus* 26:1; 36:8,35).

9. *Exodus* 26: 31–35.

10. 1 *Kings* 6:23–28; 2 *Chronicles* 3:11–13; 5:7–8.

11. 1 *Kings* 8: 6–7.

12. 1 *Chronicles* 28:18. The Cherubim themselves were "*tza'atzu'im* work" (2 *Chron.* 3:10), an expresison rather difficult to understand. In all probability, however, the word *tza'atzu'im* is derived from a root related to the Arabic verb *tzagha*, to form, to practice the art of the goldsmith, in which case the phrase means "a work of plastic form" or "work of sculpture."

13. 1 *Kings* 6:29–35; 2 *Chronicles* 3:7.

14. 2 *Chronicles* 3:14.

15. 1 *Kings* 7:29, 36,37,39. While we learn nothing positive about the shape of the Cherubim from this passage, we nevertheless can conclude something about them by elimination: since it enumerates three types of figures: lions, oxen *and* Cherubim, the latter were neither lion-shaped nor ox-shaped, as some Biblical scholars opined.

Cf. e.g., Tur-Sinai, *Enc. Miq.* s.v. Aron; Graham-May, *Culture and Conscience*, Chicago, 1936, 248–57; etc.

16. *Ezekiel* 41:18–20,23,25.

17. Cf. Raphael Patai, *Hamayim (Water)*, Tel-Aviv, 1936, p. 107.

18. ANET, p. 130, 131.

19. *Psalm* 68:5; 104:3–4.

20. *Isaiah* 19:1.

21. *Psalm* 18:11.

22. 1 *Chronicles* 13:7.

23. *Habakkuk* 3, and esp. vv. 7,8,15.

24. Cf. *Canticles* 1:9.

25. Mekhilta diR. Shimon, 51–52,54; Mid. Wayosha, 52; cf. Robert Graves and Raphael Patai, *Hebrew Myths: The Book of Genesis*, New York, 1964, p. 12.

26. *Genesis* 3:24; cf. Graves-Patai, *op. cit.*, 12.d.

27. *Ezekiel* 28:12–19; cf. Graves-Patai, *op. cit.*, 8.a., 1–4.

28. *Exodus* 40:34–38.

29. *Exodus* 24:15–17.

30. 1 *Kings* 8:10–11.

31. *Ezekiel* 9:3; 10:1–22. The details of Ezekiel's vision defy interpretation, although it is clear that his description of the wheeled quadrangular Cherub-chariot is based on certain cultic objects some of which were excavated in Babylonia. The theme of a jewel-bedecked Cherub is exclusively Ezekelian (10:1,9; 28:13–14,16), as is the idea that the bodies of the Cherubim are full of eyes. Perhaps the eyes, as the "stones of fire," are based on bejewelled Cherubim figures? The association of "glowing stones" with divine beings is found already in *Isaiah* (6:6) who calls his six-winged angels, not Cherubim but "Seraphim," i.e. "fiery beings."

32. *Exodus* 25:22.

33. The dates commonly given for Philo's birth and death used to be 30 B.C. and 50 A.D., respectively. Recently, however, this birth-date has been proved to be too early and ca. 15 B.C. has been substituted for it, while his death date has been moved down to ca. 45 A.D. Cf. Moses Hadas and Morton Smith, *Heroes and Gods*, New York, 1965, p. 129.

34. Philo, *De Spec. Leg.* I. XIII, §72, Loeb Class. Libr. p. 141.

35. Philo, *De Vit. Mos.* II. XVI, §76ff., Loeb Class Libr. p. 487. A late echo of this interpretation is found in *Zohar Hadash*, Tiqqunim (Warsaw: Levin-Epstein, no date), p. 95a: "They are Wisdom and Understanding, which are the faces of the Cherubim."

36. Philo, *On the Cherubim* VII. 21–24; IX. 27–30; Loeb Classical Libr. ed. pp. 21–27; cf. also *De Vit. Mos.* II. 98–99.

37. *Exodus* 25:19.

38. *Proverbs* 8:22.

39. Philo, *On Drunkenness*, VIII. 30 and IX. 33, Loeb ed. pp. 333–335; cf. p. 337; *De Spec. Leg.* 1.96, p. 155.

40. Philo, *On the Cherubim* XIV. 49, Loeb p. 39.

41. Philo, *Vit. Mos.* 3:8; *Quaest. in Gen.* 57.

42. *Psalm* 103:13.

43. *Proverbs* 30:17; *Ezekiel* 19:2. The attribution of softness to the father and toughness to the mother seems to go back in the Near East to a much earlier period than that of Philo. In the mythology of ancient Ugarit (14th century B.C.), the father of a mythical group of griffons or vultures is designated by a name which is interpreted by Th. Gaster as "softie," while the name of the mother of the griffons means, according to him, "toughie." Cf. Th. Gaster, *Thespis*, New York, Doubleday Anchor Books, pp. 362–63. In ANET, 154, H. L. Ginsberg makes no attempt to translate or interpret the Ugaritic names of the vultures' father (*Hargab*) and mother (*Samal*).

44. G. Scholem, *Major Trends in Jewish Mysticism*, New York, 1961, p. 37.

45. Josephus Flavius, *Ant.* 3:6:5.

46. *Ezekiel* 9:3; 10:1–22.

47. Josephus, *Ant.* 3:6: 2 and 4.

48. Josephus, *Ant.* 8:3:3.

49. *Ant.* 8:3:2.

50. Contrast this with another passage, *Ant.* 8:5:2, where Josephus describes the royal palace built by Solomon and says that the fourth row of stones in its wall "would make one admire its sculptures, whereby were represented trees and all sorts of plants with the shades that arose from their branches and leaves that hung down from them. Those trees and plants covered the stone beneath them, and their leaves were wrought so

prodigiously thin and subtle that you would think they
were in motion. . ."

51. Josephus, *Wars* 5:5:5.

52. Josephus, *Contra Apionem* 2:7 and 8.

53. Midrash Tadshe, ed. Jellinek, *Bet Hamidrash* III,
p. 164.

54. *Op. cit. p.* 167.

55. In considering what the Talmudic sources have to
say about the Cherubim, one must look at the Talmudic
reports in general on the differences between the Solomonic Temple and the one built after the return from
the Babylonian exile. To begin with, it has to be pointed
out that the sages of the Talmud as a rule referred to
the Temple of Solomon as the "First House," or "First
Temple," and to the post-exilic Temple as the "Second
House," or "Second Temple." In using the latter term,
they rarely added any qualifying clause which would make
it clear whether they referred to the Temple built by the
Babylonia returnees in 520–515 B.C., to the Temple as
restored by the Maccabees in 165 B.C., or to the Temple
as completely rebuilt by Herod in 20–12 B.C. This lack
of precision in itself causes certain difficulties when trying
to place Talmudic statements into their proper historical
background.

With the above reservation in mind, let us quote the
key passage which deals with the question of whether
there were any differences in equipment between the First
and the Second Temples. According to Shemuel ben Inya
(a Palestinian Amora of the early 4th century A.D.) the
following features of the First Temple were absent from
the Second: "The Ark, the Ark-Cover, the Cherubim, the
Fire, the Shekhina, the Holy Spirit, and the Oracular
Breastplate." This opinion, however, is contradicted by
the general statement immediately following to the effect
that those enumerated features "were indeed present (in
the Second Temple) but were of no help," and by the
preceding special reference to "the Fire of the wood-
pile" on the altar, about which R. Hanina, the adjutant
high priest (2nd half of the 1st century A.D.) said that
while the Fire on the altar in the First Temple crouched
like a lion, in the Second Temple he himself saw it
crouching like a dog (B. Yoma 21b).

These and similar passages indicate quite clearly that

the Tannaim, i.e. the Palestinian sages of the 1st and 2nd centuries A.D. whose words are incorporated in the Mishna, had definite traditions concerning the Temple, which were no longer understood by their heirs and successors, the Amoraim, who lived in the 3rd to 5th centuries either in Palestine or in Babylonia, and whose words are contained in the Palestinian Talmud and the Babylonian Talmud respectively. When a sage like R. Hanina, who also happened to be a high functionary in the Temple (as his name, "Segan hakohanim," i.e., adjutant high priest, indicates), states that he himself saw the Fire on the altar, one will have to rely on him rather than on the statement of Shemuel ben Inya who lived in Babylonia almost three centuries later.

56. B. Baba Bathra 99a.

57. B. Yoma 54a. Rab Qetina's statement was found objectionable by Rab Hisda (another Babylonian Amora of the late 3rd century) on the grounds that such a procedure would have violated the Biblical commandment (*Number* 4:20) which warned: "They (i.e. the priests) shall not go in to see the holy things while they are uncovered." However, Rab Nahman (a contemporary of Rab Hisda) had an answer to this objection: a bride who is still in her father's house is bashful toward her groom; once she lives in her husband's house, she is no longer bashful toward him. Likewise the children of Israel, while they were in the desert, were bashful and would not look at the Shekhina—the visible "Presence" of God, represented by the Cherubim; once they settled in their land, they could feast their eyes on her.

This being settled, a new question arises: does Rab Qetina speak of the First or the Second Temple? If of the First, there was no veil in it (this was the accepted Talmudic view, 2 *Chronicles* 3:14 nothwithstanding, based on 1 *Kings* 6:16 which was interpreted as referring to a partition *wall* between the Holy and the Holy of Holies). If, however, he spoke of the Second Temple, in that there were no Cherubim (this in accordance with the view of R. Shemuel b. Inya quoted above). The first, anonymous, answer is that the reference is to the First Temple, and that the Veil mentioned was the Veil of one of the doors. The second answer, given by Rab Aha bar Ya'akov (a Babylonian Amora of the early 4th

century), holds that Rab Qetina spoke of the Second
Temple, and that he referred not to the Cherubim of
the Ark, but to the Cherubim engraved on the walls of
the Temple as stated in the Book of Kings (1 *Kings*
6:29,35).

This explanation is followed by a masterly reinterpretation by Rabba bar Rab Shila (an early-4th-century A.D.
Babylonian Amora) of one of the phrases appearing in
the description of Solomon's Temple. The bases of the
lavers, we are told in 1 *Kings* 7:36, were decorated by
engraved Cherubim, lions and palm trees, "according to
the space of each, with wreaths." The words in quotes,
"*k'ma'ar ish w'loyoth*" in Hebrew, are read by Rabba
"*k'ish ham'ure b'liwya (shelo),*" that is the Cherubim were
"like a man intertwined with his wife."

58. B. Yoma 54b.

59. Lam. Rab. Petihta §9; Pesiqta diR. Kahana ed.
Buber, Lyck, 1868, pp. 137b–138a; ed. Mandelbaum,
New York, 1962, I, 301; Yalqut Shimoni to Isaiah §474,
to Zephaniah §567.

In its midrashic form the tradition seems to refer to
an incident that took place at the time of the destruction
of the First Temple or somewhat prior to it. It is a midrash to *Lamentations,* Jeremiah's songs of woe over the
destruction of the First Temple, and the Ammonites and
Moabites mentioned in them figure among the peoples
who launched an attack on Jerusalem shortly before
Nebuchadnezzar besieged the city in 598 B.C. (2 *Kings*
24:1–2). However, a scrutiny of the events recorded in
the *Books of Kings, Chronicles,* and *Jeremiah* fails to
disclose any occurrence such as the one taken for granted
in the above passages, namely a penetration of gentiles
into the Holy of Holies of the Temple prior to its destruction. The only juncture at which such an event could
have conceivably taken place was the siege of Jerusalem
by Nebuchadnezzar in 598 B.C. The two accounts of this
event, contained in the *Book of Kings* and in *Chronicles*
are so different as to be irreconcilable, but historians tend
to accept the one contained in *Kings* as reflecting what
actually transpired. According to that account, King
Jehoiakim of Judah (reigned 608–598 B.C.), shortly before his death rebelled against Nebuchadnezzar, who
thereupon set out to punish him. The Babylonian army

reached Jerusalem soon after Jehoiakim's death, and laid siege to it. This was more than Jehoiakim's son and successor, the eighteen-year old Jehoiachin, could endure, and he threw himself on the mercy of Nebuchadnezzar, thereby saving his city and country from destruction, although he himself was taken into captivity to Babylon.

The narrative in *Kings* is so explicit in detailing what happened at that tragic hour in Jerusalem's history that we can be positive that had the Temple been entered by Nebuchadnezzar and thereby desecrated for the first time since it was built, this would certainly have been recounted by the historian. We are told that, when Nebuchadnezzar arrived at Jerusalem, young king Jehoiachin "went out to the king of Babylon," with his mother, princes, officers and servants, all of whom Nebuchadnezzar took to Babylon as his captives. We are further informed that Nebuchadnezzar took away all the Jewish soldiers, craftsmen and smiths, a total of ten thousand persons. (In *Jeremiah* 52:28 the more realistic figure of 3,023 is mentioned.) Finally, we are apprised that Nebuchadnezzar took all the treasures from the House of Yahweh and the king's house, and cut in pieces all the vessels of gold which Solomon had made for the Temple (2 *Kings* 24:8–16). On this latter point, *Chronicles* again has a divergent tradition; Nebuchadnezzar carried off the vessels of the House of Yahweh and put them into his temple in Babylon (2 *Chronicles* 36:6–7,10). The version of *Kings* seems here too to be more reliable: what Nebuchadnezzar was interested in was, not to acquire cult objects for his temple, but to obtain gold: he, therefore, did not hesitate to break the large golden vessels into pieces so as to be able to transport them more easily.

One can thus reconstruct what happened: Nebuchadnezzar demanded, obtained and took away all the gold vessels of the Temple and the Palace, just as the Egyptian Pharaoh Shishak had done in the days of Rehoboam (928–911 B.C.), more than three centuries previously (1 *Kings* 14:25–26). If we check back to the account of Solomon's Temple construction, we shall find enumerated a large number of "pure gold" vessels: altar, table, candlesticks, lamps, cups, snuffers, basins, pens, etc. (1 *Kings* 7:48–50), which went under the collective name "all the vessels that were in the House of Yahweh"—practically the same phrase used in connection with their removal by Nebuchadnezzar: "all the gold vessels which Solomon, King of Israel, had made in the Temple of Yahweh as Yahweh had said." The Cherubim were not touched by Nebuchadnezzar because they were not of solid gold: they were made of olive-wood, and merely overlaid with gold (1 *Kings* 6:23, 28). Even if the gold overlay of the Cherubim still existed 350 years after they were made, and was not replaced by brass, as Solomon's golden shields were by his son Rehoboam (1 *Kings* 14:27), it was of small value compared with the many solid gold vessels delivered to Nebuchadnezzar by Jehoiachin. It is, therefore, safe to assume that, whether or not Nebuchadnezzar's officials supervised the removal of all gold vessels from the Temple, the Cherubim were not disturbed, and certainly not dragged out in derision into the streets.

We thus conclude that the Cherubim-incident was merely agadically connected to the First Temple, and that the event to which it referred must have taken place in the days of the Second Temple to which all the three Amoras quoted above have reference. However, we cannot go along with them in interpreting both statements—the one referring to the showing of the Cherubim to the people during their presence in the Temple at the three feats of pilgrimage, and the one describing the dragging out of the Cherubim into the streets—as having the Cherubim-reliefs decorating the walls of the Temple as their subject. This interpretation became necessary only because several Babylonian Amoras accepted as axiomatic the view that there were no Cherubim in the Holy of Holies in the Second Temple, just as there was no Ark, Ark-cover, Fire, Shekhina, Holy Spirit, and Oracular Breastplate in it. However, as we have seen, this view is contradicted by more reliable, firsthand eyewitness accounts as to the presence of the Fire, and by the general assertion that all the enumerated features did, in fact, exist in the Second Temple as well.

As to the Cherubim, Rab Qetina's statement is unequivocal: the Veil was rolled up and the Cherubim behind it were shown to the people. The Veil is, of course, the curtain separating the Holy from the Holy of Holies. If all that had been meant by Rab Qetina was that the

Cherubim engraved on the walls of the Temple were
shown to the people, there would have been no need to
roll up any veil: The walls were not covered by veils or
curtains, and, if they were adorned with reliefs of Cherubim as were the walls of the First Temple, i.e. from
the outside as well as the inside (1 *Kings* 6:20), all the
Israelites could see them from their courtyard, without
even having to approach the Temple building itself.

Secondly, if we assume that there were no Cherubim
on the outer walls of the Temple, but there were on the
inner walls of the *hēkhal* (the Holy Hall), and that Rab
Aha bar Ya'akov (above, p. 83) referred to these, we
run up against yet another difficulty. By consulting any
modern reconstruction of the floor plan of the Herodian
Temple, one at once notices that the line of vision from
the court of the Israelites (which was the closest non-
priests were allowed to approach the Temple) through
the two doors between the *ulam* (vestibule) and the
hekhal (Holy Hall), into the *hekhal* itself was tightly
hemmed in by the large altar of burnt offerings which
stood on the southern side, and the eight tables used
for the preparation of the sacrifices which occupied the
northern side of the Court of Priests (cf. M. Avi-Yonah,
Sepher Yerushalayim, Jerusalem, 1956, vol. I, pp. 399,
406). Due to the narrowness of this line of vision, the
two side walls of the *hekhal* were not visible to people
outside, in the Court of Israelites. The only part visible
was the Veil which was stretched across the back end
of the *hekhal*. When the Veil was rolled up, the Cherubim
behind it, in the Holy of Holies (*devir*), became visible.

Thirdly, if Shimeon ben Laqish also refers to Cherubim
decorating the walls in relief, how did the foreigner
"take them out" and carry them around in the streets
in cages? Rashi (ad B. Yoma 54b), to be sure, comments, that "they folded them down from the wall" but
this explanation is forced.

Moreover, the showing of the Cherubim to the awe-
struck pilgrims, and the taking them out in sacrilegious
derision and displaying them to the profane crowd of
the marketplace, have about them the feel of a deep
mystery and its wanton desecration; they make sense
only if they refer to a unique group of statuary that was

so holy that it was normally hidden in the dark interior of the adytum.

60. *Exodus* 23:14–17; 34:23–24; *Deuteronomy* 16:16.

61. *Leviticus* 23:40; *Deuteronomy* 16:14; M. Sukka 5:1.

62. Cf. R. Patai, *Man and Temple*, pp. 24–53.

63. *Exodus* 32:6. The Hebrew verb *l'tzaheq*, translated above as "engaged in sexual intercourse," is a technical term meaning precisely this. It appears, e.g., in the story of Isaac and Abimelech, where the Philistine king is said to have learned that Rebekah was indeed the wife and not the sister of Isaac when, looking out his window, he saw Isaac *m'tzaheq*, engage in sexual intercourse, with Rebekah.

64. Nelson Glueck, *Deities and Dolphins*, New York, 1965, p. 166.

65. Cf. Patai, *Man and Temple*, pp. 13,66,70.

66. M. Sukka 5:2; Tos. Sukka 4:1; M. Middoth 2:5; Yer. Sukka 55b middle; B. Sukka 52a; Patai, *Man and Temple*, pp. 27–28.

67. Emil Schürer, *Geschichte des jüdischen Volkes*, 3rd and 4th eds., I. 197, quoting *1 Macc.* 1:20–24; Josephus, *Ant.*, XIII:5:3–4; *2 Macc.* 5:11–21; Josephus, *Contra Apionem* II:7.

68. Schürer, *op. cit.*, pp. 197–98; quoting *1 Macc.* 1:29–40; *2 Macc.* 5:23–25; Josephus, *Ant.* XII:5:4.

69. Cf. e.g., Jellinek, *Beth Hamidrash*, I. p. 31–46.

70. Cf. Moses Hadas, *Aristeas to Philocrates*, New York, 1951, p. 54. According to the earlier estimate of Emil Schürer, *op. cit.*, III. 611, it was written in ca. 200 B.C.

71. Cf. Schürer, *op. cit.*, III. 609.

72. S. Zeitlin, editorial note in Hadas, *Aristeas to Philocrates*, p. 71.

73. *Ant.* XII: 2: 5,9,10,11,15.

74. *Aristeas* 51–82 and 320; Hadas, *op. cit.* pp. 121–131,225.

75. Cf. *Exodus* 25:23–28; *1 Kings* 7:48.

76. Hadas, *op. cit.* p. 123. Aristeas and, following him, Josephus devote many pages to the description of the table. We learn that it was decorated with egg designs, garlands of all kind of fruit, visibly projecting clusters of grapes and ears of grain, also dates and apples, olives

and pomegranates, etc. "They worked stones of the colors of the several species to resemble the shapes of the fruits. . ." The legs had lily-shaped capitals; there were leaves of ivy intertwined with acanthus, and "all the parts were carefully made and fitted, the ingenius art corresponding to truth to such a superlative degree that if a breath of wind blew, the leaves stirred in their place, so closely was every detail modelled on reality" (cf. Hadas, *op. cit.* pp. 125–27.) Josephus largely repeats *Aristeas'* description of the table, adding that the intricate "sculptures" representing the many types of fruit were so life-like "that you would guess they were nowise different from real tendrils; for they were so very thin and so very far extended at their extremities that they were moved with the wind and made one believe that they were the product of nature, not the representation of art" (Josephus, *Ant.* XII:2:9). It must have been these decorations which inspired the later Talmudic legends about golden trees planted by Solomon in the Temple which brought forth fruit and thus provided nourishment for the priests (B. Yoma 21b, 39b; Yer. Yoma 41d; cf. Num. Rab. 11:3; 12:4; Mid. Tanhuma Num. ed. Buber, p. 33; Cant. Rab. 3:9; Josephus, *Ant.* VIII:5:2; cf. Patai, *Man and Temple,* pp. 90, 101).

For our present purpose it is interesting to note that the "living golden trees" motive represents another example of the attribution by the Talmudic sages to the First Temple of a feature which was introduced only into the Second Temple, and at a relatively late date at that. This strengthens our argument that the exhibition of the Cherubim in cages in the marketplace, attributed by the Talmudic sages to the First Temple period, actually took place likewise in the days of the Second Temple, during the sack of Jerusalem by Antiochus Epiphanes.

77. Josephus *Ant.,* XII:2:11.

78. Cf. Joseph Klausner, *History of the Second Temple* (in Hebrew), Jerusalem, 1952, II. 130.

79. Cf. Schürer, *Geschichte,* 4th ed., III. 362–63.

80. M. Yoma 3:10.

81. Cf. Tos. Sukka 4:6, p. 198; B. Arakhin 10b; A. Büchler, *Studies in Jewish History,* Oxford Univ. Press, 1956, pp. 51ff.

82. Philo, *De Spec. Leg.* I. 319ff.

83. According to W.W. Tarn, *The Greeks in Bactria and India*, Cambridge, 1938, pp. 414–36.

84. Hadas, *Aristeas* 83, p. 133.

85. Gen. Rab. 21:9.

86. Ex. Rab. 25.2.

87. *Deuteronomy* 6:4.

88. Maimonides, *Guide of the Perplexed*, III. 45. Transl. by S. Pines, University of Chicago Press, 1963, p. 577.

89. *Exodus* 25:18.

90. *Midrash HaGadol*, ed. M. Margulies, Jerusalem, 1956, p. 580. The original of the word translated above as "breasts" is "*vashdotam*." Margulies in a footnote states that he does not know what this word means. My suggested translation is based on the following considerations: the context shows that the word must mean a part of the human body. The *alef* inserted between the *v* and the *sh* seems to be a *mater lectionis* for *a*, as is frequently found in *Midrash HaGadol*, e.g., the name Raba is spelled, not in its usual form RBH, but RABH. The feminine plural suffix *-ot*, instead of the usual dual suffix, appears in the text in the word preceding *vashdotam*, namely *yadotam* ("their hands"), while one would expect *y'dehem* and *sh'dehem*. These deviations from standard Hebrew mask, but cannot obliterate, the meaning of the word *vashdotam*, i.e. "their breasts."

91. *Numbers* 7:89; *Deuteronomy* 32:4.

92. *Zohar* III. 59a.

93. *Exodus* 25:20.

94. *Leviticus* 18.7.

95. *Zohar* II. 176a.

96. Cf. Bahya ben Asher, *Biur 'al HaTorah*, Amsterdam, 1726 (on *Exodus 25*), folios 117b, 117d, 118c. Reference to the symbolic significance of the male and female Cherubim is also found on fol. 118d and 119a.

97. Hugo Gressmann, *Die Lade Jahves*, 1920, pp. 64–65.

98. Julian Morgenstern, "Amos Studies III," *Hebrew Union College Annual*, vol. 15, 1940, p. 121, note 98; *id.* The Ark, the Ephod, and the "Tent of Meeting," Cincinnati, 1945, pp. 95, note 159, 96, 107, 111.

Chapter IV. THE SHEKHINA

1. Cf. Chapter III, "The Cherubim," p. 51.
2. Cf. *ibid*. pp. 53–54.
3. *Exodus* 40:38.
4. *Exodus* 40:35.
5. 1 *Kings* 8:10–11; 2 *Chronicles* 5:14; 7:2.
6. 1 *Kings* 8:12–13; 2 *Chronicles* 6:1–2.
7. The technical term for the visible appearance of Yahweh in the sanctuary or in any other place chosen by Him is the verb *shakhan*, meaning to dwell, or abide. In the great and famous Sinai theophany (*Exodus* 24:16), "Yahweh's glory dwelt (*shakhan*) on Mount Sinai"; and subsequently He commanded Moses to build Him a sanctuary "that I may dwell (*w'shakhanti*) among" the Children of Israel (*Exodus* 25:8) Following the conquest of Canaan, God took up His abode on Mount Zion, and is referred to by *Isaiah* (8:18) as "Yahweh Zeboath who dwells (*shokhen*) in Mount Zion." Zion is God's holy mountain: "I am Yahweh your God, dwelling (*shokhen*) in Zion My holy mountain," says *Joel* (4:17). In the *Psalms* (135:21) this concept becomes the basis for a divine epithet: "Blessed be Yahweh out of Zion, the Jerusalem-dweller (*shokhen*), Hallelujah," just as in an older poetic context He is called "the thornbush dweller" (*Deuteronomy* 33:16).
8. The Tabernacle is often called *ohel mo'ed*, "Tent of Meeting," or simply *ha'ohel*, "the Tent," as well. It seems that the oldest Elohistic tradition used the term "Tent of Meeting," while the more recent Priestly tradition preferred the archaic term *Mishkan*, "dwelling" (cf. de Vaux, *Ancient Israel*, pp. 294–95), thereby giving emphasis to the idea that Yahweh actually "dwelt" (*shokhen*) in the desert sanctuary.
9. *Exodus* 33:9; *Numbers* 12:4–10.
10. *Exodus* 40:34–35; cf. de Vaux, p. 295.
11. *Nehemiah* 8:8.
12. *Job* 28:13–28.
13. *Proverbs* 8:22–31.
14. *Wisdom of Solomon, passim* (esp. 7:25ff.); *Sir.* 19:20; 24; *Bar.* 3:9–37; *Secr. of Enoch* 30:8.

15. *Wis. Sol.* 8:3.

16. Cf. Scholem "Zur Entwicklungsgeschichte der kabbalistischen Konzeption der Schechinah," *Eranos Jahrbuch* 1952, vol. 21 Zurich, 1953, pp. 48–49.

17. Philo, *On the Cherubim* XIV. 49. Loeb Class. Libr. p. 39.

18. Cf. Gilles Quispel, "Der gnostische Anthropos und die jüdische Tradition," *Eranos Jahrbuch* 1953, vol. 22, pp. 195–234, quoting Iren. 1.30 and Preuschen, *Adamschriften*, p. 22.

19. *Exodus* 25:8.

20. *Exodus* 29:45–46.

21. *Numbers* 5:3.

22. Cf. also *Numbers* 35:34.

23. *Deuteronomy* 32:10.

24. Cf. Siegmund Maybaum, *Die Anthropomorphien und Anthropopathien bei Onkelos*, Breslau, 1870, pp. 51–54, 63f.

25. Ex. Rab. 2:4.

26. B. Sukka 5a, quoting *Exodus* 19:20.

27. B. Sota 13a–b; cf. Mekhilta, Beshallah.

28. Num. Rab. 12:4 (pp. 46d, 47b); Pesiqta diR. Kahana, ed. Mandelbaum, p. 4.

29. Num. Rab. 12.4, p. 47b; Pesiqta diR. Kahana, ed. Mandelbaum, p. 4.

30. Num. Rab. 12.6.

31. Pesiqta diR. Kahana, ed. Mandelbaum, pp. 2–3.

32. B. Sanhedrin 103b, quoting 2 *Chronicles* 33:7, 22.

33. B. Rosh Hashana 31a; cf. Pesiqta diR. Kahana, ed. Mandelbaum, p. 234, and parallel sources listed there.

34. B. Rosh Hashana 31a and Rashi, *ibid*.

35. *Jeremiah* 3:22.

36. *Hosea* 5:15; Pesiqta diR. Kahana, ed. Mandelbaum, 235.

37. Pesiqta diR. Kahana, ed. Mandelbaum, pp. 390–91.

38. Cf. B. Yoma 21; Yer. Taanith 65a.

39. B. Yoma 9b.

40. Cf. B. Yoma 21b.

41. Rashi *ad* Megilla 29a.

42. B. Megilla 29a.

43. B. Sota 9b.

44. B. Megilla 29a.

45. B. Bekhoroth 8a.

46. Num. Rab. 12.8.

47. Pesiqta diR. Kahana, ed. Mandelbaum, pp. 396–97.

48. B. Sota 12b.

49. B. Shabbath 87a; cf. B. Pesahim 87b; Deut. Rab. 11:10 end; B. Yebamoth 62a; Aboth diR. Nathan, p. 10.

50. B. Shabbath 12b.

51. Targum to *Judges* 6:13 and *Psalm* 16:8.

52. Alpha Beta diR. Akiba, ed. Jellinek, *Beth Hamidrash* III. 29.

53. B. Sanhedrin 103b-104a.

54. B. Sota 17a.

55. B. Qiddushin 70b.

56. B. Shabbath 92a.

57. B. Nedarim 38a.

58. B. Qiddushin 70b.

59. B. Shabbath 30a; B. Pesahim 117a.

60. Pesiqta diR. Kahana, ed. Mandelbaum, pp. 110, 161; Ex. Rab. 32.4; Mid. Hagadol Shemini 10a, p. 189.

61. Alpha Beta diR. Akiba, ed. Jellinek, *Beth Hamidrash* III. 29.

62. B. Sanhedrin 39a.

63. Exodus 25:8.

64. 1 *Kings* 8:27.

65. Pesiqta diR. Kahana 20a, 62a; ed. Mandelbaum, pp. 8,33,337, and parallel sources listed *ibid*. in the footnotes.

66. Cf. Chapter III, "The Cherubim," pp. 58–60.

67. Cf. A. Marmorstein, *Studies in Jewish Theology*, Oxford Univ. Press, 1950, pp. 130–31.

68. *Proverbs* 24:28.

69. *Proverbs* 24:29; Lev. Rab. 6.1.

70. Since the passage in Lev. Rab. 6.1, quoted above, speaks of the "Holy Spirit," and not the Shekhina, Gershom Scholem is technically correct when stating that Midrash Mishle (see below) contains the first and only midrashic reference to a differentiation between God and the Shekhina. Cf. Scholem, "Zur Entwicklungsgeschichte der kabbalistischen Konzeption der Schechinah," *Eranos Jahrbuch* 1952, vol. 21, Zurich, 1953, p. 59. In substance, however, he is in error, because, as pointed out above, the differentiation between God and the Holy Spirit, found in Lev. Rab. 6.1, is essentially identical with a differentiation between God and the Shekhina.

71. Midrash Mishle ed. Buber, p. 47a, quoting *Proverbs* 22:29; cf. Mishna Sanhedrin 10.2 on the three kings (Jeroboam, Ahab and Manasseh) and the four commoners (Balaam, Doeg, Ahitophel, and Gehazi) who have no share in the World to Come, and B. Sanh. 104b.

72. Bereshit Rabbati, ed. Albeck, p. 27. The same midrash is found much earlier in a Hebrew version of the *Book of Enoch*, where, however, the crucial passage reads "I removed my Shekhina from their midst." Cf. Jellinek, *Beth Hamidrash* II. 114.

73. *Exodus* 24:10.

74. Midrash Hagadol Exodus 555; cf. B. Qiddushin 49a, and Tosafot *ibid*. beginning with "Ham'targem"; *Arukh*, s.v. Tirgem.

75. *Psalms* 103:13.

76. *Isaiah* 66:13.

77. Pesiqta Rab. 139a.

78. See above, pp. 73–74.

79. Lam. Rab. Introduction, 25.

80. Lam Rab. Introduction, 24.

81. Pesiqta diR. Kahana, ed. Mandelbaum, p. 4.

82. Aboth diR. Nathan, ed. Schechter, p. 102, and see parallel sources in the notes.

83. B. Baba Bathra 17a; cf. Cant. Rab. *ad* 1.2 (5)

84. Deut. Rab. 11.10 end.

85. B. Sota 13b; Sifre Deut. 355.

86. Cf. below, chapter VI. "Matronit."

87. Albright, *Archaeology and the Religion of Israel*, p. 85.

88. Plural: *Genesis* 18:2,4,5,8,9,16,22; singular: *Genesis* 18:1,3,10,13,14,17–21,23–33.

89. *Genesis* 19:1ff., 13. Cf. on this entire problem Aubrey R. Johnson, *The One and the Many in the Israelite Conception of God*, Cardiff, 1942. Johnson shows that the same vacillation between singular and plural is found also in other ancient Near Eastern religions, pp. 28–31.

90. Cf. above, p. 74.

Chapter V. THE KABBALISTIC TETRAD

1. Cf. G. Scholem, *Major Trends in Jewish Mysticism,*
New York, 1961, pp. 20ff.

2. *Op. cit.*, p. 229.

3. *Zohar* III. 290b. My translation in the text above
is free. It renders the sense of the passage instead of
trying to give a literal translation which would be clumsy
and difficult in English. The same procedure was followed in the rendering of most passages quoted from
Kabbalistic literature.

4. *Zohar* III. 290a.

5. *Zohar* III. 65b.

6. Cf. Scholem, *op. cit.*, pp. 211ff.; I. Tishby, *Mishnat
Hazohar*, Jerusalem, 1957, I. pp. 98ff.; Zvi Werblowsky,
Joseph Karo—Lawyer and Mystic, Oxford University
Press, 1962, pp. 206ff.

7. Cf. Rudolf Anthes, "Mythology in Ancient Egypt,"
in Samuel Noah Kramer (ed.), *Mythologies of the Ancient World*, New York: Doubleday Anchor Books, 1961,
pp. 36–37.

8. Samuel Noah Kramer, *The Sumerians: Their History, Culture and Character*, The University of Chicago
Press, 1963, p. 115.

9. *Op. cit.*, p. 118.

10. *Op. cit.*, p. 122.

11. *Loc. cit.*

12. *Op. cit.*, p. 175.

13. *Op. cit.*, p. 182.

14. *Op. cit.*, p. 258.

15. Cf. Anthes, *op. cit.*, p. 36.

16. ANET, p. 120.

17. Cf. Hans G. Guterbock, "Hittite Mythology," in
Kramer, *Mythologies of the Ancient World*, p. 155.

18. Cf. Cyrus H. Gordon, "Canaanite Mythology," in
Kramer *op. cit.*, pp. 183–217; Cf. above, chapters I and
II.

19. Cf. Roscher, *Ausführliches Lexikon der griechischen und römischen Mythologie*, s.v. Juno; H.J. Rose,
A Handbook of Greek Mythology, London, 1933, pp.
102,324.

20. Cf. M.J. Dresden "Mythology of Ancient Iran," in Kramer *op. cit.*, pp. 355–56.

21. Cf. W. Norman Brown, "Mythology of India," in Kramer *op. cit.*, pp. 305–06, 309,311–12.

22. E. Dale Saunders, "Japanese Mythology," in Kramer, *op. cit.*, 417–21.

23. Cf. Raphael Patai, *Man and Earth in Hebrew Custom, Belief and Legend,* Jerusalem, 1942, I. 134ff.

24. *Zohar* III. 290b.

25. E.g., in ancient Egyptian, Babylonian, Greek and Hindu mythologies; in Icelandic, Polynesian, Micronesian, Indonesian, Maori, North and South American Indian, African, Mongolian, Siberian, etc. mythologies. Cf. Stith Thompson, *Motif-Index of Folk-Literature*, rev. ed., Bloomington, Indiana, vol. I, 1955, p. 128: A625. World Parents: sky-father and earth-mother as parents of the universe. The sky-father descends upon the earth-mother and begets the world. A625.1. Heaven-mother—earth-father. A625.2. Raising of the sky. Originally the sky is near the earth (usually because of the conjunction of the sky-father and earth-mother). It is raised to its present place. Cf. also Patai, *Man and Earth*, I. 112ff.

26. *Zohar* I. 162a–b, explaining the secret meaning of *Psalm* 37:25.

28. *Zohar* III. 77b–78a.

29. Cf. Scholem, *op. cit.*, pp. 173–194,185.

30. The *Merkaboth* (sing., *Merkaba*) are the divine chariots which, based on *Ezekiel* 1 and 10, have become the mystical symbol of God in the early Kabbalistic doctrine.

31. "Androginos" is the term used by the author in his Aramaic text.

32. Joseph ben Abraham Gikatilla, *Sha'are Orah*, Offenbach, 1715, pp. 61b-62a.

33. Cf., for instance, Gen. Rab. p. 55; cf. Robert Graves and Raphael Patai, *Hebrew Myths*, New York, 1964, 10.1.

34. *Zohar* III. 296a.

35. *Pardes Rimmonim*, VIII. 17.

36. Cf. Gen. Rab. p. 55; Cf. Graves-Patai, *Hebrew Myths*, 10.1.

37. Cf. *Genesis* 1:26–27. A hermaphroditic creator god

figures also in ancient Greek, Egyptian, Hindu and Aztec mythologies, cf. Stith-Thompson, *Motif-Index*, A 12.

38. *Zohar* III. 77b.

39. *Zohar* I. 30b–31a.

40. *Zohar* I. 156b, Sitre Torah.

40a. Cf. Stith Thompson, *Motif-Index*, Index, s.v. Jealousy.

41. Shir Hashirim Rabba 3.11; cf. also Sepher Habahir §43, and Scholem, *Ursprung and Anfänge der Kabbala*, Berlin, 1962, p. 149.

42. *Zohar* III. 17a.

43. *Zohar* III. 88b.

44. Cf. Scholem, *Major Trends*, pp. 56,362,363.

45. The last two names are frequent in the book Bahir, the 12th-century Kabbalistic treatise, cf. Scholem, *Das Buch Bahir*, Leipzig, 1923, 49,52,61,65,131.

45a. Cf. G. Scholem, *Von der mystichen Gestalt der Gottheit*, p. 171 and p. 177 where he quotes Joseph Gikatilla, *Sha'are Orah*.

46. Tiqqune Hazohar, tiqqun 34, p. 77; quoted after Tishby, *Mishnat Hazohar*, II. 623.

47. Cf. above, p. 133.

48. *Zohar* III. 5a, 69a.

49. *Proverbs* 28:24.

50. *Zohar* III. 44b.

51. *Zohar* III. 7a.

52. Cf. Scholem, *Major Trends*, pp. 115, 229 and 403, note 75.

53. Cf. Scholem, *op. cit.*, p. 139.

54. Cf. Graves-Patai, *Hebrew Myths*, chapters 1–21.

Chapter VI. MATRONIT—THE GODDESS OF THE KABBALA

1. ANET, pp. 41,44,54,55,56,57,159,178,309; Samuel Noah Kramer, *The Sumerians*, Univ. of Chicago Press, 1963, pp. 122,140–141,153,161–62,197,205–06,262.

2. Stephen H. Langdon, *Semitic (The Mythology of All Races,* Vol. V), Boston, 1931, pp. 25–28,94,97; id., *Babylonian Liturgies*, Paris, 1913, pp. 43,95; ANET, 83,84,94,

108, 111, 113, 118, 119, 123, 205, 250, 294, 298, 299, 383, 427, 449, 451.

3. Cf. Emil G. Kraeling, *Bible Atlas*, New York: Rand McNally, 1956, p. 305 and maps iii and xi; Herodotus i. 131; Roscher, *Ausführl. Lexikon d. Griech. Myth.*, s.v. Anaitis; Strabo xi. 532c; *Enc. of Rel. and Ethics*, s.v. Anahita; G. Widengren, *Numen* I (1954), p. 72, and II (1955), pp. 92, 122–23. That Anahita was considered a daughter of Ormuzd is stated by the 4th-century A.D. Armenian historian Agathangelus, cf. Fr. Windischmann, "Die persische Anahita oder Anaitis," *Abhandl. d. philosoph.-philolog. Classe d. könig. Bayer. Akad. d. Wiss.*, München, vol. 8. (1858), pp. 85–128.

4. *Numbers* 19:2.

5. *Zohar* iii. 180b, Raaya Mehemna.

6. *Zohar* iii. 89b–90a, Raaya Mehemna.

7. *Zohar* iii. 267a, Raaya Mehemna.

8. *Zohar* iii. 189a.

9. Gordon, in Kramer (ed.), *Mythologies of the Ancient World*, 204.

10. *Zohar* i. 21b–22a.

11. *Zohar* i. 21b–22a.

12. B. Sota 13b; Sifre Deut. 355.

13. *Zohar* i. 49a, iii. 74b.

14. *Zohar* i. 30b–31a.

15. Tiqqune Hazohar, Tiqqun 34, p. 77; quoted after Tishby, *Mishnat Hazohar*, ii. 623.

16. *Zohar Hadash*, Midrash Haneelam to Ekhah, Warsaw, n.d., p. 183.

17. *Ibid*.

18. *Zohar* iii. 296a.

19. *Zohar*, ii. 89a–b.

20. *Zohar* i. 12b.

21. *Zohar* ii. 219b; i. 64a.

22. *Leviticus* 16:8–10.

23. *Zohar* iii. 79a; i. 64a.

23a. I.e., the sign of the Covenant, the circumcision. In this case the divine phallus, as above in the passage just quoted from the Zohar, I:12b.

23b. That is, his semen, which above was termed "river."

23c. In the letter *he* (ה), the left "leg" is not attached to the top horizontal part, the "beam," which stands for the body; whereas in the *het* (**ח**) it is attached to it. Note that here the imagery has changed: now the "leg" has become the son of the Matronit.

23d. Below (p. 173) we shall meet again with Metatron, chief of all angels, represented as the son of the Matronit who issues from betwixt her legs.

23e. Excerpts from folios 38b–40a of the manuscript *Sefer Tashaq* by R. Joseph, a xerox copy of which has been kindly put at my disposal by Prof. Jeremy Zwelling of Wesleyan University, Middletown, Connecticut, who is preparing a critical edition of the book, based on several extant manuscripts. My translation is from the Hebrew original.

24. *Zohar* iii. 42a–b.

25. *Zohar* i. 210a–b.

26. *Zohar* iii. 17a–b, 74b.

27. *Zohar* iii. 69a.

28. *Ibid.*

29. *Zohar* i. 84b.

30. *Zohar* i. 49b–50a, 66b; Moses Cordovero (1522–1570), *Pardes Rimmonim*, Gate 16, section 6.

30a. Jacob ben Hayyim Tzemah, *Sefer Nagid uM'tzave*, Amsterdam, 1712, pp. 5b–6a.

31. See above, chapter V, "The Kabbalistic Tetrad."

32. *Zohar* i. 84b, iii. 17a–b, 186b.

33. *Exodus* 15:3; *Isaiah* 51:9; *Psalm* 89:11; *Isaiah* 63:1–6.

34. B. Baba Bathra 17a; B. Sota 13b; Sifre Deut. §355; cf. Deut. Rabba, 11:10 end; Cant. Rab. 1 and 3.

35. *Zohar* ii. 29a.

36. *Zohar* ii. 50b.

37. *Zohar* ii. 51a–b.

37a. *Sefer Hekhalot*, included in Jellinek, *Bet haMidrasch*, 5:183–84.

38. *Zohar* iii. 75a–b.

39. An allusion to the "Behemoth on the Thousand Mountains" was found by the authors of the Midrash in *Psalm* 50:10 where God says: "For every beast of the forest is Mine, and the cattle (in Hebrew: Behemoth) upon a thousand hills." Cf. Midrash Konen 25; Pesiqta Rabbati 80b–81a; Leviticus Rabba 13.3; 22.10; Numeri Rabba 21.18; Pirqe diRabbi Eliezer, ch. 11; and see also Graves-Patai, *Hebrew Myths*, 6. n, o, and p.

40. The chief passages are *Zohar* I. 223a–b, and III. 60. *Proverbs* 5:5 is quoted in *Zohar* I. 35b, 221b, and II. 48b. Cf. G. Scholem's excellent analysis of these passages in his *Von der mystischen Gestalt der Gottheit*, Zürich: Rhein-Verlag, 1962, p. 186.

40a. Cf. Raphael Patai, *The Jewish Mind*, New York: Scribner's, 1977, pp. 134–50, and especially p. 144, quoting G. Scholem, *On the Kabbalah and Its Symbolism* (New York: Schocken, 1965, p. 107).

40b. Marvin H. Pope, *Song of Songs: A New Translation with Introduction and Commentary* (Anchor Bible series), Garden City, N.Y.: Doubleday, 1977, p. 167.

40c. *Ibid.*, pp. 317–18; cf. also pp. 191–92.

40d. Patai, *op. cit.*, pp. 147–48.

41. Cf. *Encyclopaedia Britannica*, 11th ed., s.v. Mary.

42. Cf. Evagrius, *Ecclesiastical History*, iv. 24.

43. *Enc. Brit., ibid.*

44. Hastings (ed.), *Dictionary of the Bible*, s.v. Mary, p. 292.

45. *Real-Encyclopedie für Protestantische Theologie und Kirche*, vol. 12, p. 319, s.v. Maria.

45a. Pope, *op. cit.*, pp. 170–71.

46. Hastings, *Dict.* pp. 290,292; *Real Enc.* pp. 316–17.

47. *Enc. Brit., ibid.*; *Real Enc.*, p. 316.

48. *Real Enc., ibid.*; *Die Religion in Geschichte und Gegenwart*, 3rd ed., s.v. Marienverehrung, vol. 4, p. 764 (Tübingen, 1960).

49. Cf. above, p. 55.

50. *Real Encl.* p. 315.

51. Moses Cordovero, *Pardes Rimmonim*, Sha'ar 'Erkhe haKinuyim, Koretz, 1780, ch. 3, p. 120c.

Chapter VII. LILITH

1. Thorkild Jacobsen, *The Sumerian King List*, Chicago, 1939, p. 18, n. 37, and p. 90, n. 131.

2. Bruno Meissner, *Babylonien und Assyrien*, Heidelberg, 1925, ii. 201.

3. Ebeling, *Reallexikon der Assyriology*, ii. 110.

4. Samuel N. Kramer, *Gilgamesh and the Huluppu-*

Tree, Chicago, 1939, pp. 1–2. The same story was told in the missing part of Tablet xii of the Babylonia Gilgamesh epic dating from the 7th century B.C.; cf. Alexander Heidel, *The Gilgamesh-Epic and Old Testament Parallels*, Chicago, 1946, p. 94.

5. Emil G. Kraeling, *Bulletin of the American Schools of Oriental Research* 67 (Oct. 1937), pp. 16–18.

6. Cf. William F. Albright, *Bull. of the Amer. Schools of Oriental Research*, No. 76 (December, 1939), p. 9.

7. *Isaiah* 34:14.

8. B. Nidda 24b.

9. B. Erubin 100b.

10. Rashi to B. Sanhedrin 109a.

11. These names, as shown by Moses Gaster, *Studies and Texts*, pp. 1252ff., are derived from Byzantine magic names such as Sisynios, Synithoros, and the like; cf. also H.A. Winkler, *Salomo und die Karina*, Stuttgart, 1931.

12. Alpha Beta diBen Sira, ed. Eisenstein, *Otzar Midrashim*, p. 47; cf. M. Gaster, MGWJ 29 (1880), 553ff.; Num. Rab. 16.25; *Zohar* I. 34b.

13. B. Erubin 18b; Gen. Rab. 20.11, pp. 195–96; 24.6, p. 236; Tanhuma Genesis Buber 20; etc.

14. B. Shabbath 151a.

15. James A. Montgomery, *Aramaic Incantation Texts from Nippur*, Philadelphia, 1913, pp. 77–78, and cf. pp. 75–76 which are paraphrased or summarized above.

16. Montgomery, *op. cit.*, pp. 155–56, bowl no. 8.

17. *Hosea* 2:5.

18. Jehuda L. Zlotnik, *Ma'ase Yerushalmi*, Jerusalem, 1946, p. 33.

19. *Op. cit.*, pp. 66–67.

20. Cf. G. Scholem, *Major Trends in Jewish Mysticism*, New York, 1961, pp. 40ff. In an Arabic incantation text against the Qarina (the Muslim equivalent of Lilith), King Solomon is said to have called his vezir and cousin Asaf ibn Barakhia, in whose name we recognize Joshua ben Perahia, and commanded him to write an amulet to ward off the demoness and all her helpers, cf. H.A. Winkler, *Salomo und die Karina*, Stuttgart, 1931, p. 18.

21. Gottheil, whose transcript was published by Montgomery, reads, *Yahweh Qadmonah Hayin Lilith*. It seems to me, however, that these words should be read *whawah*

qadmonah hutz Lilith, giving the famous Jewish magical incantation formula as translated above.

22. Montgomery misunderstood this name. In later Jewish magic it has become a commonplace to arrange a formal sale of a child whose life was threatened by an evil spirit and to call him Mercado, i.e., The Sold One, if a boy, and Mercada, if a girl.

23. Montgomery, *op. cit.*, pp. 258ff. My translation. A very similar incantation is reprinted in as recent a popular remedy-book as Raphael Ohana's *Mar'eh ha-Yeladim,* Jerusalem, 1908, p. 61b.

24. Cf. Montgomery, *op. cit.* pp. 252–53.

25. Cf. Cyrus H. Gordon, "Two Magic Bowls in Teheran," *Orientalia,* vol. 20, Rome, 1951, pp. 306–15.

26. Cf. Gordon, *op. cit.* pp. 306–07, whose translation was followed above, with a few slight changes.

27. Cf. Gordon, *op. cit.,* pp. 309–10. Lilith appears on numerous other bowls as well, Cf. Gordon, *Orientalia* 10 (1941), pp. 120–21, 279, 289 (where "male and female Liliths" are mentioned), 339, 340 ("Lilin," masculine plural), 347 ("Liliths"), 348 ("male and female Liliths"), 351 ("I adjure thee, O Lilith Hablas, granddaughter of Lilith Zarnay"), 353 ("bewitching female Liliths"), 354, 356.

28. *Genesis* 1:20–21.

29. *Zohar* i. 34b.

30. Yalqut Reubeni to *Genesis* 2:21, p. 68.

31. *Zohar* iii. 19a.

32. *Zohar* i. 148a, Sitre Torah.

33. Gershom Scholem, "Kabbaloth R. Ya'aqobh weR. Yitzhaq," *Madda'e haYahaduth* vol. II, Jerusalem, 1927, pp. 251, 260.

34. *Genesis* 1:3.

35. *Zohar* i. 19b, with I. Tishby's comments in his *Mishnat Hazohar* i. 372.

36. B. Sukka 5b.

37. *Zohar* i. 19b.

38. *Zohar* i. 34b.

39. *Zohar* i. 19b.

40. Cf. above p. 190, where "Lilith Buznai" is mentioned.

41. Midrash Abkir; *Zohar* iii. 76b; Yalqut Reubeni to *Genesis* 4:8, p. 95.

42. Naphtali Herz ben Jacob Elhanan, *Emeq Hamelekh,* Amsterdam, 1648, 179d–180a.

43. Cf. Bahya ben Asher ibn Halawa (d.1340), *Commentary to the Pentateuch* (in Hebrew); Venice, 1546, 15d; Manasseh ben Israel (1604–1667), *Nishmat Hayyim,* Amsterdam, 1652, 114b, ch. 12 of the Third Maamar; *Emeq Hamelekh,* 23c–d, chapter 42.

44. *Zohar* i. 19b.

45. *Emeq Hamelekh,* p. 103a; cf. the Yiddish book *Hanhagat Hassidim we'Anshe Ma'asse,* Frankfurt a.M., 1700, pp. 16a–17a.

46. *Zohar* i. 148a–b, Sitre Torah.

47. *Zohar* i. 148b, Sitre Torah.

48. *Emeq Hamelekh,* Sha'ar Tiqqune Hateshuvah, ch. 11, p. 19c. The mythical references in this incantation are clear enough. The statement that Lilith is wrapped in velvet may refer to the scarlet dress which, as we just saw, Lilith was believed to wear when trying to seduce men. The admonition that she should return to the raging sea whose waves call her, refers to the well-known myth according to which Lilith's permanent abode is in the waves of the Red Sea.

49. *Emeq Hamelekh* 84b.

50. Cf. G. Scholem, *Tarbiz,* vol. 19 (1948), p. 175.

50a. Solomon Navarro, "The Story of R. Joseph della Reina," in *Sefer Liqute Shas of Isaac Luria,* Livorno, 1790, pp. 58b–59a.

51. *Zohar* i. 19b. The turn of the flame is reminiscent of the turning of the Cherubim themselves: according to the Talmudic view (B. Baba Bathra 99a) when the Cherubim turned their faces toward each other, this showed that Israel obeyed the will of God; when Israel sinned the Cherubim turned their faces away from each other. The smile of Lilith is reflected in the smile that one can observe on the faces of sleeping children. Therefore, according to Jewish folk-belief, one should wake such a child, whereupon Lilith will flee.

52. *Zohar* iii. 19a.

53. *Zohar* iii. 77a.

54. *Zohar* iii. 77a.

55. *Meqore Minhagim,* 91f., and Raphael Ohana, *Mar'eh haYeladim,* Jerusalem, 1908, p. 52a.

56. Ohana, *loc. cit.,* quoting Liqqute Gure ha'Ari; cf.

also *Sepher Zekhirah* 53b; Grunwald, *Mitteil. zur jüd. Volkskunde*, viii, 62; similar beliefs and practices among other peoples, cf. Wuttke, *Der deut. Volksaberglaube*, 386; Ploss, *Das Kind*, ii. 851; Nyberg, *Kind und Erde*, 222; Graves-Patai, *Hebrew Myths* 10.4.

57. Ohana, *op. cit.*, 94a.

58. *Op. cit.*, 25a.

59. *Op. cit.*, 94a–b.

60. Cf. *Genesis* 4:19, 22.

61. Gen. Rab. 23.3, p. 224, and parallel sources.

62. *Pirqe R. Eliezer*, according to reading of Nahmanides on *Gen.* 4:2; cf. *Mid. Hagadol* i. 118; *Zohar* i. 55a; *Zohar* Ruth 99a, beginning with the words "R. Nehemia patah"; *Agadat Bereshit* (introd.) 38; Louis Ginzberg, *Legends of the Jews*, I. 150; V. 171: Menahem Zioni b. Meir of Speyer (15th century). *Sepher Zioni*, Cremona, 1560, p. 14b.

63. *Zohar* i. 56a; cf. 19b.

64. *Zohar* iii. 76b.

65. *Zohar* i. 9b.

66. *Zohar* iii. 76b–77a.

67. G. Scholem, *Tarbitz* vol. 19 (1948) p. 172; cf. also Mid. Tehillim 72, Buber, p. 324; *Yalqut Reubeni* to *Genesis* 4:8, p. 95, quoting Sepher Miskhan ha'Eduth. The reference to Hadad the Edomite is found in 1 *Kings* 11:14,17.

68. Targum Sheni to *Esther* 1:3.

69. Cf. Scholem, *Tarbitz*, vol. 19 (1948) p. 169.

70. Cf. Targum to *Job* 1:15.

71. Cf. above, p. 193.

72. Bahya on *Genesis*, Venice, 1546, 15d; cf. also Isaac Caro, *Toldoth Yitzhak* (Mantua, 1558), to *Genesis* 16a; *Yalqut Reubeni* Reubeni Gadol, Wilmersdorf, 1681, 53c (Parashat Toldoth); Aharon Shemuel, *Nishmat Hayyim*, Hanau, 1617, 114b (Ma'amar Gimel, ch. 12).

73. Nathan Spira, *Tubh HaAretz*, Venice, 1655, p. 19c.

74. *Psalm* 91:10; Ohana, *Mar'eh HaYeladim* 10a–b, quoting Mahari Taitazak.

75. *Isaiah* 27:1.

76. Moses Cordovero, *Pardes Rimmonim*, Cracow, 1591, Gate 25, ch. 5, p. 186d.

77. *Emeq Hamelekh*, p. 84b, cf. p. 140b.

78. Cf. e.g. *Emeq Hamelekh*, 140b, and Bezalel ben

Solomon of Kobrin, *'Amudeha Shiv'ah*, Dusseldorf, 1693, pp. 51c–d.

79. *Isaiah* 27:1.

80. *Emeq Hamelekh*, pp. 84c, 103a, 121b, 130a; *Zohar* ii, 108b.

81. *Op. cit.*, p. 84a; G. Scholem, *Tarbitz*, vol. 19 (1948), p. 173.

82. Cf. *Genesis* 36:39.

83. *Jeremiah* 1:14.

84. Cf. G. *Tarbitz*, vol. 5, p. 194.

85. Cf. Scholem, "Kabbaloth R. Ya'aqobh weR. Yitzhaq." *Madda'e haYahaduth*, vol. II, Jerusalem, 1927, pp. 251, 255, 258, 260–61. This jealousy in the family of evil divinities mirrors the jealousy the Mother Goddess feels when she sees the boundless love the Father God feels for their daughter the Matronit, cf. above, p. 141.

86. Cf. *Genesis* 28:9.

87. Moses Cordovero, *Pardes Rimmonim*, Cracow, 1591, Gate 25, ch. 5, p. 186d; Gate 26, ch. 8, p. 188d.

88. Abraham Galante, *Sepher Qol Bokhim*, Venice, 1589, p. 15, to *Lamentations* 1:5.

89. Cf. above, p. 189.

90. *Emeq Hamelekh*, 140b.

91. *Genesis* 3:34.

92. Hayyim Vital *Sepher 'Etz Hayyim*, Koretz, 1784, p. 129d.

93. *Cant.* 3:8.

94. *Zohar* ii. 163b.

95. Cf. above, p. 190.

96. *Zohar Hadash* Tiqqunim, Warsaw: Levin-Epstein, no date, p. 117a top.

97. *Zohar* i. 27b.

98. *Proverbs* 30:23.

99. *Zohar* iii. 69a.

100. Shlomo Alqabetz, *B'rith haLevi*, ch. 7, cf. ch. 6.

101. G. Scholem, *Tarbitz*, vol. 5, pp. 50,194–95; I. Tishby, *Mishnat HaZohar*, i. 299.

102. *Zechariah* 9:9.

103. *Zohar* iii. 69a.

104. *Emeq Hamelekh*, p. 84d.

Chapter VIII. THE SABBATH—VIRGIN, BRIDE, QUEEN, AND GODDESS

1. *Isaiah* 58:13–14.

2. *Genesis* 2:2–3; *Exodus* 20:8–11; *Deuteronomy* 5:12–15.

3. Cf. *Jubilees* 50:8.

4. Cf. A.Z. Aescoli, *Sepher HaFalashim*, Jerusalem, 1943, p. 37; Wolf Leslau, *Falasha Anthology*, New Haven, 1951, p. 19.

5. B. Ketubot 62b; B. Baba Kamma 88a; cf. Yer. Megilla 75a mid.

6. B. Ketubot 62b. For the Talmudic belief in the power of the word, cf. R. Patai, *Man and Temple in Ancient Jewish Myth and Ritual*, pp. 185ff.

7. Cf. Stobaeus, *Ecl.*, i. 1.10.

8. Philo, *Leg. Alleg.* i. 15 (Loeb Class. Libr. i. p. 155).

9. Philo, *De Opif. Mundi* 100 (Loeb i. p. 79).

10. Philo, *De Spec. Leg.* ii. 56–58 (Loeb vii. pp. 343, 345).

11. Philo, *Vit. Mos.* ii. 210 (Loeb vi. p. 553).

12. Cf. the tractate *Shabbat* of the Mishna, the Babylonian Talmud and the Palestinian Talmud.

13. B. Shabbat 119a.

14. *Loc. cit.*

15. *Loc. cit.*

16. *Loc. cit.*

17. B. Shabbat 119b.

18. *Exodus* 20:8; Gen. Rab. 11:8, pp. 95–96; cf. Pesiqta Rabbati 117b.

19. The latter is remarkable in view of the fact that the Hebrew noun *Shabbat* has the masculine form and gender.

20. Leslau, *Falasha Anthology*, *op. cit.* p. 3.

21. *Op. cit.* pp. xli–xlii.

22. *Op. cit.* pp. 9,10.

23. *Exodus* 31:13.

24. Cf. *Job* 25:4–5.

25. Cf. B. Sanhedrin 65b; Pesiqta Rabbati 23, p. 120a; *Zohar* iii. 288b.

26. Cf. Graves-Patai, *Hebrew Myths*, ch. 25.

27. Cf. *Isaiah* 58:13–14.

28. Cf. B. Shabbat 118b.

29. Leslau, *op. cit.*, pp. 16,17,18,19,21,23–24,30–32, 36,37–38.

30. *Op. cit.*, pp. 42,45. A comparison between the Falasha Sabbath and the Mandaean Sunday, also personified and in many ways paralleling the former, was made by L. Troje, "Sanbat," in Richard Reitzenstein, *Die Vorgeschichte der Christlichen Taufe*, Leipzig and Berlin: Teubner, 1929, pp. 328–77. He also pointed out (p. 347) that the expression "Sabbath of God," found in the *Teezaza Sanbat*, goes back to Philo of Alexandria, *De Cherub.* 87. In that passage (Loeb Class. Libr. ed. p. 61) Philo says that "Moses often in his laws calls the Sabbath, which means 'rest,' God's Sabbath." In fact, in most of the pertinent passages, the Hebrew expression is "the seventh day is a Sabbath *unto* the Lord" (*Exodus* 20:10; 31:15; 35:2; *Leviticus* 23:3). However, in *Exodus* 31:13 and *Leviticus* 19:3 the expression "my Sabbaths" occurs, put in the mouth of God. Thus Troje's conclusion that the expression "God's Sabbath" was coined by Philo, is only partly correct.

31. *Op. cit.*, p. 143, note 9.

32. *Op. cit.*, p. 147, note 95.

33. Cf. I.L. Baruch (ed.), *Sepher HaShabbat*, Tel Aviv, 1936, pp. 333–35.

34. Cf. e.g. *Seder Avodath Yisrael*, Rödelheim, 1868, p. 200.

35. *Exodus* 20:8.

36. *Deuteronomy* 5:12.

37. *Exodus* 31:16.

38. *Exodus* 20:8.

39. *Zohar* ii. 138a; cf. J. Tishby, *Mishnat HaZohar* ii. 487–8,491.

40. *Zohar* ii. 63b.

41. *Zohar* iii. 272b.

41a. Pope, *op. cit.*, p. 175.

42. The Hebrew word *"qiddashta"* which appears in the Sabbath benediction, means both "you sanctified" and "you betrothed."

43. David ben Joseph Abudarham, *Sepher Abudarham,*
Prague, 1784, p. 45a.

44. This line alludes to the midrash according to which
the Sabbath existed in God's thought even before the
creation of the world, although, coming as it did after
the six days of creation, it was the end and completion
of the Creator's work.

45. The son of Yishai (Jesse) the Bethlehemite was,
of course, David; but the poet alludes to a more distant
son, or descendant, of Yishai, namely, the Messiah whose
early coming was a very real expectation among the
Safed Kabbalists.

46. Another allusion to the Messiah. David was a
descendant of Perez (or Pharez).

47. This is based on B. Taanith 29b. The concept of
the Shekhina as the Sacred Apple Orchard is closely
paralleled by the Catholic view of Mary as the Olive
Tree, expressed, e.g. by St. Alfonso Maria di Liguori
(1696–1787) as follows: ". . . Mary was called the olive
tree, like a fair olive tree in the plains (*Eccles.* 24:19),
for as the olive tree produces nothing but oil, the symbol
of mercy, thus from the hands of Mary nothing but
graces and mercies proceed." See Barry Ulanov (ed.),
The Way of St. Alphonsus Liguori, New York, 1960,
p. 87. This book carries the "Imprimatur" and "Nihil
obstat" of the archdiocese of New York.

47a. Pope, *op. cit.,* p. 175.

47b. Cf. e.g., Hayyim Vital (1542–1620), *Sefer ha-
Gilgulim* (Book of Transmigrations), Przemyshla, 1875,
pp. 15a–b.

48. Cf. G. Scholem, *Eranos Jahrbuch,* vol. 19 (1950),
pp. 154ff.

49. This poem is printed in the prayer books following
the Lurianic tradition, e.g. *Siddur Torah Or weSha'ar
haKolel,* Wilna 1896, pp. 55a–56a.

50. I.e., the Sabbath, who is identified with the Shekhina and is God's bride.

51. This is a daring simile: *Yesod* ("Foundation"),
one of the ten Sephirot, corresponds to the penis in the
human body. It is said to be "hers," because it is through
it that God unites with his bride, the Sabbath-Shekhina.

52. The Aramaic original has *katish* which means not

only "presses" as translated above, but also "penetrates" or "deflowers," as in Yer. Qiddushin 59a top.

53. *Siddur Torah Or,* Wilna, 1896, p. 56a.

54. M. Ketubot 5:6.

55. *Exodus* 21:10; cf. R. Patai, *Sex and Family in the Bible and the Middle East,* New York, 1959, pp. 43ff., 158ff.

56. Joseph Caro, *Shulhan 'Arukh,* Orah Hayyim §240.

57. Cf. Magen Abraham, a commentary printed in the standard editions of the *Shulhan 'Arukh,* Orah Hayyim, to §240.

58. *Isaiah* 56:4-5.

59. *Zohar* ii. 89a. The above interpretation largely follows that of I. Tishby, *Mishnat haZohar,* Jerusalem, 1961, ii. 537-38.

60. Hayyim Vital, *'Etz Hayyim* Sh'ar haKelalim, 12-13; and other passages quoted by S. W. Horodetzky *HaMistorin beYisrael;* Tel Aviv, 1961, iii. 98; cf. also Shabbetai of Rashkow, *Seder Tefilla mikol haShana,* Koretz, 1794, pp. 157b-258b. The rest of the day is also devoted to communion with the world of the divine. In the *Kiddush,* or Sanctification, of the second Sabbath meal, taken in the morning of the Sabbath, after returning from the Morning and Mussaf prayers in the synagogue, the Holy King, the Holy Ancient One, the Holy Apple Orchard (i.e. the Sabbath-Shekhina), and the Small Face are invited to participate in the meal (*Siddur Torah Or,* Wilna, 1896, p. 78b, 82a). The same invitation, in a somewhat different wording, is extended again for the third meal, taken on the afternoon of the Sabbath following the return from Minha prayer in the synagogue. According to another view, the first meal was given in honor of the "Female of the Small Face," i.e., the Shekhina; the second, in honor of the "Holy Ancient One," and the third, in honor of the "Small Face" (cf. Isaiah Halevi Horowitz (ca. 1565–1630), *Sh'ne Luhot HaB'rit,* Amsterdam edition, reprinted in New York, 1946, i. 139b).

The third meal was usually lingered over until the time came to return to the synagogue for the evening prayer. At this prayer it was customary to protract the singing of the word *Barkhu* ("Bless you") as long as one's breath allowed, because the completion of this word signified the precise moment at which the Queen Sabbath departed, and this they would try to postpone as long as possible (cf. Isaac of Vienna (12th–13th centuries), *Or Zaru'a;* Jacob Segal (15th c.), *Minhage Maharil,* as quoted in Baruch (ed.), *Sepher Hashabbat,* pp. 59, 65).

Although with the appearance of three stars on the darkening sky the Sabbath was definitely over, two more ceremonies remained which extended her felt presence far into the night. One was the *Havdalah* ("Separation"), performed by each family head in his home, in the presence of his wife and children. This consisted of lighting a bunch of elaborately woven wax candles, drinking a cup of wine, and smelling sweet herbs, all to the accompaniment of appropriate benedictions. The Polish Kabbalist Isaiah Halevi Horowitz quotes his own father to the effect that "One must sing the *Havdalah* to a good and beautiful melody in order to bid the Queen farewell in joy and in song. Also, for the same reason, it is our custom to perform the rite standing, although one could do it sitting down, because one must be standing up in order to accompany her. . . And one adds a part of the weekday to the holy day at the outgoing of the Sabbath in order to teach and to show that one is reluctant to let the Holy Guest go, and that it is difficult to part from him. Therefore one holds him back, and from most of the houses accompanies him with songs and paeans. . ." (*Sh'ne Luhot HaB'rit, op. cit.*).

It was the custom of the Hassidim of East Europe "to spend the time from sunset to the hour of the evening prayer (on the Sabbath afternoon) in songs and praises of great joy, and they used to dance and frolic in their great happiness in honor of the Queen Sabbath as she was leaving, in the same manner in which she was received. This resembled the musical entertainment of a bridegroom and bride. And this is what every wise man would do in his congregation to honor the Queen, and this is a wonderful charm (*segulla*) to reduce the disturbers of their souls and to assure themselves of a happy and joyous week. . ." (Baruch, *op. cit.*, p. 82).

Following the Havdalah, several traditional songs were sung, and then came the time for the last ceremony regarded as part of the Sabbath observances although the Sabbath itself had ended at nightfall. This was the festive

meal called *Seudat Melawe Malka* (Meal of Farewell
to the Queen"), which, like the three earlier Sabbath
meals went back to Talmudic tradition (cf. B. Shabbath 117b-118a, 119b) and was regarded by Joseph
Caro as a religious duty (*Shulhan 'Arukh,* Orah Hayyim,
§300, and the commentary of Sha'are Teshuva *ad loc.*).
Among the Hassidim, who regarded the time spent at this
meal and its attendant merriments as part of the Sabbath, the *Melawe Malka* was the occasion for much
gaiety, feasting, and dancing protracted far into the night.

CONCLUSION

1. Mother Earth and the city (Zion) as the mother of
the people are discussed in detail in Raphael Patai, *Man
and Earth in Hebrew Custom, Belief and Legend* (in
Hebrew). Vol. II. Jerusalem, 1943, pp. 65-120.
2. Cf. C.G. Jung, *Gesammelte Werke* Zurich-Stuttgart,
1958, vol. 16, pp. 263ff., "Die Conjunctio."
3. Cf. *Real Encyclopedie für protestantische Theologie
und Kirche,* s.v. Maria, vol. 12, pp. 316-17.
4. Cf. Hastings (ed.), *Dictionary of the Bible,* s.v.
Mary, p. 290.
5. *Leviticus* 18:5; *Numbers* 21:8-9.

APPENDIX

1. A. R. Bellinger, F.E. Brown, A. Perkins, and C.B. Welles (eds.), *The Excavations at Dura Europos Conducted by Yale University and the French Academy of Inscriptions and Letters, Final Report*, Vol. VIII, Pt. 1: *The Synagogue* by Carl H. Kraeling, with contributions by C.C. Torrey, C.B. Welles, and B. Geiger (New Haven, 1956).

2. Erwin R. Goodenough, *Jewish Symbols in the Greco-Roman Period*, Vols., IX,X,XI, *Symbolism in the Dura Synagogue* (New York, 1963–64).

3. *Op. cit.* IX. 202.

4. *Op cit.* IX. 202.

5. *Op. cit. pp.* 202–03.

6. *Op. cit.* p. 209.

7. *Op. cit.*, 202; cf. also Goodenough, "The Rabbis and Jewish Art in the Greco-Roman Period," *Hebrew Union College Annual* vol. XXXII, (1961), pp. 270–71.

8. Cf. above, pp. 156–57.

9. Cf. above, chaps. I and II.

10. Cf. Jacob Neusner, "Judaism at Dura Europos," *History of Religions*, vol. 4, No. 1 (Summer 1964), p. 101.

11. Cf. Mishna 'Avoda Zara 3.4; Bab. 'Avoda Zara 44b; cf. Yer. Shevi'it 38b-c.

12. Goodenough, *op. cit.* X. 76.

13. *Op. cit.* X. 138.

14. Cf. *History of Religions*. Vol. 4, No. 1 (Summer 1964), pp. 85–91.

15. Cf. Goodenough, *op. cit.*, X. 121; Neusner, *op. cit.*, p. 90.

16. Cf. above, pp. 114ff., 158ff.

17. Cf. *Zohar*, I. 21b-22a; cf. above, p. 161.

18. Cf. B. Sabbath 87a; cf. B. Pesahim 87b; Deut. Rab. 11.10 end; cf. above, p. 117f.

19. B. Sota 13b; Sifre Deut. 355; cf. above, p. 117.

20. B. Sota 12b; Cf. Ex. Rab. 1.23.

21. B. Sota 12b; Cf. Exodus Rabba 1.22–1.23.

22. Cf. "The History of Moses our Master," in Jellinek, *Beth Hamidrash* ii. 2; *Sepher Hayashar* 242.

23. Exodus Rabba 1.25; Pirqe Rabbi Eliezer 48.

24. B. Sota 12b. cf. Ex. Rab. 1.22–25.

25. Pirqe Rabbi Eliezer 48.

26. Pirqe Rabbi Eliezer 48; Sepher Hayashar 241–42; "The History of Moses our Master," in Jellinek, *Beth Hamidrash* ii. 2.

27. Tanhuma Exodus 8.

28. Cf. above, p. 92.

29. Cf. above, pp. 92–93 and sources quoted there.

30. Septuagint to Job; Ginzberg, *Legends of the Jews* ii. 236–37; V. 389; Jack Finegan, *Light From the Ancient Past*. Princeton, 1959, p. 498.

31. Sifre Num. 78; B. Sota 11b; Exodus Rab. 1.15; cf. Ginzberg, *Legends of the Jews,* ii. 251, 253; v. 393.

32. Goodenough, *op. cit.* IX. 211, 214–17.

33. Cf. *Encyclopaedia Judaica,* Berlin, 1929, iii. 390–92; *Israel: Ancient Mosaics,* New York, UNESCO, 1960, p. 10 and plate VI.

34. *Exodus* 40:38.

35. Cf. R. Patai, *Man and Temple in Ancient Jewish Myth and Ritual,* Edinburgh, 1947 (new edition, New York, 1967), pp. 186; Robert Graves and R. Patai, *Hebrew Myths: The Book of Genesis,* New York, 1964, *passim.*

BIBLIOGRAPHY

In addition to the Hebrew Bible, the Apocrypha, the New Testament, the Talmuds, and Midrashic and Kabbalistic literature, the following works were consulted and quoted:

Abudarham, David ben Joseph, *Sepher Abudarham* (in Hebrew), Prague, 1784.

Aescoli, A. Z., *Sepher HaFalashim* (in Hebrew), Jerusalem, 1943.

Aharon Shemuel, *Nishmat Hayyim* (in Hebrew), Hanau, 1617.

Albright, William F., in *American Journal of Semitic Languages and Literatures,* Jan. 1925.

————, *Archaeology and the Religion of Israel,* Baltimore, 1942.

————, *The Archaeology of Palestine,* Pelican Books, 1949.

————, *The Archaeology of Palestine and the Bible,* New York, 1932.

————, in *Bulletin of the American Schools of Oriental Research,* 76 (Dec. 1939).

————, *The Excavations of Tell Beit Mirsim,* vol. III (Annual of the American Schools of Oriental Research), New Haven, 1943.

————, *From the Stone Age to Christianity,* Baltimore: John Hopkins Press, 1940.

————, in *Journal of the Palestine Oriental Society,* 1931, pp. 123–24.

Alqabetz, Sh'lomo, *B'rith HaLevi* (in Hebrew), Lemberg, 1863.

ANET. See Pritchard, James B., *Ancient Near Eastern Texts*.

Avi-Yonah, Mordecai, in *Sepher Yerushalayim* (in Hebrew), Jerusalem, 1956, vol. I.

Bahya ben Asher, *Biur 'al HaTorah* (in Hebrew: Commentary to the Pentateuch) Venice, 1546, and Amsterdam, 1726.

Baruch, Y. L. (ed.), *Sepher HaShabbat* (in Hebrew), Tel Aviv, 1948.

Bellinger, A. R., F. E. Brown, A. Perkins and C. B. Welles (eds.), *The Excavations at Dura Europos Conducted by Yale University and the French Academy of Inscriptions and Letters, Final Report*. Vol. VIII, Pt. 1: *The Synagogue* by Carl H. Kraeling, New Haven, 1956.

Bezalel ben Solomon of Kobrin, *'Amudeha Shiv'ah* (in Hebrew), Düsseldorf, 1693.

Büchler, Adolf, *Studies in Jewish History*, Oxford University Press, 1956.

Caro, Joseph, *Shulhan 'Arukh* (in Hebrew). Numerous editions.

Caro, Yitzhak, *Toldoth Yitzhaq* (in Hebrew), Mantua, 1558.

Cassuto, Umberto, *The Book of Exodus* (in Hebrew), Jerusalem, 1959.

Cordovero, Moses, *Pardes Rimmonim* (in Hebrew), Cracow, 1592, and Koretz, 1780.

Danelius, Eva, "Shamgar ben Anath," *Journal of Near Eastern Studies*, July, 1963.

de Vaux, Roland, *Ancient Israel: Its Life and Institutions*, New York, 1961.

Die Religion in Geschichte und Gegenwart, 3rd ed., Tübingen: Mohr, 1957–65.

Ebeling, Erich, and Meissner, Hugo, *Reallexikon der Assyriologie*, Berlin, 1929–34.

Eleazar ben Judah ben Kalonymos of Worms, *Sepher Raziel* (in Hebrew), Amsterdam, 1701.

Emeq haMelekh. See Naphtali Herz.

Enciqlopedia Miqrait (Biblical Encyclopaedia, in Hebrew), Jerusalem, 1955–

Encyclopaedia Britannica, 11th ed., New York, 1910–11.

Encyclopaedia Judaica, Berlin: Eschkol, 1928–34. 10 vols. (Aach-Lyra.)

Evagrius, Scholasticus, *Ecclesiastical History*, London: Methuen, 1898.

Finegan, Jack, *Light from the Ancient Past*, Princeton, 1959.

Galante, Abraham, *Sepher Qol Bokhim* (in Hebrew), Venice, 1589.

Gaster, Moses, "Beiträge zur vergleichenden Sagen und Märchenkunde," MGWJ, 29, 1880.

————, *Studies and Texts in Folklore, Magic*, etc., London: Maggs Bros. 1925–28. 3 vols.

Gaster, Theodor H., *Thespis*, New York: Doubleday Anchor Books, 1961.

Gikatilla, Joseph ben Abraham, *Sha'are Orah*, Offenbach, 1715.

Ginzberg, Louis, *The Legends of the Jews*, Philadelphia: Jewish Publ. Soc. of Amer., 1911–38. 7 vols.

Glueck, Nelson, *Deities and Dolphins*, New York, 1965.

Goodenough, Erwin R., *Jewish Symbols in the Greco-Roman Period*, vols. IX, X, XI, *Symbolism in the Dura Synagogue*, New York: Bollingen Foundation, 1963–64.

————, "The Rabbis and Jewish Art in the Greco-Roman Period," *Hebrew Union College Annual*, vol. 32, Cincinnati, Ohio, 1961.

Gordon, Cyrus H., "Aramaic Incantation Bowls," *Orientalia*, 10, Rome, 1941, pp. 116ff., 272ff., 329ff.

————, "Two Magic Bowls in Teheran," *Orientalia*, vol. 20, Rome, 1951, pp. 306–15.

Graham, W. Creighton, and Herbert G. May, *Culture and Conscience: An Archaeological Study of the New Religious Past in Ancient Palestine*. University of Chicago Press, 1936.

Graves, Robert, and Raphael Patai, *Hebrew Myths: The Book of Genesis*, New York, 1964.

Gray, John, *I and II Kings: A Commentary*, Philadelphia: Westminster Press, 1963.

————, *The Legacy of Canaan*, Leiden: Brill, 1957.

Gressmann, Hugo, *Altorientalische Bilder zum Alten Testament*, 2nd ed., Berlin-Leipzig, 1920.

————, *Die Lade Jahves*, Berlin-Stuttgart-Leipzig, 1920.

————, "Josia und das Deuteronomium," *Zeitschrift für die Alttestamentliche Wissenschaft*, 1924, pp. 313–37.

Grunwald, Max, in *Mitteilungen zur jüdischen Volkskunde*, vol. 8, Vienna, 1905.

Hadas, Moses (ed. and tr.), *Aristeas to Philocrates*, New York, 1951.

————— and Morton Smith, *Heroes and Gods*, New York, 1965.

Halévy, J., in *Revue des Etudes Juives*, vol. 12, Paris, 1886, pp. 112f.

Hanhagath Hassidim we'Anshe Ma'asse (in Yiddish), Frankfurt a.M., 1700.

Hastings, James (ed.), *Dictionary of the Bible*, New York, 1898–1902.

—————, (ed.), *Encyclopaedia of Religion and Ethics*, Edinburgh, 1908–26.

Heidel, Alexander, *The Gilgamesh-Epic and Old Testament Parallels*, Chicago, 1946.

Herodotus, Works of. Various editions.

Horowitz, Isaiah Halevi, *Sh'ne Luhot HaB'rit*, Amsterdam ed., reprinted in New York, 1946.

Horodetzky, S. W., *HaMistorin beYisrael* (in Hebrew), Tel Aviv, 1961.

Isaac ben Moses of Vienna, *Or Zaru'a* (in Hebrew), Zhitomir, 1862–90. 4 vols.

Israel: Ancient Mosaics (Preface: Meyer Shapiro; Introduction: Michael Avi-Yonah), New York, UNESCO, 1960.

Jacobsen, Thorkild, *The Sumerian King List*, Chicago, 1939.

Jellinek, Adolph, *Bet haMidrash*, 6 vols. (reprint), Jerusalem: Bamberger & Wahrmann, 1938.

Johnson, Aubrey R., *The One and the Many in the Israelite Conception of God*, Cardiff, 1942.

Josephus Flavius, Works of. Various editions.

Jung, C. G., *Gesammelte Werke*, Żurich-Stuttgart, 1958.

Karo, Isaac. See Caro, Yitzhaq.

Karo, Joseph. See Caro, Joseph.

Klausner, Joseph, *History of the Second Temple* (in Hebrew), Jerusalem, 1952.

Kraeling, Emil G., *Bible Atlas*, New York: Rand McNally, 1956.

—————, in *Bulletin of the American Schools of Oriental Research*, 67 (Oct. 1937).

Kramer, Samuel Noah, *Gilgamesh and the Huluppu-Tree*, Chicago, 1939.

————, *The Sumerians: Their History, Culture and Character*, University of Chicago Press. 1963.

———— (ed.), *Mythologies of the Ancient World*, New York; Doubleday Anchor Books, 1961.

Landgon, Stephen H., *Babylonian Liturgies*, Paris, 1913.

————, *The Mythology of All Races*, vol. 13, *Semitic*, Archaeological Institute of America, Boston, 1931.

Leslau, Wolf, *Falasha Anthology*, New Haven, 1951.

Lewysohn, Abraham, *Meqore Minhagim* (in Hebrew), Berlin, 1846.

Lucian, *De Dea Syria. The Syrian Goddess* . . . ed. by J. Garstang, London: Constable & Co., 1913.

Maimonides, *Guide of the Perplexed*, translated by S. Pinnes, University of Chicago Press, 1963.

Manasseh ben Israel, *Nishmat Hayyim* (in Hebrew), Amsterdam, 1652.

Maybaum, Siegmund, *Die Anthropomorphien und Anthropopathien bei Onkelos*, Breslau, 1870.

Meissner, Bruno, *Babylonien und Assyrien*, Heidelberg, 1925.

Meqore Minhagim. See Lewysohn, Abraham.

MGWJ *Monatschrift für Geschichte und Wissenschaft des Judentums*. Frankfurt a.M. 1851–1939.

Moelln, Jacob ben Moses, *Maharil* . . . *Minhage* . . . *Ashk'naz* (in Hebrew), Cremona, 1565 and subsequent editions.

Montgomery, James A., *Aramic Incantation Texts from Nippur*, Philadelphia, 1913.

Morgenstern, Julian, "Amos Studies III," *Hebrew Union College Annual*, vol. 15, Cincinnati, Ohio, 1940.

————, *The Ark, the Ephod, and the "Tent of Meeting."* Cincinnati, Ohio, 1945.

Naphtali Herz ben Jacob Elhanan, *Emeq Hamelekh* (in Hebrew), Amsterdam, 1648.

Navarro, Solomon, "The Story of R. Joseph della Reina," in *Sefer Lique Shas of Isaac Luria*, Livorno, 1790.

Neumann, Erich, *The Great Mother*, New York: Pantheon Books, Bollingen Series XLVII, 1955.

Neusner, Jacob, "Judaism, at Dura Europos," *History of Religions*, vol. 4, no. 1, Summer, 1964.

Nyberg, Bertel, *Kind und Erde*, Helsinki, 1931.

Ohana, Raphael, *Mar'eh HaYeladim* (in Hebrew), Jerusalem, 1908.

Patai, Raphael, *Hamayim* (Water; in Hebrew), Tel-Aviv, 1936.

————, *Man and Earth in Hebrew Custom, Belief and Legend* (in Hebrew), 2 vols. Jerusalem, 1942–43.

————, *Man and Temple in Ancient Jewish Myth and Ritual,* Edinburgh, 1947; new ed., New York, 1967.

————, *Sex and Family in the Bible and the Middle East,* New York, 1959.

————, "The 'Control of Rain' in Ancient Palestine," *Hebrew Union College Annual,* vol. 14, Cincinnati, Ohio, 1939.

————, *The Jewish Mind,* New York: Scribner's, 1977.

Philo of Alexandria, Works of. Loeb Classical Library.

Ploss, Hermann Heinrich, *Das Kind in Brauch und Sitte der Völker,* 3rd ed., by B. Renz, Leipzig: T. Grieben (L. Fernau), 1911–12, 2 vols.

Pope, Marvin H., *Song of Songs: A New Translation with Introduction and Commentary* (Anchor Bible series), Garden City, N.Y.: Doubleday, 1977.

Preuschen, Erwin, *Adamschriften—Die apokryphen gnostischen Adamschriften* etc., Giessen: J. Ricker, 1900.

Pritchard, James B., *Ancient Near Eastern Texts,* Princeton, 1955.

————, *Palestinian Figurines in Relation to Certain Goddesses Known through Literature,* New Haven, 1943.

Quispel, Gilles, "Der gnostische Anthropos und die jüdische Tradition," *Eranos Jahrbuch 1953,* vol. 22. Zurich, 1954.

Ranke, H., in *Studies Presented to F. L. Griffith,* London, 1932.

Real-Encyclopedie für protestantische Theologie und Kirche. Ed. by Johann Jakob Herzog. 3rd ed., Leipzig: J. C. Hinrich.

Reed, William L., *The Asherah in the Old Testament,* Texas Christian University Press, Forth Worth, Texas, 1949.

Roscher Wilhelm H. (ed), *Ausführliches Lexikon der griechischen und römischen Mythologie,* Leipzig, 1884–1934.

Rose, H. J., *A Handbook of Greek Mythology*, London, 1933.

Schmidt, Wilhelm, *The Origin and Growth of Religion*, London: Methuen, 1931.

Scholem, Gershom, *Das Buch Bahir*, Leipzig, 1923.

————, in *Eranos Jahrbuch*, vol. 19 (1950).

————, "Kabbaloth R. Ya'aqov weR. Yitzhaq" (in Hebrew), *Madda'e HaYahaduth*, vol. II, Jerusalem, 1927.

————, "L'Heqer Qabbalat R. Yitzhaq ben Ya'aqov HaKohen" (in Hebrew), *Tarbitz*, vol. 5, Jerusalem, 1934.

————, *Major Trends in Jewish Mysticism*, New York, 1961.

————, *On the Kabbalah and Its Symbolism*, New York: Schocken, 1965.

————, *Ursprung und Anfänge doer Kabbala*, Berlin, 1962.

————, "P'raqim Hadashim Me'Inyan Ashm'dai w'Lilith" (in Hebrew), *Tarbitz*, vol. 19, Jerusalem, 1948, pp. 160–75.

————, *Von der mystischen Gestalt der Gottheit*, Zurich: Rhein-Verlag, 1962.

————, "Zur Entwicklungsgeschichte der kabbalistischen Konzeption der Schechinah," *Eranos Jahrbuch 1952*, vol. 21, Zurich, 1953.

Schrader, Eberhard *Die Keilinschriften und das Alte Testament*. New ed. by Heinrich Zimmern and H. Winkler, Berlin, 1902–3.

Schürer, Emil, *Geschichte des jüdischen Volkes*, 3rd and 4th ed., Leipzig, 1901–11.

Seder 'Avodath Yisrael (Prayerbook), Rödelheim, 1868.

Sefer Tashaq, by R. Joseph. Annotated edition by Jeremy Zwelling. (In preparation.)

Segal, Jacob, *Minhage Maharil*. See Moelln, Jacob ben Moses.

Shabbetai of Rashkow, *Seder Tefilla mikol haShana* (prayerbook), Koretz, 1894.

Siddur Torah Or weSha'ar haKolel (prayerbook), Wilna, 1896.

Spira, Nathan, *Tuv ha Aretz* (in Hebrew), Venice, 1655.

Tarn, W. W., *The Greeks in Bactria and India*, Cambridge, 1938.

Thompson, Stith, *Motif-Index of Folk-Literature*, revised ed., Bloomington, Ind., 1955–57. 4 vols.

Tishby, Isaiah, *Mishnat haZohar* (in Hebrew), vol. I, Jerusalem, 1957.

Troje, L., "Sanbat," in Richard Reitzenstein, *Die Vorgeschichte der Christlichen Taufe*, Leipzig and Berlin, 1929.

Tzemah, Jacob ben Hayyim, *Sepher Nagid uM'tzave*, Amsterdam, 1712.

Ulanov, Barry (ed.) *The Way of St. Alphonsus Liguori*, New York, 1960.

Views of the Biblical World, vol. I, Chicago–New York, 1959–61. Jerusalem, 1960.

Vital Hayyim, *Sepher 'Etz Hayyim* (in Hebrew) Koretz, 1784.

————, *Sefer haGilgulim* (in Hebrew: Book of Transmigrations), Przemyshla, 1875.

Werblowsky, Zvi, *Joseph Karo—Lawyer and Mystic*, Oxford University Press, 1962.

Widengren, G., "Stand und Aufgaben der iranischen Religionsgeschichte," *Numen*, vol. I, Leiden, 1954, pp. 16ff., vol. II, 1955, pp. 46ff.

Windischmann, Fr., "Die persische Anahita oder Anaitis," *Abhandl. d. philosoph.-philolog. Classe d. könig. Bayer. Akad. d. Wiss.*, München, vol. 8, 1858.

Winkler, H. A., *Salomo und die Karina*, Stuttgart, 1931.

Woolley, Charles Leonard, "The Excavation at Ur, 1924–1925," *Antiquaries Journal*, vol. 5, London, 1925, pp. 347–402.

Wuttke, Adolf, *Der deutsche Volksaberglaube der Gegenwart*, 3rd ed. by E. H. Meyer, Berlin: Wiegandt & Grieben, 1900.

ZATW—*Zeitschrift für die alttestamentliche Wissenschaft*.

Zimmern, Heinrich, *Keilinschriften und das Alte Testament*, 3rd ed. See Schrader, Eberhard.

Zioni, Menahem ben Meir of Speyer, *Sepher Zioni* (in Hebrew), Cremona, 1560.

Zlotnik, Jehuda L., *Ma'ase Yerushalmi* (in Hebrew), Jerusalem, 1946.

INDEX